GW00630904

To my dear wife Ann
who thinks I am all at sea.

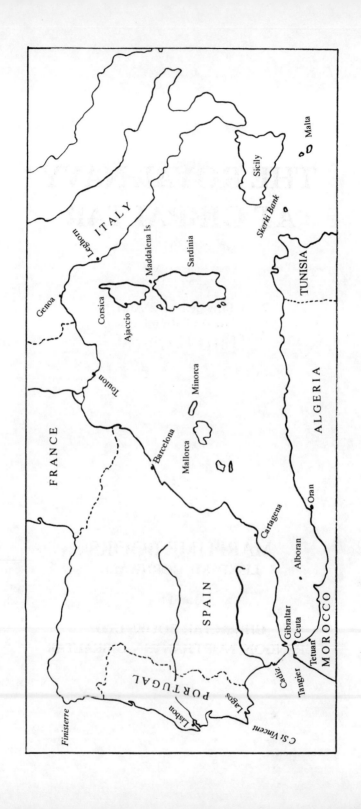

THE ROYAL NAVY
AT GIBRALTAR

Tito Benady

MARITIME BOOKS
LISKEARD, CORNWALL

and

GIBRALTAR BOOKS LTD
GRENDON, NORTHANTS - GIBRALTAR

1992

This book was first published in Great Britain in 1992 by
Maritime Books
Lodge Hill, Liskeard, Cornwall PL14 4EL

A catalogue record for this book is available from the British Library.

ISBN 0 9077771 491

Typeset by Priory Publications, Haywards Heath, West Sussex
Printed in the UK by Antony Rowe Ltd,
Bumper's Farm, Chippenham, Wiltshire SN14 6QA

CONTENTS

Maps and plans

Engravings

List of plates

Sailors and Royal Marines take part in the Ceremony of the Keys at
   Casemates on 8 January 1942. *(Photo Imperial War Museum)*
HMS *Ark Royal* entering harbour 1940. *(Photo Imperial War Museum)*
A 6-inch coast defence gun from Devil's Gap Battery overlooks Force H in the
   harbour in 1941. HMS *Argus* is tied up at the South Mole with either the
   Rodney or *Nelson*. The cruiser at anchor to give her AA battery a wide arc
   of fire was probably HMS *Hermione.*. *(Photo Imperial War Museum)*
Force H, HMS *Renown, Malaya,* and *Ark Royal* sail past the east side of the
   Rock in 1940. *(Photo Imperial War Museum)*
Force H at sea in November 1940 whilst engaged in Operation White to fly
   off Hurricanes to Malta. Photograph taken from *Sheffield* of *Argus,*
Renown, and *Ark Royal. (Photo Imperial War Museum)*
Sailors joining the Army and civilians in the VE Day celebrations in the
   Grand Parade. *(Photo Imperial War Museum)*
U-541 is brought into the harbour after surrendering on 12 May 1945. *(Photo
   Imperial War Museum)*

Plates between pages 208 and 209

The Naval Picket House at the entrance to Main Street. The shore patrols
   operated from here and drunks invariably ended up here. On this
   occasion in 1953 the drunks seem to be in charge as the White Ensign is
   flying upside down. *(Photo Stuart Brown)*
The Bland ferry SS *Gibel Tarik* remembered by many as the Tangier ferry
   between 1949 and 1954. She figured in the Alec Guiness film 'Captain's
   Paradise'. Originally HM minesweeper *Ford* of the Hunt class, she was
   converted to a car ferry and renamed *Forde* in 1928. During World War II
   she served as a salvage vessel. *(Photo courtesy John Gaggero)*
The old Naval Hospital. *(Photo John Farmar)*
The entrance to the Victualling Yard with Parson's Lodge behind. *(Photo John
   Farmar)*
The explosion in the barge alongside the *Bedenham. (Photo Elio Bado, courtesy
   Gibraltar Museum)*
The explosion seen from New Camp. *(Photo Norman Cummins, courtesy
   Gibraltar Museum)*
The *Bedenham* after the explosion. *(Photo courtesy Gibraltar Museum)*
The wreckage on Gun Wharf after the explosion. *(Photo courtesy Gibraltar
   Museum)*
HMS *Childers.*
HMS *Gambia.*
HMS *Vanguard* at the New Mole.
HMS *Hermes* in the Bay.
The boom defence vessel RMAS *Moorland.*
The harbour tug RMAS *Dexterous.*
The French destroyers *Guepratte* and *Kersaint* astern of HMS *Jutland* with two
   Dutch destroyers of the Friesland class alongside.
The RFA *Eddybeach* leaves harbour in 1962 for the last time.
The Mediterranean Fleet in harbour.

HMS *Bulwark* comes alongside.

A fine aerial view of one of the last concentrations of big ships in the harbour.

The ships of Exercise Spring Train in the harbour, April 1982, before news of the Argentinean invasion of the Falklands was received.

HMS *Plymouth* returns from the Falklands.

HMS *Boxer*, a type 22 frigate of the Broadsword class.

HMS *Beaver*, a sister ship.

HMS *Active*, a type 21 frigate.

Sister ship HMS *Avenger*.

HMS *Invincible*.

HMS *Ark Royal*.

HMS *Hart* with the Admiralty Tower behind; the quay alongside is reserved for use by the Royal Navy. *(Photo John Farmar)*

HMS Rooke and the new extension to Coaling Island. *(Photo John Farmar)*

The new reclamation in the harbour. *(Photo John Farmar)*

PREFACE

This book is a description of how the Royal Navy became aware of Gibraltar and its advantageous position for an overseas base, and the role the Rock has played in its history over a period of three centuries. Although at times I have found it necessary to sketch in some of the events that took place in Gibraltar and refer to the continuing political differences with Spain, it is not meant to be a history of Gibraltar or of the Anglo-Spanish dispute about the possession of the Rock.

The idea of the book was Lt Commander Mike Critchley's of Maritime Books and I should like to thank him for his help and advice which give the book whatever merits it may possess. The errors and faults are all my own. I should like to thank my daughter Susannah Benady for editing the manuscript, Helen Sharp for drawing the maps and George Felipes for drawing the plan of the original settlement in the 12th century.

I must express my gratitude to all who have helped me in my researches. The Reading Room staff of the Public Records Office, the British Library and the Biblioteca Nacional, Madrid. Joaquin Bensusan, the former Curator of the Gibraltar Museum, and Dr Clive Finlayson the present curator. Mrs L M Huart, formerly Librarian of the Garrison Library. Tommy Finlayson, the Gibraltar Government Archivist, and his predecessor, the late Bill Cumming; as well as Manuel Ravina, Director of the Provincial Archives of Cadiz. I should also like to express my thanks to the many individuals who have gone out of their way to assist me with advice and information, Commander Joe Ballantine RNR, Mark Benady, Dr Sam Benady, Marylou Benson, Orlando Bossino, Charles Cabedo, Adolphus Canepa, Lt Commander John Craven RN, Commander Bob Cribb RN, Lt Commander John Farmar RN, Lt Commander Maurice FitzGerald RN, John Gaggero, Sir Joshua Hassan, Captain Anthony Hazell RN, Commander C A Howeson RN, General Sir William Jackson, Commander Richard Mitchell RN, David Penman, Dr Anthony Seymour, Vice-Admiral Sir George Vallings, Lt Commander

Bob Williams RN; and last but not least Professor Luis de Mora-Figueroa and Tony Gilbert who drew my attention to a number of sources that I would otherwise have missed.

This volume would not have been as interesting without the work of the numerous authors I mention in the bibliography whose books I have scrutinised for references to Gibraltar. My thanks are particularly due to Mrs Ann Monsarrat for permission to quote from Nicholas Monsarrat's autobiography *Life is a Four Letter Word*; to Peter C Smith for permission to quote from his book *HMS Wild Swan*; to Conway Maritime Press Ltd for permission to quote from *Wings at Sea* by Gerard A Woods; to the Doubleday division of Doubleday, Dell Publishing Group Inc for permission to quote from Dwight D Eisenhower's *Crusade in Europe*; to W Foulsham & Co Ltd for permission to quote from *Out Sweeps!* by Paul Lund and Harry Ludlam; to Harper Collins Publishers (New Zealand) Ltd for permission to quote from *HMNZS Achilles* by Jack S Harker; and Scolar Press for permission to quote from *The Beaty Papers* edited by B McL Ranft.

Tito Benady, Grendon, 1 October 1992

GLOSSARY

The number given after the name of sailing warships denotes the number of guns carried. This does not mean that the weight of their broadsides and fighting strength was proportional to the number of guns, as the largest gun of a 14 gun sloop was probably a 6 or 9 pounder, that of a 36 gun frigate a 24 pounder, and of a ship of the line a 32 pounder (and in the 19th century a 68 pounder).

It was usual to refer to a sailing ship of war by the number of guns she was designed to carry, for example a ship of the line of 74 guns would be referred to as 'a 74', and the number 74 was put after her name.

Letters of marque was the licence to fit out a private vessel and employ it in the capture of the enemy's shipping.

Levanter is the local name for the east wind.

Madcat was a Catalina flying boat fitted with Magnetic Anomaly Detector equipment.

Polacre was a Mediterranean three-masted brig, with lateen sails on fore and mizen, and square sails on mainmast.

Praam was a flat-bottomed boat which originated in Scandinavia, used for shipping cargo or as a gun platform.

Settee was a small, fast single-decked merchant vessel with two or three lateen sails.

Vice Admiralty Court was the tribunal with admiralty jurisdiction in British colonies.

Xebec was a three-masted Mediterranean ship with lateen sails (though some carried square sails) which varied in size and could carry anything from 8 to 28 guns.

ABBREVIATIONS

AA	anti-aircraft
AACR	Association for the Advancement of Civil Rights
AACU	Anti-Aircraft Cooperation Unit
ABS	armed boarding ship
AMC	armed merchant cruiser
A/S	anti-submarine
ASDIC	sonar (Anti-Submarine Detection Investigation Committee)
BL	breech loading
CAM	Catapult Aircraft Merchant ship (fitted with catapult for a fighter aircraft)
CBF	Commander British Forces
CinC	Commander-in-Chief
CINCAFMED	CinC Allied Forces Mediterranean (NATO designation)
CNS	Confederate Navy Ship
COMGIBMED	Commander Gibraltar-Mediterranean Area
COMNAVSOUTH	Commander Naval Forces South (NATO designation)
DEPFA	Defence of port and anti-sabotage
DNI	Director of Naval Intelligence
FAA	Fleet Air Arm
FHQ	Fortress Headquarters
FO	Flag Officer
GSLP	Gibraltar Socialist Labour Party
HG	convoy designation, Gibraltar to Britain (Home from Gib)
IFF	Identification Friend or Foe - electronic identification device which identified friendly aircraft on a radar screen
KMF	convoy designation (UK to Mediterranean - Fast)
KMS	convoy designation (UK to Mediterranean - Slow)
MAD	Magnetic Anomaly Detector

MEW	Ministry of Economic Warfare
MHQ	Maritime Headquarters
MKF	convoy designation (Mediterranean to UK - Fast)
MKS	convoy designation (Mediterranean to UK - Slow)
ML	motor launch
MS	motor ship
M/S	minesweeper
NI	Naval Intelligence
NRS	Navy Records Society
NS	New Style: dates according to the Gregorian calendar of 1582 which corrected a discrepancy in the Julian calendar which had made the year 11 minutes too long. The error was rectified by making century years not to count as leap years unless divisible by 400. NS was not introduced into Britain until 1752. Before that, the Gregorian NS was eleven days ahead of the OS Julian calendar.
OE	convoy designation, Britain to Port Said (Outwards East)
OG	convoy designation, Britain to Gibraltar (Outwards Gib)
OS	Old Style: dates according to the Julian calendar (introduced by Julius Caesar) which Britain retained until 1752. OS was eleven days behind NS from 1600 onwards. Under the Julian calendar the year started on 1 April.
OSS	Office of Strategic Services (US version of SOE)
PAS	Port Auxiliary Service (became RMAS in 1976)
PSW	Private Ship of War - designation of a merchant ship commissioned as a privateer.
QF	quick firing gun: a gun designed to be closed up by means of the cartridge rather than the breach - a much faster operation.
RFA	Royal Fleet Auxiliary
RML	rifled muzzle loader
RMLI	Royal Marine Light Infantry

RMAS	Royal Maritime Auxiliary Service
RNAS	Royal Navy Air Service (incorporated into RAF on 1 April 1918)
RNR	Royal Naval Reserve
SACEUR	Supreme Allied Command Europe (NATO designation)
SLC	Siluro a Lunga Corsa = long range torpedo (Italian human torpedo)
SNO	Senior Naval Officer
SOE	Special Operations Executive (in charge of undercover operations in occupied Europe during World War II)
SS	Steam Ship
USN	United States Navy
USS	United States Ship
VE Day	Victory in Europe Day, 8 May 1945
VJ Day	Victory over Japan Day, 15 August 1945

(Overleaf) Sir Henry Sheeres was an engineer who supervised the building of the mole at Tangier from 1669 and organised its destruction in 1683. He published a number of books. In 1703 he produced *A Discourse on the Mediterranean Sea and the Streights of Gibraltar* and in 1705 he brought out a second edition which was prefaced by this map of Gibraltar. There is no supporting evidence for his statement that 'Cromwell ..... would have cut this neck of land to make Gibraltar an Island &c,' but in the spring of 1656, the merchant ship *Industry,* on its way to Blake in the Mediterranean loaded with ammunition and entrenching tools, was captured by Spanish privateers and taken into Bayonne. *(Baumber p219)*

A New and Exact Map of the City and Bay of
GIBRALTAR in Spain Taken by Sᴿ G. ROOKE
Vice-Admiral of England The 24 of July 1704. By H.M.

0   1   2   3   4
Engliſh Miles

PART OF ANDALUSIA

High Hills

BAY OF GIBRALTAR

Old Mole

Road

3   4   4

10

GIBRALTAR

25   10

Fort that blew op.
Sᵗʰ mole Head here
the Seamen landed
The Gr. Platform

Redout

Here yᵉ Prince of Heſſe
landed wᵗʰ 1800 marines.
Ol. Cromwel had a deſign
upon this place, and would
have cut this neck of
land to make Gibral-
tar an Iſland &c.

Calpe
Mons

Old
Gibraltar

Ballaſt
Place

6
36   30

C. Cabrita

Gibraltar Pt.

MEDITERRANIAN SEA.

Straits   of   Gibraltar.

The Bay is very fair and almoſt like a Haven landlockt for a Weſt wind: but a South
Weſt wind bloweth right in, a South wind comes from yᵉ top of yᵉ Mountain of Gibral
tar, to Anchor in this Bay you muſt ſail so far in that yᵉ innermoſt Point of Gibraltar
bears about Eaſt from you, then you will have 5 or 6 Fathom Clear ground yᵉ Ebbing and
Flowing is about 3 or 4 Foot. in ſailing with an Eaſterly wind from yᵉ Road of Gibral-
tar, you ſhould bear up toward yᵉ Weſt shore; for tis scarce poſſible you can get out of yᵉ
Bay along yᵉ high land becauſe yᵉ Eaſterly winds fall with ſuch whirlings from the
Hills of Gibraltar .

xvi

CHAPTER I

THE ROYAL NAVY AND THE MEDITERRANEAN.

The story of the Royal Navy at Gibraltar is part of the story of the growth of British trade - and the need to protect that trade - which led to the creation of the British Empire. Gibraltar was one of the first places to become known to English sailors when trade with the Mediterranean was being pioneered. It was captured during the first century of the creation of the Empire, becoming the first permanent foothold in the area. Now that the Empire no longer exists and Gibraltar's imperial role has disappeared, it remains a powerful reminder of the past.

The early commercial contacts between the British Isles and the Mediterranean were across the Channel and overland through France. The Phoenicians had pioneered trade routes by sea from the Strait of Gibraltar along the Atlantic coast of Portugal and across the Bay of Biscay but after their time, this route fell into disuse. A thousand years later, from about 1317 onwards, the Venetians and Genoese started sailing annual fleets of galleys to the Low Countries, carrying spices, silk, wine and oil, and other luxury merchandise. Towards the end of their journey, some of these galleys would be detached to English ports such as Southampton, Sandwich and London and they would return south with cargoes of wool, hides and metals.[1]

Trading voyages in the opposite direction were slow in starting. A Bristol merchant, Robert Sturmy, tried to initiate a trade in wool, lead and tin, in 1446 and again in 1457, but did not succeed in completing a round journey.[2] However, Richard Hakluyt assures us that 50 years later, in the reign of Henry VII, 'divers tall ships of London, were regularly conducting trade with Italy and the Levant. They took out cloth and calf-skins and returned with silk, spices, wine, oil and rhubarb.[3] This commerce faced a temporary interruption in the middle of the 16th century because of the rise of Ottoman sea power. But when the political situation in the eastern Mediterranean stabilised, the Levant Company was formed in 1581 to regulate what had become an important trade for English merchants.[4]

The opening of the direct routes to the east round Africa brought an end to the spice trade through the Mediterranean. But by then the trade between England and the Mediterranean countries had developed in other directions and the English had acquired a new habit which had to be catered for. By the beginning of the 17th century, the inhabitants of England had developed a strong attachment to plum puddings made with currants and raisins instead of the traditional dried plums. As one contemporary writer puts it, the English 'forsooth can hardly digest bread, pastries, broth and bag puddings without those currants.' The import of currants was to become for many years the most lucrative part of the Levant Company's business. In addition, the Mediterranean became an important market for manufactured goods from England.[5]

The important trade between England and the Mediterranean gave English sailors an intimate knowledge of the area round the Strait of Gibraltar. They got to know Cadiz well, for this was the main port for the export of wine and the other products of southern Spain, and also Jubalterra, as Gibraltar was known to the Elizabethans. The Rock was an important landmark, and also one of the ports from which the products of the country were exported to England.[6] In time it became notorious as a place to be avoided. For here a squadron of Spanish galleys guarded the passage of the Strait and menaced English shipping during the long years that England and Spain were at war. In 1563, Alvaro de Bazan (later made Marquess of Santa Cruz), who was Governor of Gibraltar and Captain General of the Ocean Sea (the Atlantic Coast), captured eight small English sailing ships which pursued a French vessel into the Bay of Gibraltar. The crews were sent to row in the King of Spain's galleys at Cadiz; and although the following year 90 of the men were released another 150 had died in the intervening time.[7]

As the sailing ships became bigger and more heavily gunned they proved that they were more than a match for the lighter galleys. Their high sides and heavy armament could prevent the large crews of the galleys from boarding and they were able to fight them off. In July 1586, five 'tall ships' from London, led by the *Marchant Royall* beat off an

The original foundation of Gibraltar by Ábd al-Mummin in 1160

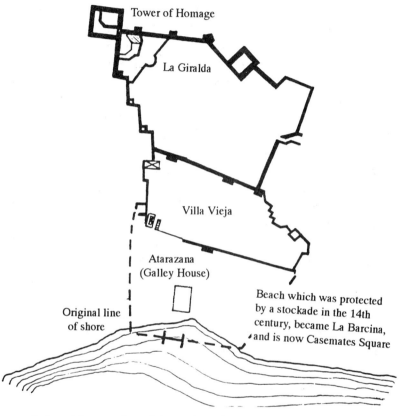

Tower of Homage

La Giralda

Villa Vieja

Atarazana
(Galley House)

Original line
of shore

Beach which was protected
by a stockade in the 14th
century, became La Barcina,
and is now Casemates Square

attack by thirteen Spanish and Maltese galleys off the coast of Pantellaria.[8] Four years later, another convoy of London ships led by the *Salomon* defeated a force of twelve galleys commanded by Giannandrea Doria, within sight of Gibraltar; and on Easter Sunday 1591 there was, in the same place, an epic five and a half hour fight between the *Centurion* of London 'a very talle shippe of burden' with a crew of 48, and five Spanish galleys carrying a thousand men, and 'by spoyling and overwearing of the Spaniards, the Englishmen constrained them to ungrapple themselves, and get them going'.[9]

The galleys were too weak to defeat the 'tall ships' and were replaced in the Spanish Strait guard by galleons. But by that time Queen Elizabeth was dead and James I had signed a peace treaty with Spain. It fell to the Dutch (who were nearing the successful end of their long fight for independence from the Spanish crown) to confront the new menace. In March 1707, a Dutch fleet of 26 ships sailed under the command of Jacob van Heemskerk to tackle the galleons, commanded by Don Juan Alvarez de Avilés, which were guarding the navigation of the Strait. On 25 April, he found the Spanish fleet anchored by the walls of Gibraltar.

The city of Gibraltar had been founded in 1160 by Abd al-Mummin, Emperor of Morocco. The original settlement was built on the western slope of the Rock, close to the steep and forbidding north face. It covered the small area that stretches from the Tower of Homage down to Casemates Square. The new city was easy to defend from attack by land; as in those days, before the reclamation of land from the sea, the entrance to the isthmus from the mainland was a very narrow stretch of land between the Rock and the Bay. It was of course possible for enemies to climb the Rock and attack the town from above. There was always a danger that an enemy might encamp on the Rock above and thus threaten the defenders in the town below. The extraordinarily strong Tower of Homage was built in the 14th century to defend this weak point.

Being on the western side of the Rock, in the sheltered waters at the head of the Bay, the harbour of the new town was protected from easterly and westerly winds but open to the south-westerlies. The galley harbour was therefore built within the walls, in a small inlet which ran right into Casemates Square. Next to the Water Gate there was a special gate through which the galleys were hauled into the large Galley House. The arch of this gate was later bricked up but was visible until the line wall was rebuilt in the 18th century.[10] The building of the Old Mole (which ran out from Montagu Bastion towards the Customs at Waterport) and the North Bastion, blocked the currents that scoured the shore and the inlet became silted up and unusable. By 1588 the area of the Old Mole was so silted up with mud and rubbish that only small boats and light vessels could use it. Deep draught sailing ships had to anchor well away.[11]

Heemskerk found Alvarez's ten galleons anchored in two rows of five, at some distance from the walls of the town, under the exiguous protection of the guns mounted on South Bastion and the fort of El Tuerto, which were built to protect the south of the town from attack from the sea.[12]

The Dutch admiral formulated a plan which was to foreshadow Nelson's tactics at the Nile. He ordered his twenty largest vessels to pair up and each pair was to grapple one of the large galleons as they lay at anchor, one on each side. The remaining six Dutch ships were detailed to deal with the eleven smaller Spanish vessels. In fact the Dutch ships borne in by a brisk south-westerly were able to surround each of the five galleons on the seaward line with three or four vessels. After hours of heavy cannonading at close quarters, the numerical superiority of the Dutch began to tell and by evening they had destroyed five of the galleons. The Spanish ran the other five galleons ashore to avoid them being captured too. Heemskerk, who had grappled Alvarez's flagship, died in the combat; the Spanish admiral was also killed at the beginning of the action.[13]

The Battle of the Bay of Gibraltar showed the need for a proper protected harbour for warships. After a number of engineers had studied the project, the construction of the New Mole at the Torre del Tuerto, was begun in 1615. Gibraltar was at that time a small agricultural town without great wealth. Shortage of funds caused the work to proceed very slowly. Ten years later the Mole was only 26 yards long. However, under the energetic direction of Luis Bravo de Acuña, who was appointed governor of Gibraltar in 1626, it was greatly extended. Work continued for a number of years, and by 1670 it had reached a total length of some 120 yards, with a battery at the head. The old pentagonal fort of El Tuerto was completely reconstructed to provide a strong defence; and the Old Mole was rebuilt and extended. The New Mole, or South Mole as it is more commonly known today, was to become the home of the Royal Navy at Gibraltar, for most of the 18th and 19th centuries.[14]

The Royal Navy appears on the scene

The Moslem corsairs operating from the ports of North Africa (known to history as the Barbary Corsairs) presented a threat to Christian shipping right through the 15th and 16th centuries, and when they changed their small galleys and other row-boats to European style sailing ships at the beginning of the 17th century, this threat intensified. Eventually even that normally pacific monarch, James I, was forced to prepare and send out a squadron of 18 ships under the command of Sir Robert Mansell. This fleet was intended to operate in conjunction with the Dutch and Spanish navies against Algiers, which was the main and strongest base of the corsairs. It is recorded that when the fleet called at Gibraltar in November 1620, Mansell landed his sick and lodged them in quarters specially prepared for them.[15] These were probably in the grounds of the Hospital of St. John of God, which had been founded in 1567 by an inhabitant of Gibraltar, Juan Mateos, in order to care for sick sailors, particularly those suffering from syphilis. This hospital was used by the Royal Navy in the 18th century until the Old Naval Hospital, overlooking Rosia, was built. Today, St. Bernard's Hospital is built on the site of the old building.[16]

This was the first time that an English fleet had been sent to the Mediterranean, and Mansell's success in maintaining his fleet safe in this station for almost 12 months, was to lead to other occasions when this was done.

In 1625, when England once again was at war with Spain, a fleet was sent under the command of Viscount Wimbledon, to attack the Spaniards in the Strait. The venture was not successful as Wimbledon was not a vigorous or inspired leader. But it became memorable because in a Council of War held on 25 October off Cape St. Vincent, Sir Robert Bruce suggested that the best objective for the expedition was Gibraltar, because it had a good harbour for the fleet. Though the town was poor,

> yet the place was of great importance as being such by the advantage whereof the trade from all partes of the Levannt might be brought under our commands; That being but a small peice, it was the easier to be manned, victualled, and holden if once taken.

This sets out succinctly the merits from the British point of view of holding Gibraltar, in that it could command the trade of the Mediterranean and be held with a relatively small garrison and at minimum cost. When eventually the expedition returned to England after being defeated in its attack on Cadiz, Wimbledon was denounced for not having given proper consideration to Bruce's proposals.[17]

The Royal Navy operated intermittently in these waters from now on, and proposals for the capture of Gibraltar were to be made again. When Cromwell went to war with Spain in 1655, a fleet - under Generals-at-Sea Blake and Mountagu - was sent to operate against the southern Spanish ports the following year. After the fleet had reached its destination, Cromwell wrote to the admirals, that if it was not possible to take Cadiz, they should consider some other place

> especially that of the town and castle of Gibraltar, - which if possessed and made tenable by us, would it not be an advantage to our trade and an annoyance to the Spaniard; and enable us, without keeping so great a fleet on that coast, with six nimble frigates lodged there do the Spaniard more harm than by a fleet, and ease our charge?[18]

Once again, the attraction was not only that Gibraltar was strategically situated but it could also be held cheaply. Mountagu had a look at the Rock and wrote back suggesting that the best way to reduce the garrison of Gibraltar was to cut it off from the mainland by digging a canal across the isthmus,

> I perceive much desire that Gibraltar should be taken. My thoughts as to that are in short these that the likeliest way to get it is by landing on the sand, and quickly cutting it off between sea and sea or so to secure our men there as that they may hinder the intercourse of the town with the main; frigates lying near to assist them and it is well known that Spain never victualeth any place for more than one month. This will want Four or Five thousand men, well formed and officered.[19]

Without a substantial landing force of soldiers, nothing could be achieved and the Navy would have to wait for another occasion when these requirements would be met.

Within a few years Cromwell was dead, the Commonwealth dissolved into anarchy and the monarchy was restored. Charles II married Catharine of Braganza, the daughter of the King of Portugal and received an ample dowry in money as well as the Portuguese held ports of Bombay and Tangier. Tangier was occupied in 1662 by Mountagu, now Earl of Sandwich, and from then on a Royal Navy squadron was to be based in the Western Mediterranean to protect British trade and imperial interests. However, being at the Atlantic end of the Strait, the open Bay of Tangier was by no means a safe port and the construction of a mole was started. The work went on for more than 20 years and eventually the mole reached a length of 475 yards, but the harbour was still open to both westerly and Levanter storms, and the heavy swell made conditions so unpleasant, that ships at anchor might be isolated from land for days on end; careening often took place in the Bay of Gibraltar rather than in the harbour at Tangier. [20]

Though Gibraltar was often used during this period, for careening ships and obtaining supplies, for both Tangier and the Royal Navy, captains preferred to make Cadiz their home port in the Strait. Not only were facilities better there than at Tangier, but they also found opportunities to hire themselves out to carry bullion and precious cargoes for the Cadiz Merchants, to their private benefit and the detriment of the service. The readiness of Royal Navy captains to abandon their duties in order to engage in private trading, or change their route for the convenience of paying passengers, was an evil which Samuel Pepys fought against as long as he was Secretary of the Navy, but without much success. [21]

Staying at sea all the year round was a hazardous affair in those days and there were the inevitable casualties. The Strait squadron of nine ships under Sir Thomas Allin, which was in pursuit of a Dutch convoy, anchored in Backstrap Bay in order to replenish its supply of drinking water from the River Guadiaro, on 1 December 1664. That night the ships set sail in a light north-easterly, but the night was pitch dark and the rain heavy, and some of the ships lost sight of the light carried by the Admiral; they turned west too soon and were carried onto the rocks on the east side of the Rock. HMS *Nonsuch* 34 and *Phoenix* 38 were total losses. HMS *Portsmouth* 46 and *Bonaventure* 42 also went aground but were saved. When Allin, in HMS *Plymouth* 60, returned to look for his squadron he too went aground 'in a sandy bay', probably Catalan Bay, but was able to kedge his ship off. The wind then veered to the west, and after they were carried as far as Fuengirola, the fleet was able to enter Gibraltar harbour on 12 December. After making running repairs they salvaged what they could from the wrecks of the *Nonsuch* and *Phoenix*. The *Bonaventure* was so badly damaged that she had to go into Cadiz for a more extensive overhaul. [22]

A Naval Depot at Gibraltar

In 1679, Vice-Admiral Arthur Herbert (later Lord Torrington) became Commander-in-chief of the Mediterranean squadron and he started looking around for a better base than Tangier, for his campaign against the Algerine pirates. After trying out Cadiz and Leghorn he eventually decided to use Gibraltar and by April 1681 he had, by judicious use of largesse, persuaded the governor of the place to allow him to careen his ships in the Bay and to station a hulk to hold the supplies for his fleet. Balthazar St Michel, Pepys' feckless brother-in-law who was the victualler at Tangier, had also reluctantly been moved to Gibraltar, although the townsmen refused to rent him warehouses on shore and resented the presence of the Royal Navy. Herbert ascribed this to their not being used to much trade and were therefore fearful of strangers. The following year the stores were returned to Tangier as the use of Gibraltar had only been granted for the duration of the campaign against the Algerines. [23]

In spite of its shortcomings as a naval base, Tangier had proved a most timely and useful acquisition in the development of the Empire and for British influence in the Mediterranean, but it suffered from the disadvantage that it was in the personal possession of the King. It was expensive to maintain and the privy purse was not up to it, nor would the King allow Parliament to wrest from his grasp control of this important commercial port and its substantial military garrison. As Charles II neared the end of his reign and the conflict between the Court and the Protestant interests in Parliament came to a head, Charles and his brother the Duke of York (later James II) decided they required the Tangier garrison back in England in order to assist them in the impending conflict. The mole was blown up, the garrison and inhabitants hurriedly evacuated and the deserted town reverted to Moroccan rule. [24]

The evacuation of Tangier was entrusted to Lord Dartford and Samuel Pepys went along to help determine the amount of compensation to be given to each of the civilian inhabitants who would be forced to give up their property. This enabled Pepys to study the problem of maintaining the Royal Navy's presence in the Mediterranean, and he recorded a conversation he had with one of the engineers who had worked on the mole. This was a Major Beckmann, a Swedish artillery officer, who had entered English service, and for part of his time in Tangier had acted as a spy in Spain on behalf of the garrison.

Pepys noted in his papers:

> Major Beckmann do speak to me greatly in commendation of Gibraltar as the place which above all others our King ought to have for the keeping an entire command in the Straits, and which he says he might have without the loss of one man's life, no cost, fortified very cheap, [no] possibility of loss with 500 or 1,000 men at most, it being capable of being attacked but in one place, which to prevent the possibility of being prevented in as to the King's service ... he will keep to himself, not communicating it to the King himself. [25]

Beckmann may have kept his opinions to himself but naval officers who called regularly at Gibraltar and knew it well must also have reached the same conclusion independently. An Italian merchant who was residing with the English consul in Algiers in 1662 remembered Royal Navy captains discussing at dinner how their admiral, Sir John Lawson, had written to England asking for a cargo of spades and other tools to be sent to the fleet in order to dig up the isthmus and isolate the town of Gibraltar before capturing it. [26]

The Royal Navy's chance to put these ideas into effect would come twenty years later when a fleet would be in the neighbourhood with the time and opportunity to carry out the plan. This time the fleet had on board the landing force, that Mountagu had stipulated in 1655 as being essential for the successful capture of the Rock. But in the meantime the Royal Navy was faced with the problem of how to carry out its tasks in the area, now that it could no longer operate from Tangier.

A new port had to be found where a squadron for the protection of merchant shipping, could be based, and to serve as a base for the continuing operations against the Barbary Corsairs. Cadiz could have been the obvious choice but Pepys, who was at the time in control of the Navy, was concerned that the rich contracts for transporting bullion, that Naval captains could obtain in that important commercial centre, would jeopardise discipline and efficiency. So he tried to stop the ships of the Royal Navy entering Cadiz, Lisbon and other important commercial centres. By the end of the 17th century Gibraltar had lost its old importance, both as a commercial port and as a naval base. A visitor in 1659 wrote:

> In the old days there were many galleys based at Gibraltar, but today there are none and no commerce either, even though it is considered to be the key to Spain and its arms bear a key. [27]

Another visitor found that there was so little commercial movement in the town that the fishermen could not dispose of their plentiful catches. [28]

In spite of his forebodings, Pepys established a base at Lisbon and in 1686 he sent John Gauden to be victualler at Gibraltar. Gauden operated there with the permission of the local governor although once again he was not allowed to rent store houses within the town walls. But in 1688 the Salé squadron was withdrawn to guard the Channel against the impending invasion by William of Orange, and Gauden returned to England. [29] When William III joined Austria, Holland and Spain, in the War of the League of Augsburg in 1689 (to confront the growing power of the France of Louis XIV) Cadiz became the main base for the English fleet. The war lasted until 1697.

Gibraltar was satisfactory as a base in peacetime but its deficiencies in time of war were demonstrated in 1693. In that year the main French fleet surprised the Smyrna convoy of 400 sail in Lagos Bay, which was guarded by a weak force under Admiral Rooke, and scattered it. A number of the merchant vessels and their escorting warships took refuge in the Bay, and some of the warships landed guns to supplement the eight serviceable pieces in the Torre del Tuerto. They were cannonaded by a French squadron, some twenty strong, for two days. Four of the warships were badly damaged and thirteen of the merchantmen were captured and towed away. A number of the sailors who took refuge ashore, later complained of ill-treatment by the townspeople. [30]

This event demonstrated clearly to the Royal Navy how vulnerable Gibraltar really was, because of its weak garrison and the small number of guns that were mounted on its ancient walls.

Notes and References

1   Wood 3, *Encyclopaedia Britannica* 1973 6:144c.
2   Wood 1-2.
3   Hakluyt 3:2-3.
4   Hakluyt 3:50-51; Wood 3-5.
5   Wood 24, 67.
6   In October 1559 an Englishman whose name is given as 'Thomas Homaslevi' (Hammersley?) chartered the ship *San Juan* in Marbella to transport two cargoes of raisins to Gibraltar. (Cabrillana 72.)
7   Duro 2:59-60; Froude 42.
8   Hakluyt 3:362-367.
9   Hakluyt 4:380-386.
10   Bertaut 105.
11   Mariategui 85,99.
12   Portillo f 38.
13   Duro 3:232-236; Vere 25-28; Mariategui 99; see also the contemorary account given in Appendix 1.
14   Portillo Ms f 13; Gonzalez 23-24; Ayala 269,273; Mariategui 97-99.
15   Corbett *England in the Mediterranean* 1:117.
16   Ayala 256-258.
17   Corbett ibid 1:156-161; Granville 5; Grossart 33-37.
18   Carlyle 2:489, 503.
19   Powell *Blake* 406-407.
20   Corbett ibid 2:30,134,136; Chappell 274.

21 Bryant *Years of Peril* 344, 360; *Saviour of the Navy* 41, 57-59; Anderson 2:x1; Chappell 79. See Lantery pages 95 and 100 which tells how he hired HMS *Tiger* to call especially at Mallorca in order to transport his family to Cadiz.

22 Anderson 1:184-189, 2:218-221.

23 Hornstein 179-194.

24 Chappell xxii-xxiii.

25 Chappell 231-232.

26 Lantery 127.

27 Bertaut 107.

28 Lantery 127.

29 Hornstein 194-204.

30 Hills 153-154.

CHAPTER II

GIBRALTAR IS CAPTURED.

The short alliance between Britain and Spain ended with the death of the Spanish king Carlos II in 1700, who died leaving no direct heirs. The crown of Spain therefore had to revert to one of his cousins, either Louis XIV of France or the Emperor Leopold I of Austria. Carlos chose Louis XIV who passed the throne of Spain to his grandson Philip with the promise that the two kingdoms of Spain and France would never be united. But this was not acceptable to England, Holland and other countries, who feared the strength of the new political union of the two strongest European powers. William III committed England and Scotland to support the claim to the Spanish throne of the Archduke Charles, the younger brother of the Emperor Leopold; though Louis XIV tried to buy William off, making him offers of Gibraltar, Minorca, Oran and Ceuta.[1] From May 1702, a state of war existed between France, Spain and Bavaria on the one hand and a coalition of Holland, Britain, and Austria on the other. Portugal, Savoy and a number of German states, including Hanover, eventually joined the coalition.

The strategy formulated by William III, and continued by the great Duke of Marlborough after the king's death in 1702, was to attack France in the north with the massed armies of the allies, and to use their superiority at sea to threaten the southern flank in Spain and along the Mediterranean coast. In 1703 a combined Anglo-Dutch fleet was sent to the Mediterranean under the command of the stalwart and dependable, but not particularly gifted, Admiral Sir George Rooke. The fleet was repulsed when it attacked Cadiz but was successful in capturing part of the Spanish treasure fleet that had taken refuge in Vigo Bay. The following year Rooke was back with 60 ships of the line and frigates, as well as smaller vessels. The fleet was based at Lisbon, but Rooke was looking for a base nearer the proposed theatre of operation.

Aboard the fleet was Prince George of Hesse Darmstadt, the commander in chief of the Archduke Charles' army. George was well connected, as he was related to the Emperor by marriage. In his younger days he had been a colonel in the English army and had fought at the Battle of the Boyne, but had resigned his commission when he became a Catholic and entered the Imperial army. He was sent to Spain with two Imperial regiments during the War of the League of Augsburg, and after the war was made Viceroy of Catalonia, a post he vacated when Philip V was declared king. Prince George was on board the fleet to look after the interests of the Archduke, to command any force the fleet landed, and to take over the rule of any Spanish territory that surrendered or was captured.

The fleet sailed to Barcelona where there was strong support for the Archduke and George had many friends, but Rooke's inability to act decisively in a situation which required him to take risks, led to a repulse; and the arrangements for a combined attack with the army of Savoy against the French naval base of Toulon also fell through. At the end of July the fleet was back in the Strait, at anchor in Tetuan Bay.[2]

Rooke had by now run out of ideas on what action to take next and he convened a council of war on 28 July to decide on the future actions of the fleet. (I follow present day historians in giving all dates in NS - see list of abbreviations). Prince George pressed for an attack on Gibraltar and this course was accepted by the council. The Prince was to command a force of marines which was to be landed to attack the town from the isthmus and to prevent relieving forces entering the besieged fortress. The command of the ships that were to bombard the town was given to Rear-Admiral George Byng by Rooke, for no better reason than that he had opposed the operation in the council of war.

On the evening of 31 July, Byng made his way to Gibraltar from Tetuan and came to anchor the following morning close to the town walls, but the mast of Byng's flagship HMS *Ranelagh* was hit by a cannon ball and he therefore withdrew to about a mile away. Byng was reinforced by seven ships of the line. This brought his bombardment force to 22 ships and three Dutch mortar boats. That afternoon the rest of the fleet anchored at the head of the Bay. Prince George then landed with 1,800 English and Dutch marines and the handful of Spanish

15

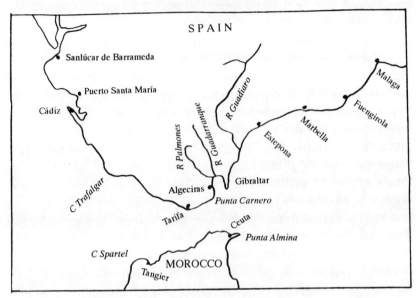

Map of the Strait

volunteers he had with him, at the mouth of the Guadarranque. The only resistance was from some 50 horsemen who were easily driven off, and the Prince summoned the town to surrender. The town refused and the following day Byng warped his ships as close as he could to the town walls against a light easterly wind.

North of the South Mole the water shoaled and it was impossible to approach nearer than 700 yards. The wind was fitful and not all ships were able to reach their appointed stations but they were instructed to position themselves as best they could. The order of battle from south to north was as follows: to bombard the New Mole, HMS *Yarmouth* 70 (Captain Hicks), *Lenox* 70 (Captain Jumper), *Kingston* 70, *Burford* 70, *Monck* 60, and *Berwick* 70. To bombard the South Bastion and town, HMS *Swiftsure* 70, *Nassau* 80, *Nottingham* 60 (Captain Whitaker), *Eagle* 70, *Montagu* 60, *Grafton* 70, *Ranelagh* 80, (Byng's flagship), *Essex* 70, *Suffolk* 70, and *Monmouth* 70. The six Dutch ships and two of the 'bombs' under Rear-Admiral Van der Dussen operated against the old Mole and North Bastion. That evening Byng got the Dutch mortar boats to fire a few shells into the town, and at midnight, as the ships were being warped into position, he ordered Captain Whitaker to send boats to burn a French privateer that lay off the Old Mole.

The following morning, 3 August, the guns of the fortress started up at 5am but did not continue firing long. The number of guns in the fortress had been increased to about 100 since 1693 and there was plenty of powder, but there were only 80 soldiers to service them. The town militia (350 strong) had been called up, but most of them were positioned along the northern fortifications, facing Prince George's marines. At 6am the ships started their bombardment, and many of the inhabitants fled from the town and took refuge on the Upper Rock or at the shrine of Our Lady of Europa at Europa Point. After a while, Byng ordered his ships not to fire unnecessarily and only to use their lower deck guns which were the heaviest. At noon he ordered a complete cease fire so that he could study the effect of the bombardment when the smoke had cleared. It was seen that some of the guns in the New Mole fort of El Tuerto had been dismounted and Byng sent Captain Whitaker to Rooke to request reinforcements from the rest of the fleet for a landing. At the same time he ordered all the boats he had available to be manned under the command of Captain Jasper Hicks the commander of the southern bombardment division.

As the boats neared the New Mole, Sir Clowdisly Shovell who was on board Rooke's flagship saw that a large number of women and children who had taken refuge in the shrine of Our Lady of Europa in order to escape the bombardment had now started to make their way back to town so as not to be cut off. Shovell did not want them to get involved in the fighting so he ordered guns to be fired in their direction, and forced them to return to the safety of the shrine.[3]

By the time Whitaker had arrived with reinforcements, Hicks and Captain William Jumper of HMS *Lenox* had landed at the New Mole, and their sailors had entered the fort there. There was then a tremendous explosion and the fort blew up, 42 sailors were killed, including two lieutenants, and 60 were wounded and many of the boats were destroyed. It is possible that the defenders sprang a mine, but it in more likely that some of the sailors had entered the gunpowder store room carrying lighted fuses for their muskets and there was an accidental explosion.

The result was confusion and the sailors started to retreat. Whitaker arrived just in time to rally the dazed attackers. The fighting was resumed and the New Mole and the redoubt, which was half-way between the Mole and the South Bastion, were soon in English hands and the Union Flag was raised over the redoubt.

Rooke then ordered Byng to go to Southport to summon the town, by drum, to surrender. Byng went ashore and did as he was ordered. While he waited for an answer he mounted guards round the Chapel of Our Lady of Europa, to protect the women and children who had taken refuge there, from insult by the sailors. That evening, Don Diego de Salinas, the Governor of Gibraltar, sent back the drum with the answer that he would give up the town the following morning and produce hostages, provided he was allowed honourable terms. Byng dined that night in the Chapel of the Knights of Malta which stood where the South Barracks were subsequently built.[4]

The following morning, Byng went to see Prince George, who was encamped on the isthmus, to explain to him the situation at Southport and the New Mole. While they were talking, the hostages came from the town to make their capitulation and Byng was asked to protect the women at the Shrine of Our Lady of Europa from the rudeness of the sailors. Byng assured them that he had posted sentries to protect them and the articles of capitulation were then agreed. The garrison was allowed to depart with its arms and baggage, and three brass cannons with 12 charges of powder and ball, as well as food and wine for 6 days' march. The inhabitants were allowed to depart freely or to remain secure in their rights, possessions and religion, provided that they took an oath of allegiance to the Archduke as King of Spain. The French in the town were not allowed to leave but were made prisoners.

After the capitulation had been signed, Prince George took possession of the northern defences and gates, and Byng hurried to the south to arrange for the women to return to the town. The sailors were then embarked to prevent looting, apart from 200 who stayed at the New Mole and 50 more in the redoubt (now Jumper's Bastion), until they were relieved by marines. Although sailors and marines had taken part in disorders and looting ashore, order had been quickly restored by the senior officers.[5]

When Rooke landed at Waterport that 4 August for the formal ceremony of possession he found that Prince George had raised his flag (the flag of the House of Hapsburg) over Landport Gate. What followed next has been the subject of controversy between British and Spanish historians as no mention of it appears in the British accounts, but the dispute has been settled by the Spanish historian José Carlos de Luna who found an eyewitness account by a certain Antonio Sanchez de Ita in the archives of the Marqués de Olmeda.

This states that the astonished bystanders saw Rooke hand a Union Flag to Captain Hicks, who, accompanied by a colour party of six armed sailors preceded by a fife and drum, traversed the place of arms at Landport Gate and disappeared up an internal staircase. He reappeared at the top of the gate, lowered George's flag and raised the Union Flag in its place. The Spanish witness misunderstood the meaning of this and presumed that this meant that Rooke was trying to usurp the sovereignty of Gibraltar from the Archduke.[6] This of course

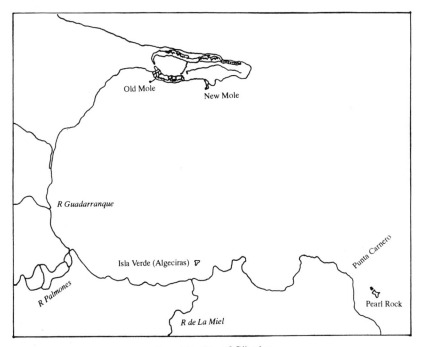

Map of the Bay of Gibraltar

was not the case, as Rooke's instructions from the government were to make sure that the inhabitants of any city captured in Spain took an oath of fidelity to the Archduke.[7]

However, a layman could hardly be expected to understand naval flag etiquette. Whenever a ship was captured by the French Navy the colours were hauled down, reversed and raised again; the Royal Navy's practice was different; they lowered the captured colours and then raised their own. What was at issue was not the sovereignty of Gibraltar (for Prince George was left to exercise the command in the name of the Archduke) but the importance of acknowledging who had captured the fortress. It certainly was not Prince George, who had remained on the isthmus with the marines. The fortress had been secured by the sailors' landing at South Mole, without the participation of the military. Rooke felt it was right that their heroism and sacrifices (they had 100 dead and 260 wounded) should thus be publicly acknowledged.

The significance of this incident was that if prize money was awarded by Parliament for the capture of Gibraltar, the evidence of who captured it and which flag was raised would affect the share that went to the Navy. The Royal Marines had only recently been formed and formed part of the Army at the time and not the Royal Navy. In the event, no prize money was awarded, for Gibraltar was not a captured enemy city but a possession that had been restored to an ally. However, a number of officers and men who went ashore had helped themselves unofficially to abandoned property and Byng embarked twelve brass guns from the fortress.[8]

The Royal Marines did not play a very active part in the capture of Gibraltar, but they gave ample demonstration of their tenacity and heroism in the siege that was to follow. Most of the inhabitants left when the Spanish troops marched out and only 20 families and some priests stayed behind. After a few days of tidying up Rooke sailed away to water his ships again, and Prince George was left in command of Gibraltar. The marines stayed with him.

In spite of Byng's forebodings, Gibraltar had been captured easily. The fortifications were so strong that the 14,000 cannon balls fired at them during the bombardment had made no impression, but the lack of a proper garrison was decisive. Philip V had been unable to garrison properly all the places that were threatened by Rooke's marauding fleet, and in the Strait area had concentrated on defending the important commercial port of Cadiz, attacked by the Royal Navy many times before, to the detriment of Gibraltar. The Spaniards were unaware that the Royal Navy had an interest in Gibraltar which went back for three quarters of a century, as it had never been manifested publicly. The plans of Bruce, Cromwell, Beckmann and Pepys had finally come to fruition.

Van der Dussen had been detached to Lisbon with five sail of the line, and the fleet was watering at Tetuan, when news reached Rooke on 20 August that the French fleet had sailed out of Toulon under the Count of Toulouse, the 26 year old illegitimate son of Louis XIV, and was on its way. Rooke immediately held a council of war and it was resolved that the fleet should lie to the east of Gibraltar to protect it from attack by the French and at the same time stop the enemy from getting through the Strait. The fleet re-embarked half the marines that had been landed at Gibraltar. The wind was easterly and the French had the weather gauge, but they were in no hurry to engage in combat as they first wanted to collect the 22 galleys which were sheltering in Malaga harbour. This delay enabled the embarkation of the marines to be conducted without hindrance.

The enemy had not yet appeared on the 23rd although their signal guns were heard in the distance. Another council of war was held and it was determined that the allied fleet should go in search of them, but only as far as Malaga. It was important not to leave Gibraltar uncovered and the fleet was short of supplies and could not afford to conduct another sweep deep into the western Mediterranean. At 11 in the morning the fleets finally met south of Malaga. The allies formed their line of battle 24 miles south-west of Fuengirola and the French formed theirs to the east. Both fleets were bearing south. The wind then dropped and nothing more happened that day.

The morning of the 24th dawned with the two lines lying nine miles from each other. They were equal in strength with 51 ships of the line each. The allies were stronger in frigates but the French had their galleys. In the engagement that followed the van under Sir Clowdisley Shovell did well, as did the outnumbered Dutch in the rear, under

Lieutenant-Admiral Callenburgh, but the fight in the centre under Rooke was inconclusive. The battle continued until 7 that evening when the fleets broke off the engagement 21 miles south of Fuengirola. Many of the allied ships which had taken part in the bombardment of Gibraltar had run out of ammunition. For the next two days the fleets lay just out of range of each other, repairing damage, and in the case of the allies, sharing out the remaining ammunition with those ships that were short. The fitful wind veered from east to west and then backed again to the east.

The 27th dawned hazily and Rooke could not make out the French so he set sail for the Strait in case the enemy had gone to the east of him during the night; but Toulouse had withdrawn and was on his way back to his base at Toulon. Both fleets were badly battered and had many casualties and both sides claimed the Battle of Malaga as a victory. The French had inflicted the greater damage, but Gibraltar had been saved from attack and Prince George had a chance to consolidate his position.[9]

It was a severely damaged allied fleet that entered Gibraltar Bay after the battle. The naval campaign for the year was now over, but before he set sail on 8 September, Rooke left the garrison of Gibraltar all the reinforcements he could spare. The marines and Spanish volunteers were left behind with enough provisions for three months. Sixty large guns were landed with their gunners, and a number of carpenters to help repair and strengthen the defences. Fresh supplies were obtained from Morocco - 50 heifers, some sheep and 2,000 quarters of corn; and some small vessels were left behind to assist the garrison - two small bomb ships, a fire ship and two victuallers.[10]

Although Gibraltar was now under the rule of the Pretender Charles III, its garrison was mainly British, and money supplied by Methune (the English minister in Portugal) and arms and ammunition from England sustained the place. Above all, Prince George depended on the Royal Navy for protection and supplies, so when Rooke sailed for England with the fleet, he left Sir John Leake at Lisbon with eleven sail of the line and half a dozen smaller ships.

Engineers and masons were required to repair and strengthen the fortifications and an engineer, Captain Joseph Bennett, with a party of masons and carpenters was sent from Lisbon. They were unable to get to Gibraltar as a French squadron of 19 sail (under Baron de Pointis) had arrived on 4 October and was blockading the Bay. The reinforcements were therefore landed at Tangier and had to slip through the blockade in small local craft.[11]

The Spaniards under the Marquess of Villadarias now tried to retake Gibraltar, but the poor roads of the area delayed the concentration of their forces. On 20 October they started opening their trenches in the isthmus, and on 26 October they commenced their bombardment. By the time Leake arrived with an augmented squadron of 24 sail on 9 November, the siege was in full swing. Both Colonel Fox who commanded the marines and Henry Nugent, an Irish Catholic who had been appointed Governor by Prince George, had been killed. But de Pointis had gone into Cadiz leaving only six ships to watch the Bay. Leake's squadron therefore had no difficulty in capturing one of the French frigates and the others were run ashore and burnt. Pending the arrival of further reinforcements Leake landed 300 seamen every morning to assist in the work of repairing the fortifications. They returned to their ships every evening. With the Royal Navy now controlling the waters of the Strait, supplies started to flow in, including a strong detachment of the Grenadier Guards under Brigadier Shrimpton, who was given the rank of major-general in Charles III's army and was appointed governor.

The siege continued. The garrison was now well supplied and reinforced, and with Leake's ships controlling the sea, Gibraltar was safe. But on 3 January 1705, after being on station for two stormy winter months, Leake was forced to return to his base in Lisbon to replenish and carry out repairs. With Leake away the enemy, now strongly reinforced with French troops commanded by Marshal Tessé, redoubled their efforts to recapture Gibraltar. On 16 February, de Pointis was back with 26 men of war. The garrison thought that they were now to be assaulted by sea as well as by land, and morale, after almost three months of constant fighting, was at a low ebb. After landing supplies de Pointis' ships were forced by severe storms to take refuge in nearby Spanish ports.

As soon as the news arrived in Lisbon of the renewed attack, Leake (flying his flag in HMS *Nottingham* 60) set out for Gibraltar. On 21 March he entered the Strait with a south-westerly gale and off Punta Carnero encountered de Pointis emerging from the Bay with only five ships of the line, as the others had been driven into the Mediterranean by the tempest. Leake had a substantial fleet of 35 sail - 23 English, 4 Dutch and 8 Portuguese. De Pointis' flagship the *Magnanime* 80 was driven ashore to the west of Marbella, as was the *Lys* 88 and both ships were burnt by their crews. The *Arrogant* 58 was captured by a squadron under Sir Thomas Dilke in HMS *Revenge* 70, and the *Ardent* 64 and *Marquis* 58 were captured by the Dutch. The Battle of Marbella showed how hopeless the Spanish prospects were for the siege of Gibraltar as long as the Royal Navy controlled the sea. After Leake anchored in the Bay on 31 March the enemy forces started to withdraw and the siege was lifted.[12]

A British naval base

The Rock was now safe in English hands, although officially it was held in trust for the Pretender to the Spanish throne. Prince George decided however that Gibraltar was not the proper place from which to launch an invasion of the centre of the peninsula. In August 1705 he left for Barcelona with an invasion force commanded by Sir Clowdisley Shovell and the Earl of Peterborough, and he was killed during the attack on the Castle of Montjuich at Barcelona. Gibraltar became a backwater forgotten by everybody except the Royal Navy, and when Shrimpton, who was the Archduke's appointee as governor, died in December 1707 Queen Anne selected Colonel Roger Elliott as the next governor.

Gibraltar's deficiencies as a naval base now became clear. Its short mole could only shelter a few ships and careening was difficult. The anchorage at the head of the Bay, by the Old Mole, was dangerously exposed to the winter Levanter storms. What was more, Gibraltar did not produce anything and all supplies had to be imported. There was not even enough drinking water for a large fleet which had to go to Tetuan for supplies. The war zone now shifted to the southern French coast and in September 1708, Minorca was captured for the sake of its great natural harbour of Port Mahon. From now on this was to be the main naval base in the Mediterranean, though Lisbon was still used and there was a victualling agent there until 1733.[13]

Gibraltar was still useful as a base to protect merchant shipping in the Strait, particularly against the Barbary pirates, and also for blocking the main French fleet from leaving the Mediterranean. But after the Battles of Malaga and Marbella, the larger French vessels were laid up and the fleet did not come out in strength again. Instead of trying to wrest control of the sea from the allies, France now adopted the policy of commerce raiding advocated by the engineer Vauban. Nevertheless it was felt to be in the Navy's interest to continue to hold Gibraltar, and although it was the Army that held the place, the Navy acknowledged its obligations by making itself responsible until 1715 for the supplies for the garrison and the Spanish civilians who had remained behind.[14]

The years of fighting brought no definite results. Madrid was twice occupied by the allies, and twice lost. The allied forces in the Peninsula suffered heavy defeats at Almansa in 1707 and Brihuega in 1710, and it became obvious that a stalemate had been reached as the bulk of the population of Spain (with the exception of the Catalans) closed ranks behind Philip V and the house of Bourbon. In 1711 the Emperor of Austria died and the Pretender Charles abandoned Spain to succeed his brother. Both France and England were exhausted financially and were tired of the war so peace negotiations were started.

After 18 months of discussion the Treaty of Utrecht was signed in April 1713. Under the treaty both Minorca and Gibraltar were ceded to England. Gibraltar, which had been effectively under British control for almost eight years, now became legally a British possession.

Notes and References

(1)   Francis 109-110.
(2)   Francis 32,109.
(3)   Laughton 142.
(4)   Clowes 2:392-396; Francis 109-115; Luna 307-319; Laughton 137-145, 189-194.
(5)   Laughton 144-145, 194.
(6)   Luna 319-320.
(7)   Leadam points out that this was in accordance with the instructions Nottingham had given the Duke of Ormonde before the capture of Cadiz the previous year: 'Her majesty is resolv'd that upon taking or surrender of that or any other place, the burghers shall take an oath of fidelity to the Archduke, tho' the garrison left by your grace shall be entirely under her majesty's orders and commands.' (page 60)
(8)   Hills 180-181.

(9) Clowes 2:396-404.
(10) Francis 119; *An Exact Journal*
(11) Kuenzel 482; Francis 129.
(12) *An Exact Journal*, Clowes 2:404; Jenkins 100-101; Martin-Leake 1:239-270; The London Gazette No 4093, Monday 29 Jan 1704 OS.
(13) Baugh *Naval Administration 1715 - 1750*, 326.
(14) Merriman 249; Baugh ibid 401; CO 91:5 letters of J Conduit, Commissary of Stores at Gibraltar, 30 July and 7 August 1714 OS.

CHAPTER III

THE EIGHTEENTH CENTURY.

With Minorca as well as Gibraltar in British hands, the Rock became of secondary importance for the Royal Navy, and the magnificent harbour of Port Mahon in Minorca was made its main Mediterranean base. It was there that the Navy established its facilities, including the first hospital for serving seamen. Sickness was rife in the ships of the Mediterranean squadron as a result of the salt diet and the ships' system of replenishing water supplies from insalubrious sources. The building of a hospital to replace the hired accommodation (which had proved totally inadequate) was authorised in 1709, but money was not forthcoming. Admiral Jennings and his officers had to finance the project out of their own pockets, and as the Admiralty was reluctant to reimburse them they only obtained their money after petitioning Queen Anne.[1]

In Gibraltar, the Army took over the old seamen's hospital of St. John of God, above the town, which had been built by Juan Mateos in the 16th century. It was described as two 'sheds or Hutts, capable of receiving about Thirty Men', and Admiral Jennings arranged for the Surgeon General of the Garrison to admit sick sailors. For each sailor he received an allowance of bread and coals and a cash allowance for their food, care and funeral if required,[2] and this appears to have become its main purpose. During the 1727 Siege, the hospital was given over entirely to the Army, but the following year it was returned to the Navy.[3]

This small hospital was totally inadequate; a single ship of the line could have more than 100 sick. Ships were therefore sent to land their sick at Port Mahon, but in emergencies sheds and warehouses were sometimes rented and converted for temporary use. In 1743, for example, before the new Naval Hospital was completed, Edward Hawke arrived in command of HMS *Berwick* 70; he had so many sick among the

Head of New Mole in 18th century

crew (mostly from scurvy) that he asked to be sent to Minorca to hospitalise his men. When he arrived at Port Mahon on 12 November, he immediately 'sent to the Hospital 100 Seamen and 20 Marines'. By 19 December he had sent almost another hundred, and smaller numbers continued to be sent to the hospital until the end of the month. The small hospital at Gibraltar was hardly able to cope with such demands even from a single ship.[4]

The main office and supply depot for the Victualling Agent and his two clerks was established in the old Convent of Mercenary Fathers (known as the White Cloisters to differentiate it from the Great Cloisters of St Francis - now the Convent - where the governor had established his residence). The offices of Bland and Gibraltar Motorways are today situated where the White Cloisters stood, and until recently you could see some of the old columns in the offices of Gibraltar Motorways. Some of these pillars have been resited at the entrance to Trafalgar House. The Victualler had his dwelling and garden in College Lane; and the triangle between Cooperage lane and Casemates was known as the Navy Yard. Here there were a number of small warehouses, and a cooperage for water casks (which gave the Lane its name) near the Water Gate. The absence of a building large enough for a mast-house meant that spare masts did not last long when protected only by 'boards and tarred canvas.'[5]

A report to the Navy Board in 1724 describes the Navy's storage facilities:

All the small stores are in the White Convent being situate in the middle of the town, near the Parade, which are always landed at the Old Mould, being near half a mile distance from the Convent. It was granted for that service by the Right Honourable the Earl of Portmore in March 1720/21, he being Governor of Gibraltar. When there were cables in store, they were lodged in a Store House near the Water Gate or Old Mould, hired of Mr. Thos: Chambers.

The Careening Geer, with what hawsers there are for hawling ships in and out of the New Mould, are lodged in the Soldiers'

Barracks, in the Fort which commands the New Mould, by the licence of the Governor.

Memo.

There is no matter of Conveniency for securing Masts, Yards, Timbers or Anchors, but, humbly presume there may be Sufficient Ones near the Fort at The New Mould.[6]

[Spelling as original!]

Gibraltar was mainly used as the base for a few cruisers to protect British shipping from the Salé corsairs, and for this the shelter offered by the New Mole was adequate as half-a-dozen ships of the line could shelter comfortably behind it protected from the south-westerly storms. Ships could even be careened in this shelter and have their keels hauled above the waterline by means of ships' capstans placed on the mole so that their bottoms could be cleaned and caulked. At the time of the 1727 Siege, Captain George Purvis made the harbour more commodious by blowing up rocks which might damage ships laid on their beam ends to careen, and by 'scalping' and smoothing the side of the mole so that there were 5 fathoms of water close alongside. Additional capstans, careening hawsers and blocks were sent out from Portsmouth and transported to Gibraltar by the relieving fleet under Sir Charles Wager. Brushwood was needed for the cleaning work and in time of peace permission was sometimes obtained from the Spanish commander to cut it from the beaches at the head of the Bay. Otherwise it had to be imported from Tetuan as the Rock had been totally denuded during the 1704 - 1705 Siege.[7]

Drinking water was normally obtained from the Red Sands (the Alameda) and the full barrels were taken down the hill by the South Bastion to a gate in a stockade on the waterside. To facilitate the loading of the barrels into the ships' boats a small wharf was built in 1736. The boats sent to collect the barrels carried a small stump mast that was used as a crane for handling them. This type of mast was known to seamen as a 'ragged-staff' and this name was given by sailors to the wharf and to the gate in the stone wall that replaced the stockade. Eventually water tanks were constructed close to the wharf which were fed by pipes direct from the springs above, so that the boats could fill their casks more easily.[8]

The duty of protecting trade, which fell on the Navy, not only required them to escort merchant ships but also to engage in diplomatic negotiations with the Moroccan authorities and establish and enforce treaties which would protect British merchant ships. When these failed, it was the duty of the naval officers to arrange for the ransoming of British nationals captured by the corsairs. In 1713 Captain George Paddon who was Commodore on the station, negotiated a satisfactory renewal of treaties with Morocco. However, Vice-Admiral Cornwall, who became commander-in-chief in the Mediterranean in 1716, decided to take a strong stand against the Salé pirates and this led to a total breakdown of relations and a state of war. In 1720 Commodore Charles Stewart was sent out with a squadron to negotiate a new treaty and he went on to Mekenes the following year to ransom

296 English being what were left alive (and had not turned Moors) of those who had been taken in the ... war.[9]

War clouds were looming again over Europe and Spain made it clear that she was going to make another attempt to regain Gibraltar, so in 1726 a small squadron was sent out under Vice-Admiral Edward Hopsonn to protect Gibraltar. He was followed in January the following year by Vice-Admiral Sir Charles Wager, who arrived in the Bay with seven ships of the line on 2 February OS. As the Spaniards only had small lateen-rigged craft, the Royal Navy controlled the waters round Gibraltar, and ships were sent to Eastern beach to throw a flanking fire on the Spanish trenches. The Navy was able to ensure that supplies reached the garrison, and was also able to interrupt supplies reaching the besieging army by sea. This was a serious matter for the besiegers, as the roads leading from Cadiz and Malaga were very bad and the wet weather made them almost impassable, so the Siege was abandoned after three months. The Royal Navy also captured a number of Spanish supply ships that the garrison found extremely useful, as well as *Nuestra Señora del Rosario* 46, a new man-of-war on her way from Santander to Cadiz. One diarist records that the weather was very bad during the months from February to May, and on 28 February OS, three prizes anchored in the Bay were wrecked. The normal anchoring place, apart from the restricted area inside the New Mole, was between the Old Mole and the isthmus, but as this was directly under the Spanish guns it obviously could not be used during the Siege, so these prizes must have been anchored off Rosia.[10]

After peace had been restored and the Spaniards had lifted the Siege and dispersed their army, the fleet returned home on 19 March 1728 OS. The final entries by our diarist giving an account of the return of the fleet to Britain are amusing:

> 19 - This Day Sir Charles with 5 other ships sail'd out of the Bay
> with a small breeze at East & was saluted with 21 Guns by the
> other Squadron & with the same Number by ye Garrison which
> the Admiral Return'd with 21 more.

After all that noisy saluting the fleet sailed to the west, but:

> 20 - This morning at 4 we found ourselves off Malaga 12 Leagues
> to the East of Gibraltar, drove by the current tho' an E. breeze.
> 21 - Came into Gibraltar Bay again and went on shore.
> 22 - Set sail again Wind E. & a Strong Gale.
> They anchored at Spithead on 9 April.[11]

This incident demonstrated the problems of navigating the Strait in the days of sail when contrary winds might keep many vessels becalmed or 'backstrapped' (ie with the sails slack against the masts) in the lee of the Rock for weeks on end gave the name Backstrap Bay to the sweep of Mediterranean coast between Europa Point and Punta Mala. This name was also acquired by the cove between Catalan and Sandy Bays because of its complete lack of wind in a westerly. Sometimes the name is given as 'Blackstrap' and is supposed to refer to the cheap dark red wine sold to the sailors by boats from the shore while their ships were becalmed.[12]

War of the Austrian Succession

During the remaining 73 years of the eighteenth century Britain went to war with Spain and/or France on four separate occasions and Gibraltar played its due part as a base during each of these wars. The first was the War of Jenkins' Ear. This was precipitated by the contraband trade that British merchants persisted in conducting with the Spanish colonies in South America, and the strenuous, and sometimes violent, efforts that Spain made to stop this illicit trade. It later merged into the War of the Austrian Succession which involved most of the European powers.

In 1731 a Spanish privateer captain named Juan de Leon Fandino captured the Jamaican ship *Rebecca*, and used Richard Jenkins, the captain, 'in a most barbarous and inhuman manner, taking all his money, cutting off one of his ears, plundering him of those necessaries which were to carry the ship safely home.' This incident went virtually unnoticed at the time but became a *cause célèbre* a few years later when tempers on both sides had reached breaking point. As war seemed imminent a fleet was sent to the West Indies and another, under Admiral Nicholas Haddock was sent to reinforce the small Strait squadron in 1738.[13]

Haddock had to keep his fleet in the Strait to keep apart the two Spanish squadrons at Cadiz and Cartagena and he therefore had to use Gibraltar and not Minorca as his main base. Its deficiencies soon became apparent. The ships' bottoms became foul and it was impossible to careen and clean all of them in the restricted area of the New Mole. The nearest friendly harbour where this could be done was Faro in the Algarve. Haddock did not in fact get his ships careened until a threatened Spanish invasion of Minorca caused him to move his base of operation to that island. When, however, work had to be done on a ship at Gibraltar, local labour was poorly paid and inefficient and the rates of pay were not sufficiently high to attract skilled labour from Lisbon. So at times gangs of workmen had to be sent out from the English dockyards. There was also a great amount of sickness in the ships and the hospital at Gibraltar was completely inadequate. In July 1739 Haddock had rented the only house to the southward, to accommodate 160 sick, and when in December typhus-ridden ships entered the harbour the sick men had to be 'lodged either in the House, Sail Loft, ... [or] Tents erected by the respective ships'. It was therefore decided to build a new hospital for the Navy. In October 1739 the Duke of Newcastle wrote to the Lieutenant-Governor of Gibraltar instructing him 'to appoint a certain piece of Ground ... for the erecting a Naval Hospital for their sick and wounded.'[14]

The place chosen for the new hospital was on a cliff to the south of the town, well away from the effects of the humid Levanter winds that tend to hang over the Rock, and also sheltered from the Spanish land batteries by a shoulder of rock. The plans for the new hospital were eventually approved in 1741 and by November craftsmen were being recruited from Portsmouth dockyard for the work. The plans provided for a hospital that could accommodate a thousand patients in a two storey building constructed round a quadrangle with deep verandahs overlooking the courtyard. The wards ran the full depth of the building but could be isolated by using the verandahs as corridors. An entrance gate and staff quarters were added on the north side. The new building was completed in 1744 at a cost of £20,898, and the old building was handed over to the Army and turned into the 'Blue Barracks'.[15]

The war lasted until 1748 but did not produce any spectacular battles, as the leadership of the Royal Navy at sea was not very inspired and battles tended to be set pieces and inconclusive. After France entered the war on the side of Spain, the theatre of war in the Mediterranean moved to the Riviera coasts of France and Italy. Port Mahon once again became the important naval base in the area. Gibraltar was, however, used intermittently for watching the main Spanish base at Cadiz; and for launching attacks upon the ships from the Spanish colonies that normally came laden to that harbour with the treasure of the silver mines of South America. In 1741 the Spanish admiral, Navarro, showed that he could traverse the Strait at night, with a following wind, without being sighted by the British fleet refitting at Gibraltar. His feat was made possible by the poor performance of the Royal Navy frigates on guard outside Cadiz.[16]

The war brought about changes in the jurisdiction of some of the colonies, including Gibraltar and Minorca, that were to have an important influence on future developments. This was the setting up of a Court of Vice Admiralty. The reason for this was the desire of the British Government that the colonies should arm and send out privateers. Before letters of marque could be issued to them, they had to present sureties before a court of Admiralty; though until 1759, owners of privateers could act as their own guarantors. Any captures had also to be presented to an Admiralty Court before it could be condemned as a lawful prize. In the beginning the powers of these colonial Vice Admiralty Courts in this respect, were severely restricted, as under the Prize Act of 1739 all Spanish galleons and register ships taken could only be condemned by the High Court of Admiralty in London. It was expected that galleons bearing large quantities of treasure would be involved and this would be too important a matter for inferior courts to handle.[17]

Seven Years War

The peace that was ushered in by the Treaty of Aix-la-Chapelle of 1748 was soon broken by French military activity on the western frontier of the American colonies along the Valley of the Ohio. In July 1755, Major-General Braddock who had gone from the command of Gibraltar to that of the Western frontier was defeated and killed by the French at the Battle of the Monongahela although Britain and France were officially at peace. Britain retaliated by imposing an Atlantic blockade, to stop the French sending reinforcements to Canada, and the Royal Navy captured a large number of French merchant ships.

In the same month, two French privateers cruising in the Strait stopped a Gibraltar boat, *La Concepcion*, which was making a voyage back from Tetuan, laden with supplies, on the pretext that it was carrying enemy (Moroccan) nationals and goods. The master of the *Concepcion*, Agustin Berrio, acted in a spirited manner in the face of overwhelming force. He refused to hand over his Moroccan passengers or their goods - or to haul down his colours - saying that he would rather 'Choose to be sunk than to consent in the doing such an affront to the King of Great Britain his Master'. The French privateers decided to take their prize back to Toulon. On the voyage back they called at Malaga, and while by international law, privateers could take their prizes into neutral ports and even sell them in wartime, Britain and France were not yet at war, so the British Consul intervened and the *Concepcion* was freed.[18]

War was inevitable. The French threatened an invasion of Britain, but in reality massed their forces for an invasion of Minorca. The garrison of that island was in a very sorry state, 41 of the senior officers, including the Governor, Lord Tyrawley, and the colonels of the three regiments stationed there, were absent. The command was in the hands of the Lieutenant-Governor, Lieutenant-General Blakeney, an 82 year-old veteran in a poor state of health. When the possibility of invasion became known in London, a fleet was prepared and placed under the command of Vice-Admiral John Byng, who sailed for the Mediterranean on 6 April 1756 and arrived at Gibraltar with nine ships of the line in May. He was there joined by the two ships of the line already on station. He was supposed to take one of the Gibraltar regiments on board and land it at Minorca, but Lieutenant-General Fowke, the Governor of Gibraltar, refused to part with it because he feared a Spanish attack. Byng now learnt that the French had landed a force of 14,000 men in the north of Minorca, outnumbering the defendants five to one. He therefore set sail for Minorca on 8 May and when he arrived on the 19 he found the British fortress of Fort St. Philip in Port Mahon, heavily invested. The enemy fleet was then sighted and both fleets manoeuvred to obtain the weather gauge. Byng was successful in this, but when battle was joined the following morning his strict adherence to line ahead formation meant that the battle was indecisive as both fleets were fairly evenly matched. Then, despairing of being able to assist the beleaguered garrison he returned to Gibraltar leaving Minorca to its fate. The garrison of Fort St Philip surrendered shortly after.

The news reached London through France in an exaggerated form, before Byng's dispatches could arrive. As a result Vice-Admiral Edward Hawke was sent out in the frigate HMS *Antelope* to replace him, and with him came Lord Tyrawley, the absent Governor of Minorca, who had orders to relieve Fowke at Gibraltar. Byng was subsequently court martialled and was found guilty under the 12th Article of War, of not having done his utmost, through negligence, to destroy the enemy's fleet and save Minorca from capture. There was only one penalty for this under the Articles of War and that was death. The Court dutifully passed sentence never expecting that it would be carried out. But the Duke of Newcastle, then Prime Minister, and Anson, the First Lord of the Admiralty, were determined to focus the guilt on Byng in order to deflect attention from their own maladministration which had resulted in the Minorca fiasco. George II stubbornly refused to exercise the prerogative of mercy in spite of being pressed to do so by William Pitt, and Byng died bravely on the quarterdeck of HMS *Monarch*, in front of a firing squad of marines. This led Voltaire to pass the sardonic comment 'In this country it is thought well to kill an admiral from time to time to encourage the others.'[19]

Hawke stayed on in the Mediterranean using Gibraltar as his main base. A French privateer captured an English merchant ship and took refuge in Algeciras. This was quite legitimate although Spain was neutral at the time, but the sight of this enemy ship just across the Bay from his main base was too much of a provocation. Hawke asked the Spanish authorities to order the French ship and her captive out of the port and, when they refused to do so, sent in the boats of the fleet to cut out the captured ship. This they succeeded in doing, in the teeth of the deadly fire poured out by the privateer and the Spanish battery. The merchant ship was towed to Gibraltar, but the boats suffered 150 casualties between dead and wounded.[20] Hawke returned to Britain in December leaving Rear-Admiral Charles Saunders in command.

Once again Gibraltar's inadequacy as a base was to be tested, but in spite of its shortcomings it proved quite effective in controlling the entrance to the Mediterranean and the passage into the Atlantic of the French fleet from their main base at Toulon. When Saunders heard, in April 1757, that a French force was anchored outside Malaga, he left Gibraltar to intercept them. He caught up with them at sunset on 5 April but the French ships were better sailers and got away during the night and slipped through the Strait aided by a brisk Levanter.[21] In May he was succeeded by Vice-Admiral Osborne.

British trade was well protected and the exit from the Mediterranean secured, but there were no important fleet actions for several years. Gibraltar's most active part was as a base for privateers, particularly now that Minorca was not available and they all had to operate from the Rock.

Many masters of small Mediterranean vessels had come to live in Gibraltar and Minorca in order to take advantage of the Mediterranean Passes, issued to ships of British register, which protected them from capture by the Barbary corsairs. They now became enthusiastic privateers. Saunders was suspicious of ships which had no British crews and were commanded 'by a Jew or a Genoese' whom he considered bad characters and a disgrace to their commissions.

The privateers were active and successful and of course attracted their share of complaints, as Naval officers did not like them. Saunders was no exception and though he fulminated against them he was unable to level any specific charges. Naval officers, including Nelson, objected to privateers because at times they had been known to turn to piracy against neutral vessels instead of confining their attention to enemy shipping. But they were also in competition with the Royal Navy for the capture of lucrative prizes, and this was resented as it deprived Naval officers of prize money. Also there was the more serious charge that they attracted men away from the warships' crews; as most seamen preferred the short cruises, laxer discipline, and higher rewards they could obtain in ships carrying letters of marque, to conditions in HM ships. In time of war a Royal Navy ship might be abroad for years at a time, with the crews confined to the vessels and never allowed ashore.

The privateers brought a period of great prosperity to the colony. John Ward, the leading merchant at Gibraltar, reputedly became 'as rich as Croesus'. When Spain joined in the war in 1762, Spanish coastal trade was open to their attacks and additional privateers were licensed in Gibraltar. The new Prize Act of 1759 no longer required Spanish ships to be taken to England in order to be condemned as legitimate prizes.[22]

The disasters of 1756 - the loss of Minorca and the Black Hole of Calcutta - led to a change in the Ministry and William Pitt took over as Prime minister. Under his inspiring leadership and war-winning strategy Britain doubled the size of its overseas empire. In 1759 the Army won victories in Montreal and Minden, and the Navy in Lagos and Quiberon Bay. In far away India, Clive and Eyre Coote had already decisively defeated the French and 1759 became known as the Year of Victories, and, such was the sense of national pride and self-confidence it engendered, it inspired the actor David Garrick to write the stirring words of *Heart of Oak*,

... 'tis to glory we steer,
to add something more to this wonderful year; ...
We'll fight and we'll conquer again and again.

During the Seven Years War the Royal Navy produced an outstanding list of admirals - Anson, Hawke, Boscawen, Keppel, Saunders, Rodney and Howe, all of whom were imbued with the feeling that there was no task too difficult for the Navy and that they could not be defeated whatever the odds against them. They founded a naval tradition that made Britannia the ruler of the waves. In future wars this supremacy was to be assured by two technical innovations.

First, during the War of the American Revolution (1775-1783) it became general practice in the Royal Navy to sheath ships' bottoms with copper, this slowed down the growth of marine organisms on the hull and meant that ships did not become sluggish even after long periods at sea. Second, in 1779, the Carron foundry in Glasgow introduced the 'carronade', a light gun firing a heavy shot over a short distance which was ideal for hammering and holing the hulls of enemy vessels. It had long been the practice in the Royal Navy to aim at the hulls of enemy ships though the French usually aimed at the rigging. Shooting down a ship's masts could stop it dead in the water but it would only be sunk or forced to surrender by having its hull battered to pieces. The problem had been that English ships tended to mount lighter guns than the French or Spanish, and the addition of carronades to the armament after 1779 corrected this weakness. Thus Nelson was to inherit both the tradition and the means to annihilate his enemies and this enabled him to set the seal on the Royal Navy's supremacy at sea.

The efficacy of Gibraltar in guarding the entrance to the Mediterranean was demonstrated in November 1757. The fleet, under Vice-Admiral Osborne, had given up its blockade of the French Mediterranean coast and had fallen back on its winter quarters at Gibraltar. The French admiral La Clue sailed with six ships of the line from Toulon, but on reaching the Strait he found Osborne waiting for him with an overwhelming force. He fled back to Cartagena, where Osborne's cruisers kept a close watch on him. The main fleet lay at

Gibraltar so that the French could not slip past them. Whenever the wind was easterly and fair for the French to try to pass the Strait, Osborne went to sea and stationed his ships between Gibraltar and Ceuta, and, whenever it turned westerly he returned to port to careen and replenish supplies. The following February Osborne sailed for Cartagena when he received news that La Clue was being reinforced by an additional squadron from Toulon under the Marquis Duquesne, the former French Governor of Canada. The wind was westerly and it was therefore impossible for the French to slip through the Strait. Osborne was lucky for the gale drove Duquesne's squadron towards the English fleet. He himself stayed off Cartagena in case La Clue should come out, but he detailed a number of his ships to pursue the French reinforcements. The *Orphée* 64 was quickly taken and the *Oriflamme* 50 was driven ashore. Duquesne in the *Foudroyant* 80 was pursued by Captain Arthur Gardiner in HMS *Monmouth*, a much smaller ship carrying 64 guns. Two hours later Gardiner was killed in the running fight, but the command devolved on Lieutenant Robert Carkett, who doggedly pursued his larger adversary for a further three hours until he was joined by HMS *Swiftsure* and *Hampton*. Duquesne hauled down his flag and surrendered.[23]

The finest hour of Gibraltar as a base during this war was undoubtedly the part it played in the Battle of Lagos Bay. La Clue was unable to slip past the Royal Navy at Gibraltar so he returned to Toulon where he was watched by the fleet under Vice-Admiral Broderick.

In April 1759, Edward Boscawen arrived at Gibraltar with reinforcements, to take over command. As the French fleet was ready for sea he set up a close blockade of Toulon but, at the beginning of July, he had to return to Gibraltar for provisions and repairs. On 17 August HMS *Gibraltar* 24, which was patrolling off Estepona, sighted the French fleet of twelve sail of the line and three frigates off the Moroccan coast.

The news was promptly conveyed to Gibraltar but the fleet was not ready and Boscawen and several of his senior officers were dining with the Spanish general at San Roque at the time. The French slipped past them, but Boscawen set out in pursuit during the night. The following morning La Clue had only seven ships with him, the others having taken refuge in Cadiz contrary to orders. The British fleet was also divided because of the haste with which it had sailed, Boscawen was in the van with only eight sail. However, luck was with him as the wind started freshening in the east and reached him some time before it reached the fleeing French. Boscawen ordered his leading ships to set all sail and pursue the enemy without forming line of battle. At 2.30 pm HMS *Culloden* began to fire on the French, and very soon afterwards other ships joined in. At this stage the breeze began to fall and Boscawen in HMS *Namur* did not come into action until 4 pm. HMS *Namur* went alongside the French flagship *Océan*, the French firing high as they normally did, disabled her after half an hour by bringing down her mizenmast and topsails. Boscawen transferred to the *Newark* by boat, but by then the battle had turned into a chase some fifteen miles from Lagos. Although La Clue took refuge in that neutral port, Boscawen's ships pursued them right inside. The flagship and *Redoutable* were burnt, and the *Centaure, Temeraire* and *Modeste* were captured. Only two of the French ships managed to get away. Boscawen returned to England with his prizes and Broderick remained on guard outside Cadiz, blockading the other four ships and three frigates.[24]

Boscawen's reward was to be made a Privy Councillor and a general of Marines. Captains Bentley, of the *Warspite* and Stanhope, of the *Swiftsure*, were knighted for their part in the battle. The three prizes were purchased and added to the Navy under their French names.[25]

Broderick stayed on watch outside Cadiz for several weeks until a fierce storm drove him to seek shelter inside Cadiz harbour as Spain was still neutral. Two of his ships were so badly damaged by the storm that he had to send them to Gibraltar for repairs, the others anchored close by the French squadron. As the French gave no sign of wanting to sail, Broderick left the harbour on Christmas day, but was hit by another severe gale and had to take the rest of his ships to Gibraltar for repair. On New Year's day 1760, the French left Cadiz and sped through the Strait in the darkness of night. Broderick, busy with his repairs, was badly let down by his scouting frigates and did not find out what had happened until after the enemy squadron had reached Toulon two weeks later.[26]

Sir Charles Saunders, back from having convoyed and supported Wolfe's army for the invasion of Canada, was sent to the Mediterranean to take over as CinC. He set sail from Spithead on 21 May 1760. He was appointed a Knight of the Bath four days later, as a reward for his services in Canada. The news reached him after he arrived at Gibraltar and an investiture ceremony was conducted there by Major-General Parslow who commanded the garrison. This was the first time that such an investiture had been held in Gibraltar. General Eliott was to be similarly honoured after the Great Siege, and Saumarez after the Battle of Algeciras.[27]

Spain entered the war on the side of France at the beginning of 1762 and although Saunders had plans to attack the Spanish Navy in Cadiz harbour, these came to nothing. On the other hand, the trade war was quite successful and both the privateers and warships made numerous captures. Two of Saunders' frigates, HMS *Active* and *Favourite* captured the Spanish treasure ship *Hermiona* on 15 May, off the coast of the Algarve. The Spanish ship had sailed from South America before news of Spain entering the war had arrived. The total value of the treasure was valued at over £500,000 and when landed in London it was conveyed in 20 wagons, which flew the Union Flag over the Spanish colours, with an escort of military bands and a regiment of dragoons, and was cheered by a prodigious concourse. The two fortunate captains and the admiral each received £65,000. Every officer on board the two frigates received £13,000 and every seaman nearly £500, which would have been worth 30 times as much in today's money.[28]

The war was now coming to an end. Peace negotiations started at the end of the year, and the Peace of Paris was signed in march 1763. Britain made large gains of territory, on the West Coast of Africa and the West Indies, as well as obtaining Canada and all other French possessions in North America east of the Mississippi. France also accepted her primacy in India. Britain recovered West Florida in exchange for returning Havana, and France restored Minorca in exchange for Belle Isle off the French coast, which had been captured in 1760.

Notes and References

(1) Coad *Historic Architecture of the Royal Navy* 143-145.
(2) CO.91:1 Report of the Inspectors of the Army, General Sir Harry Belasyse MP and Edward Stowell, 1713.
(3) Dalton 2:349.
(4) Ayala 257-258; R Mackay 21-22; Coad *Historic Architecture* 145; Baugh *British Naval Administration in the Age of Walpole* 221.
(5) 1753 map of the town; Baugh *Naval Administration 1715 - 1750* 326, in page 56 he gives the naval establishment at Gibraltar as consisting of an Agent, two clerks and a cooper, costing £581 a year.
(6) Adm/A/2129.
(7) Baugh *Naval Administration 1715 - 1750* 337-338; Charnock 4:16.
(8) *Oxford English Dictionary*; Ad Ms 15152 f 23; *Gibraltar Directory 1939* 204.
(9) Charnock 2:411, 3:305, 313; Benady *Settlement of Jews* 92-94.
(10) *SH*; Clowes III:46-47.
(11) *SH*.
(12) These terms were current in the 18th century. The anonymous diarist of the Great Siege noted on 14 November 1779: 'All Barcelo's ships are *blackstraped*, that is, they are dropped behind the hill [Rock], and unable to recover their stations, so that we remain masters of the Bay.' (*Authentic Journal* 15.)
(13) Richmond 1:4, 8-10; Clowes 3:50-52, 265-266.
(14) Richmond 1:9-10; CO.91:10 Columbine to Newcastle 7 Dec 1739; Baugh *Naval Administration 1715 - 1750* 381; *British Naval Administration* 221-22.
(15) Coad *Historical Architecture* 145-146; Baugh *Naval Administration 1715 - 1750* 490.
(16) Richmond I:167-169.
(17) CO.91:10 Columbine to Newcastle 7 Dec 1739; Pares 24,49.
(18) CO.91:11 Fowke to Robinson 25 July 1755.
(19) *Candide* chapter 23.
(20) Clowes 3:292.
(21) Charnock 5:123; Clowes 3:169-170.
(22) ADM.1:384 9 Apr, 2 Aug, 7 Nov 1762; CO.91:14 Parslow to Egremont 28 Feb 1762; Sherrard 116.
(23) Corbett *Seven Years War* 1:237-238, 255-260.
(24) Clowes 3:211-215; Corbett ibid 2:31-39.
(25) Clowes 3:215.
(26) Corbett ibid 2:87-88.
(27) CO.91:14 Parslow to Egremont.
(28) Corbett ibid 2:321; Salmon 190.

CHAPTER IV

THE GREAT SIEGE.

The peace made in Paris in 1763 carried within it the seeds of the next great contest. French power in North America was completely neutralised and the thirteen American colonies straggling along the eastern seaboard no longer had to depend on the mother country for protection. The Seven Years War had been costly and George III and his government felt that it was only fair that the colonies should contribute to the cost of their own defence. The British Government imposed taxes on colonial trade and attempts were made to impose them on the colonies. Resistance was immediate and widespread, and soon turned into armed rebellion. In 1774 the first Continental Congress was held and henceforward the 13 colonies made common cause. On 4 June 1776 they declared themselves to be an independent nation in the face of a substantial body of loyalist opinion in America and conciliatory voices in England. War followed.

France saw an opportunity to humiliate Britain and make up the losses she had suffered in the Seven Years War. In March 1778 she entered the fray. The following month the Toulon fleet was sent to America under the Comte d'Estaing to cooperate with Washington; whilst the Brest fleet, which was fitting out, had to be blockaded by the Royal Navy in case they embarked a force for an invasion of Britain. When the Brest fleet got to sea in July there was an indecisive encounter off Ushant.

Gibraltar was fitting out privateers against American trade, as early as 1776, and from 1778 they also operated against the French. As the Toulon fleet had passed into the Atlantic there was no need for the Royal Navy to blockade that port and only a small squadron was stationed in the Mediterranean. In May 1779 two French 74s, newly fitted-out at Toulon and on passage to Brest, met two 32-gun British frigates in the

Strait. HMS *Thetis* was a fast sailor and managed to get away but HMS *Montreal* struck her flag in the face of such overwhelming odds.[1]

After conducting negotiations with France for some months, Spain entered the war in June 1779 with the specific aim of regaining Gibraltar and Minorca. The communication with Gibraltar was closed on the 21st and the Great Siege commenced on that date. The garrison of 5,000 under the command of the governor, General Sir George Eliott, was to hold out for three and a half years against superior forces in the face of severe privation and suffering. That Gibraltar continued to remain British was due to a large extent to the support given by the Royal Navy.

The first thing that was required was to move the merchant ships from their normal anchorage off Waterport, which was directly under the Spanish batteries (though it was useful in peacetime because they could sail in and out easily), to the New Mole (which required warping in and out); and a new battery was built with heavy guns landed from HMS *Panther*. The Gibraltar squadron at this time consisted of HMS *Panther* 60, the flagship of Vice-Admiral Robert Duff, the frigate HMS *Enterprise* 28, and the sloops HMS *Childers* 14 and *Fortune* 10, and *Gibraltar*. This last ship was not the frigate that had served in the previous war, but an American 12-gun brig which had been captured earlier in the year and commissioned into the service. It was not the last time it changed flags; in July 1781 it was captured by the Spaniards while still serving at Gibraltar and renamed *Salvador*; it was eventually recaptured by the Royal Navy in July 1800![2]

On 11 July the Spanish Admiral Antonio Barceló appeared in the Strait with a few xebecs convoying 40 settees from Malaga, loaded with provisions. The British squadron got in among the Spanish ships and captured a dozen of them.

Barceló was to conduct the naval blockade for the rest of the Siege. On 13 July he was reinforced by two ships of the line, two frigates, some xebecs and a number of galleys and armed boats. He established a small shipyard at the mouth of the Palmones River, and there built a number of gunboats including some flat-bottomed galleys of his own design. These vessels were over 50 foot long at the waterline, drew six feet, and carried a long 24-pounder. Above the gunwales they had movable bulwarks which were lined inside and out with thick layers of cork to make them impervious to the smaller shots of the besieged. The top sides curved inwards, particularly at the bows and stern, to give better protection for the crews, and at a later stage a number had their sides lined with plates of iron from the top of the bulwarks to below the waterline. These armoured gunboats were extremely manoeuvrable, sailing well with their large lateen sail, and were rowed with 14 oars on each side. They proved a thorn in the side of the garrison, and were used not only to attack shipping and intercept blockade runners, but also to steal up to the town walls at night and lob shells into the unsuspecting fortress.[3]

Barceló stationed his force around Gibraltar: a 70-gun ship, a frigate and two xebecs at Algeciras, a similar force at Ceuta, and a blockading force of six small xebecs, 12 galleys and 20 armed boats, in the Bay.[4]

There are a number of contemporary printed accounts of the Great Siege, the best and most complete is undoubtedly John Drinkwater's *A History of the Siege of Gibraltar*, but from a naval point of view the most interesting is *An Authentic and Accurate Journal of the Late Siege of Gibraltar*, which is anonymous but obviously written by somebody who could watch ship movements carefully, as it is virtually an eyewitness account of these movements.

Gibraltar was now blockaded but some supplies still came in. Small boats slipped in from Morocco with livestock and vegetables; and what was more remarkable, from Spain, with vegetables and fruit which were exchanged for tobacco. On 18 August 1779, for example, a Spaniard came into Waterport from Spain in an open boat, with onions and fruit, having a pass for Ceuta. He was not permitted to land but he was allowed to sell his cargo and buy tobacco. He returned home under the cover of darkness. Neutral vessels passing Europa Point either came in unaware of the blockade or else were forced to, by British guns and gunboats, and sold their cargoes of rice or wheat or barley to the garrison.

As the year came to an end, Barceló's blockade became increasingly effective and more and more of the blockade runners were stopped and taken into Algeciras. After six months of blockade, supplies began to run short, bread was limited and rationed, and fresh meat was ten times the normal price. On 4 November the PSW *Peace and Plenty* from

Leghorn, was stopped from entering the Bay by the Spanish gunboats and was eventually driven aground on Eastern Beach. Duff was not able to come to her assistance with his heavy ships but his boats took off her crew, after which she was destroyed by the Spanish forces.[5]

Relief by Rodney January 1780

With the French fleet operating in America and threatening an invasion across the Channel, the Royal Navy concentrated on these two theatres and control of the Mediterranean was lost. Gibraltar, which had only had supplies for six months at the beginning of the Siege, obviously needed relieving. In October 1779, Admiral Sir George Rodney was ordered to take reinforcements to the Caribbean and assume the command, and it was decided that on the way he should convoy ships for the relief of Gibraltar and Minorca. In order not to alert the enemy the whole fleet was said to be bound for America and the fact that almost half the victuallers were destined for the Mediterranean was kept a secret until after they had sailed. The fleet was not ready until December (and then it was delayed by persistent westerly winds) so it did not set sail down the Channel until Christmas Eve.

Rodney's squadron was reinforced by a strong detachment from the Channel Fleet under Rear-Admiral Digby, who became his second in command. He had more than 150 vessels under his command, including the convoy. There were 22 ships of the line, 8 frigates, 66 storeships, transports and victuallers, and over 50 merchant ships. By 4 January the fleet was well south in the Bay of Biscay and the section of the convoy proceeding to the West Indies, consisting of 37 storeships, victuallers and transports, and all the merchant vessels, was detached under an escort of frigates. The rest of the fleet ploughed on southward.

By daybreak on 8 January when they were off the Portuguese coast, some twenty ships were seen silhouetted to the north east. This was a convoy of 16 merchantmen of the Royal Commercial Company of Caracas, loaded with naval stores, provisions and bale goods, on its way from San Sebastian to Cadiz under the escort of one ship of the line, four frigates and two sloops. The Spaniards started firing as soon as they saw Rodney's fleet, but the Admiral ordered his ships to chase and by noon they were among the convoy. Within a few hours all the convoy and their escort had struck their colours. The ship of the line *Guipuzcoana* was a brand new 64, built by the Caracas Company as an escort for their convoys and did not form part of the regular Spanish Navy. Rodney renamed her *Prince William* and incorporated her immediately into his fleet. He also decided to take to Gibraltar the twelve victuallers which were carrying supplies for the Spanish army besieging it. The other four merchant ships and the frigates were sent back to England under escort.[6]

The *Guipuzcoana* had been renamed in honour of the fifteen year-old third son of George III. Prince William was serving on board HMS *Prince George* (Digby's flagship), he was rated as midshipman a week after this action and served afloat until 1789, reaching the rank of post captain. When the captured Spanish Admiral Langara visited Rear-Admiral Digby on arrival at Gibraltar and was taking his leave, the royal midshipman reported to the Admiral that his barge was ready. The Spaniard, astonished to see the son of the king acting as a junior officer exclaimed, 'Well does Great Britain merit the empire of the sea when the humblest stations in her navy are supported by princes of the blood.' In 1830 the Prince ascended the throne as William IV.[7]

The convoy now consisted of 42 vessels, one transport, twelve victuallers, four storeships and the twelve captured victuallers for Gibraltar, and nine transports, two victuallers and two storeships for Minorca. The escorting ships had to heave to every evening to allow the plodding merchant vessels to catch up.

At midday on the 16th as they were rounding Cape St Vincent, an enemy fleet was reported to the south-east. Rodney ordered the formation of line ahead but at 2.30 when it became obvious that the enemy was fleeing he ordered a general chase. The fleet that had been sighted was that commanded by Don Juan de Langara y Huarte and consisted of nine ships of the line and two frigates. Rodney ordered his ships to keep to leeward of the enemy so that being heeled over to port they could open the lower row of ports on their starboard side and use all their tiers of guns on that side against the Spaniards. At 4 pm HMS *Edgar* was the first ship to start firing at the enemy and others joined shortly after. The *Santo Domingo* blew up within an hour and the *Princesa* struck her flag at 5 pm. Langara's flagship the *Fenix* had her bowsprit and mizen mast shot away, she lost steerage way and her lower gun-deck was awash as she wallowed in the heavy seas. She struck shortly after 7pm; and the *Diligente* followed soon after. It was now dark, but there was a bright moon, and the remaining ships were remorselessly pursued in what became known as the Moonlight Battle, though Spanish historians refer to it as the first Battle of St Vincent. Three more ships were taken and only two ships of the line and the frigates managed to get away. But the following morning two of the captured liners were driven ashore by the gale and only four were eventually brought into Gibraltar.[8]

On 13 January, Vice-Admiral Duff at Gibraltar had placed his small squadron on alert, having somehow received advance warning of the approach of Rodney's fleet. On the 15th a brig, one of the ordnance storeships that had become separated from the convoy, anchored off Rosia and confirmed the good news. After that, individual ships started straggling in. Rodney arrived in the Strait with the convoy on the 18th but the combined effects of the westerly gale and the strong current carried his ships past the Rock and the following morning they were off Marbella. HMS *Edgar* which was escorting the *Fenix* and some other ships that were sailing behind Rodney, managed to make their way in the following day, but the Admiral and the main fleet did not manage to beat their way back until the 25th.[9]

Rodney was suffering from gout and gravel, but from his sick bed he arranged for the newly captured Spanish ships to be incorporated into the Royal Navy. The name of the *Fenix* was changed to HMS *Gibraltar* but the others were commissioned under their old names. 'The Spanish men-of-war we have taken,' he wrote to his wife, 'are much superior to ours.' He also arranged for an exchange of prisoners with the Spanish authorities.[10] The victuallers and store ships for Minorca were sent off under escort but Governor Eliott insisted on retaining the 73rd Regiment which had been posted to that garrison. This action was subsequently approved by the British Government. The relief had been most timely, for the garrison had been placed on short rations and the civilians had been without bread for two weeks. With the addition of the supplies on the captured Spanish ships, originally intended for the Spanish army, the garrison's stocks now amounted to bread and flour for 607 days, beef for 291 days and pork for 487, and other supplies for an average of six months. Thanks to the Navy, Gibraltar was no longer in immediate danger of being starved into surrender.[11]

Rodney's fleet lay at anchor in the Bay for almost three weeks and during this time Barceló kept his outnumbered squadron behind the boom in Algeciras harbour. But what was remarkable was that Admiral Cordoba, lying in Cadiz with a superior force of 24 ships of the line (20 Spanish and 4 French), did not come out to give battle, although Rodney had only 20 of the line (17 after he had detached the Minorca convoy) and the five prizes. When the Minorca escorts returned, Rodney set sail on 13 February and three days later set his course for the West Indies with four ships of the line, a frigate and a sloop. The rest of the fleet returned to Britain under Digby. Vice-Admiral Duff, who had expressed a desire to be relieved, returned to England on HMS *Prince George.* Rodney detailed Captain John Elliot with HMS *Edgar* 74 to stay as commodore in his place. However when the Admiralty heard of this they ordered the *Edgar* home, and from 20 April 1780, the command of the Gibraltar station devolved on Captain Harvey of HMS *Panther.*[12]

Fire ships

After Rodney's departure the blockade was resumed. The supplies which had been landed at Gibraltar commanded very high prices and this encouraged blockade runners from Morocco, Minorca and Leghorn as well as from Britain. Some reached the Rock safely, but many were captured. Drinkwater's *History* and the *Authentic Journal* are full of accounts of these ships. Their success depended largely on the state of the weather and the degree of alertness of the blockaders at any given moment.

Barceló next decided to employ a new stratagem against Gibraltar. In the early hours of the morning of 7 June the frigate *Enterprise* which was moored off the entrance to the New Mole, saw a ship sailing towards her out of the dark. She hailed her and the reply was 'Fresh beef from Barbary.' The *Enterprise* decided that the stranger was rather suspicious and fired at her and gave the alarm. The approaching ship then burst into flames, as did a second and third vessel behind her, and others, to a total of nine; Barceló was sending in his fireships. The batteries and the ships started firing at them and boats were sent to tow them away. Two of the fireships drifted into Rosia Bay close to where HMS *Panther* lay at anchor, the others were too far out. The fireships burnt for three hours, and it was an awesome sight for the garrison which had a grandstand view. The masts of some of fire-ships stood till the last and the sheets of flame shooting up their rigging looked like lighted sails. The enemy's plan was to destroy the stores and shipping at the New Mole (there were 20 ships sheltering there at the time). It miscarried only because the wind was light and the ships were set on fire too early, not because of the effectiveness of the defensive fire, for there was a delay of an hour before Gibraltar's batteries started firing. The hulls of the fireships proved most useful, as the next day they were towed in, broken up and sold to the inhabitants who were very short of fuel.[13]

On 2 July the *Panther* left for Britain, leaving Captain Leslie of HMS *Enterprise* as senior officer on the station. Gibraltar continued to be closely blockaded and large ships with no freedom of manoeuvre were only sitting targets for the Spanish gunboats. Sometimes they were even attacked at their moorings by the enemy's ships of the line. The other ships that formed the squadron at this time were the sloops HMS *Gibraltar* and *Fortune*, and the *St Fermin* which had been captured, by Rodney, off the Portuguese coast with the convoy on 8 January. A new battery was mounted on Parson's Lodge to protect the anchorage and work was started on a boom that stretched from the head of the New Mole to the shore.[14]

Occasionally some vessel broke the blockade and reached the New Mole but, more often than not, the besieged were mortified to see the blockade runner stopped and taken to Algeciras by the besiegers. The writer of the *Authentic Journal* felt that this was largely due to the attempt being made by vessels that were too recognisably British, and types more common in the Mediterranean would have had a better chance of running the blockade. On 22 December 1780 he made the following entry,

In the afternoon a small sloop was taken into Algeciras, which, I fancy, is from Ireland. It is astonishing that people at home should venture to send out sloops, cutters, or schooners, to this place, as they are the most suspicious vessels of any that swim. The moment one is discovered, at whatever distance, the alarm is given along the enemy's coast, and the cruisers post themselves accordingly, so that it is a hundred to one that neither, sloop, cutter, nor schooner, escapes. Ships, snows, doggers, and such like vessels, are most likely to escape, especially if they keep towards the southward [of the Strait], and have foreign colours to hoist, in case of a cruiser's passing them; but I fear our people do not think it worth their while to furnish their vessels with any but English colours, so that they have it not in their power to deceive the enemy.

Things got worse when two Moroccan vessels were escorted to Gibraltar by the Spaniards. On board were the British consul from Tangier and all the British subjects resident in Morocco, who had been expelled because the Emperor had farmed the revenue of his ports to Spain for the duration of the war. Henceforth there were no more supplies to be expected from that quarter. To add to the other privations the Spanish gunboats had taken to patrolling the fishing grounds, and fresh fish, which had been an important standby was no longer available.[15]

Relief by Darby April 1781

And so into 1781. The town bakers ran out of flour before the end of February and the civilian population was again left without bread. The small Royal Navy Squadron left Gibraltar for Minorca carrying the incurable invalids of the garrison. Captain Leslie also had orders to collect a convoy and bring in supplies which were urgently needed, for it was now a year since the relief by Rodney's fleet.[16]

The British Government also realised that another effort had to be made to supply the Rock if it were to be retained. The Channel fleet was at the time much inferior to the combined forces of France and Spain, and in addition, war had (rather recklessly) been declared on Holland. Nevertheless, an effort had to be made and a fleet of 28 ships of the line sailed with a large convoy on 13 March, under the command of Admiral George Darby.

Groups of ships for other destinations joined the convoy but were detached before they reached the Strait. On 10 April the fleet reached Cape Spartel without any interference by the main Spanish fleet which lay in Cadiz Bay. A cutter arrived at Gibraltar the following day with news of the impending relief, and when the mist had cleared on the morning of the 12th the inhabitants were overjoyed to see the large convoy standing into the Bay in a compact and orderly body led by several men-of-war. The bulk of the fleet stayed cruising off the Moroccan coast in case the main Spanish fleet made an appearance. The wind was light and the sails of the ships filled just enough to give them steerage. As the relieving force made their stately advance into the Bay, 15 Spanish gunboats, each mounting a long 24-pounder gun (which enabled them to outrange the largest men of war) came out and started cannonading the convoy. The land batteries joined in, but this did not deter the relieving fleet which came to anchor off the New Mole and Rosia Bay.

For the past year the Spaniards had been hoping to starve Gibraltar into surrender. But just in case this did not work they had been busy constructing a large number of batteries on the isthmus and at the head of the Bay, to batter the fortress into submission. At noon that day they started a bombardment which was to continue with hardly any respite for 21 months, although within a few weeks the 3,000 shots fired in the first 24 hours had dropped to an average of 600 a day. By the end of the Siege the enemy had fired a quarter of a million shot and shell at the garrison and not a single building in the town was left intact.

The bombardment uncovered stores of wine and spirits which the soldiers found and the town became a scene of drunkenness, rioting and general looting. Even the Navy's stores in Irish Town were sacked. Eliott had to hang a number of the looters, among the ruins of the White Convent, before he could restore order. The military wounded and sick also had to be removed from the town and the Naval Hospital was taken over for their use.

All the while the work of unloading the store ships went on unceasingly in spite of the bombardment and the constant harassment by the gunboats. All the government stores were disembarked but when the fleet took advantage of an easterly breeze on 20 April, to set sail for the west, many of the ships with private cargoes sailed unloaded. They had not discharged their cargoes because they were not able to secure the high prices they were asking. Many of the inhabitants sailed with the fleet. They had seen their property destroyed by the bombardment before they left and were now destitute refugees seeking asylum in Britain.[17]

A week later HMS *Enterprise* arrived from Minorca with a convoy of 20 ships loaded with victuals and wine. The convoy was under Captain Roger Curtis of the frigate HMS *Brilliant* 28 which with HMS *Porcupine* 24 formed part of the escort. The new arrivals had no idea that the fortress had been relieved by Darby the week before and were pleasantly surprised at the low key reception they got from the Spanish blockading force. From now on The Spanish gunboats stepped up their night attacks and a number of civilians were killed, so when the *Enterprise* sailed for Britain on 29 May, with a convoy of 15 ships, many more of the inhabitants left.

However, they did not all get away, some of the ships were captured by American privateers and more than 140 of the refugees were returned to the garrison the following month.[18]

The two frigates HMS *Flora* 42 and *Crescent* 34 (which had been part of the escort to the supply ships sent by Darby to Minorca) were returning to Gibraltar when they encountered a much superior force off the south-west coast of Spain, but managed to get away after a sharp skirmish. They arrived off Europa Point just as the *Enterprise* was setting off with her convoy and, after signalling the garrison crossed the Strait to investigate two ships near Ceuta. They turned out to be Dutch frigates. The *Flora* engaged the *Castor* 36, a considerably smaller ship, and after two and a quarters hours forced her opponent to strike her colours. Meanwhile the *Crescent* had been fighting the *Briel* 36, a larger and more stoutly built vessel and had the worst of the encounter. All her main deck and four of her quarter deck guns were disabled and her sails and masts were shot away. She struck her flag but before the *Briel* could take possession the *Flora* came up and drove her off. The *Briel* made off to Cadiz and the two RN ships and the captured *Castor* repaired their damage as best they could and sailed for England. In their battered condition they were no match for two French frigates they met in the

Pastora Junk Ship—Don Buena Ventura Moreno, Admiral.

Gun Boat.   Mortar Boat.   Gun Boat under sail.

Fortune, Prame.   Vanguard, Prame.

Repulse, Prame.   English Gun Boat.   A Moorish Galley.

Junk Ship as it appeared 6th September, 1782.

Craft that took part in the Siege, from contemporary drawings by Captain John Spilsbury

Bay of Biscay which captured the *Crescent* and *Castor* though the *Flora* managed to get away.[19]

Roger Curtis

Curtis now became the senior naval officer and took a very active part in the defence. He raised a naval brigade and Eliott awarded him the honorary army rank of 'brigadier' and always addressed him by this title. It also fell on Curtis to organise another body which was to prove most useful in assisting the defence of Gibraltar. Since the beginning of the siege, the government had been pressing Eliott to organise a force of gunboats to counter Barceló's armoured galleys, but he had been unable to do so for lack of resources. In the summer of 1781 he had two brigs, the *Vanguard* and *Repulse* and the sloop *Fortune*, cut down and fitted with heavy guns, but although they were rigged with lateen sails, they were usually moored off the New Mole as floating batteries to fend off the gunboats.

The storeship *St Anne* storeship arrived on 25 February 1782 with a miscellaneous collection of much needed stores and the ready made timbers and frames for two gunboats. Another ten kits arrived in the *Vernon* a month later. The Navy started work assembling these boats and the first one was ready on 24 April. By 4 June the flotilla consisted of twelve boats - each of them with a crew of 21. The *Brilliant* manned *Revenge, Defiance, Resolution, Spitfire, Dreadnought* and *Thunder*, the *Porcupine* manned the *Europa, Terrible, Fury, Scourge*, and *Terror*, and the cutter *Speedwell*, the *Vengeance*. The *Revenge, Defiance*, and *Europa* mounted a 24-pounder, and the other gunboats an 18-pounder gun.[20]

The Grand Attack

The gunboats soon proved their value but they were not commissioned a moment too soon, for the Spanish Navy was making new plans for attacking Gibraltar. On 9 May our diarist noted:

> This afternoon arrived at Algeciras, from the west, a Spanish line of battle ship, with eight large empty storeships. Their appearance is very shabby, their rigging quite dry, and they seemed to be poorly manned.[21]

These storeships together with another two which arrived later, were merchant ships of between 600 and 1,200 tons; they had been brought to the Bay to be converted to floating batteries in accordance with the proposal and plans prepared by the French engineer d'Arcon. Four days later our diarist added:

It is reported with some degree of probability, that those ships are lined with cork, &c. and intended to operate against this place, in the course of the summer; we are therefore preparing to give them a suitable reception when ever they come.

The preparation made by the garrison was the placing of furnaces in all the batteries, which were to be used for heating the cannonballs before they were fired. It was hoped to set the attacking ships on fire through the use of these hot shots or 'roast potatoes' as they were jocularly known.

However, the plans of d'Arcon took this possibility into account, and not only were the floating batteries to be heavily protected, but they were also to be fitted with fire-fighting equipment to cope with the hot shot. The garrison watched the work being carried out on the floating batteries day by day. Masts were removed and the upper works cut down, the decks were strengthened, and new strong roofs were fitted. The roofs and one side of the hulls were heavily reinforced with sandbags and cables enclosed behind oak boards to stop cannonballs penetrating them. To cope with the hot shot, d'Arcon designed a system of pumps which continually circulated water over the outside like 'blood through the human veins'. Other pumps also circulated water on the inside surface, but, as the caulking was bad, water dripped over the guns and gunners; the pumps were turned off before the ships went into battle in order that the powder for the guns should remain dry.[22]

All this time the Spaniards continued working on the land batteries which were being extended and strengthened. Ships were sometimes successful in breaking the blockade to bring much needed supplies to the garrison. Supplies were continually arriving for the Spanish forces by sea. In the middle of June 1782 the Spanish guns fell silent for several weeks, they were husbanding their ammunition for the great attempt.

On 17 July the Duke of Crillon, fresh from having conquered Minorca, took over the command of the Spanish forces and the French troops that had been sent to assist them. By the end of August naval reinforcements started arriving for the besiegers, ships of the line and flat-bottomed boats, obviously intended for landing troops on Gibraltar's southern beaches.

On 9 September seven Spanish and two French ships of the line formed line of battle at Europa Point, and sailed northward as far as the New Mole, bombarding the British batteries. In the afternoon 16 of Barceló's gunboats took over the bombardment, and after midnight the ships of the line again attacked the Line Wall from Europa Point to Parson's Lodge. The following day there was a repeat of the attack from the sea and the bombardment from the land rose to a crescendo. By the 11th the British fortifications began to show the effect of the continuous bombardment - a number of parapets and walls had been demolished. The main attack was obviously imminent and HMS *Brilliant, Porcupine* and the other ships were scuttled at the New Mole to save them from being set on fire by the enemy. The next day the combined fleets of Spain and France entered the Bay, 40 sail in all, including half a dozen three-deckers, under the command of Admiral Luis de Cordoba. Everything was now ready for the Grand Attack, after three years of preparation and blockade.

The morning of 13 September dawned with a light north-westerly breeze, that enabled the lumbering floating batteries to make their slow way across the bay from their anchorage off the mouth of the Palmones - all ten of them. Ranging from the *Pastora* of 24 guns, the flagship of Admiral Buenaventura Moreno who commanded the squadron, to the smallest, *Los Dolores* of six guns. The ten floating batteries sailed slowly towards the town until just after 9am they were anchored in a rough line stretching from the Old Mole to the New Mole, between 900 and 1,100 yards from the Line Wall. The *Pastora* and the *Talla Piedra* anchored opposite King's Bastion. The furnaces at the batteries had been lit, but for the first couple of hours the shots that were fired were cold.

The floating batteries seemed impervious to the largest cannon balls which rolled off their sloping roofs and did not penetrate their reinforced sides. By midday the British gunners were able to start employing their hot shot, and as the furnaces could not cope with the large number of cannon balls needed, fires were also lit around heaps of shot piled in corners of the Line Wall. After a couple of hours the *Talla Piedra*, which took the brunt of the fire from King's Bastion, started smoking but the fire was put out. The floating batteries showed amazing resistance to the red-hot shot fired at them at point blank range but by evening some of them were beginning to burn and the firing from all of them had been silenced by the superhuman efforts of the British artillery.

The Spanish gunboats had been unable to reinforce the work of the floating batteries because the wind had veered to the south-west and the sea became very rough. It was impossible for Moreno to sail his battered, cumbersome ships away from the town in these conditions and he sent a message to Crillon asking to be towed away. Crillon passed the request on to Cordoba, but the Admiral did not react.

That night 'Brigadier' Curtis abandoned his post ashore where he commanded the southern part of the Line Wall, and rowed his twelve gunboats among the floating batteries. Moreno was faced with the possibility of having his squadron captured by the Naval Brigade and he had no option but to set fire to the batteries where they lay. Curtis chased off the Spanish boats that had come to rescue the crews of the floating batteries and brought 357 prisoners ashore. In the early hours the batteries started to blow up. By dawn there were still six of them burning as they lay at anchor, but these exploded during the morning, some of them with such force that they blew open, closed doors in the town. The Grand Attack had failed and Admiral Cordoba had limited his role to covering the attackers against a possible intervention by the British fleet - which did not materialise. He had remained a spectator to the horrific events throughout - without participating or committing any part of his large fleet.

Spain despaired of regaining Gibraltar; it was obvious that it was not to be gained by either blockade or by force, and there was nothing more to be done. A flag of truce was sent and arrangements were made for the exchange of prisoners. The bombardment from the land batteries continued unabated and the combined fleet stayed in the Bay, but it was moved from the anchorage off Palmones to Algeciras, which was better protected from the south-westerlies which now started to blow hard. HMS *Brilliant* was raised from the seabed now that the danger was over, and after being pumped out was found to be none the worse for her two weeks' immersion. The other small vessels scuttled at the New Mole at the same time were then pumped-out and raised.

Matters continued thus for almost a month until the night of 10 October when a great gale blew from the south-west. At dawn the Spanish *San Miguel* 72 was seen off Orange Bastion close reefed and trying to weather the Rock. The Gibraltar batteries opened up a desultory fire and the *San Miguel* eventually grounded near Ragged Staff. Rear-Admiral Juan Moreno who was flying his flag on the stranded vessel, seeing that he was in an impossible situation hoisted the Union Jack over his ensign as a sign of surrender. The storm was now subsiding and Captain Curtis went off in the cutter HMS *Speedwell* to take possession of the vessel. The officers and crew were landed and imprisoned on Windmill Hill.[23]

Relief by Howe October 1782

That afternoon alarm signals were seen on the enemy's watch-towers and shortly after, a large British Convoy was seen in the Strait. The news of this approaching relief had prompted Cordoba to order his ships the previous day to lie at single anchor. A three-decker had broken loose and had driven the *San Miguel*, a new ship recently completed in Havana, from her mooring, before she could set her sails. The approaching fleet was commanded by Lord Howe.

The British Government had been aware for some time of the impending attack on Gibraltar and had been preparing a relieving fleet for some months, but Howe was not able to set sail from Spithead until 11 September. As it was known that Spain and France had assembled a large combined fleet in the Strait, Howe was instructed to take the whole Channel Fleet with him. As it was, he only had 34 ships of the line as compared to the 48 that the combined fleet could muster at that date. When the convoy reached Finisterre the ships for other destinations went their own way and Howe continued to Gibraltar convoying the 31 supply ships for the fortress. On 8 October, when off Cape St. Vincent, he sent HMS *Latona* 38 ahead to announce the impending arrival of the convoy to the garrison of Gibraltar, and she anchored off Rosia on the evening of the 11th. During the night several of the victuallers made their way in but the next morning the main fleet was seen off Marbella, having been driven to the east by the westerly winds. During the day HMS *Panther* arrived with more store ships, but Howe was not keen to be caught in the narrow waters of the Strait by the superior Combined Fleet so he remained to the east of the Rock in order to remain to windward. The enemy fleet therefore set sail after him but missed him and in the morning of the 14th the watchers on Signal Hill could see Howe's ships, but not Cordoba's, which had been driven further east. The wind turned easterly the following day and the convoy made its way back to Gibraltar. All the supply ships had entered by the 18th and also some ships of the line that had embarked two regiments that were brought to augment the garrison. Howe was able to outsail the Combined Fleet because, at this stage of the war, British warships had coppered bottoms and could therefore sail faster than their opponents.

On the 19th the Combined Fleet was seen to the east and Howe set sail from Gibraltar to the west as he did not want to be caught within the Strait by a superior force, with his ships embarrassed by currents and hemmed in by land. Once he was past Cape Spartel he hove to so that the enemy could catch up with him. Cordoba finally managed to engage him at 6 o'clock on the evening of the 20th, but many of his ships were slow sailers and only 33 went into action. The fight lasted for some four hours but was inconclusive. The following day the wind died down and Cordoba's ships were now so widely scattered he could not bring them into action as an organised force, so he did not renew the attack. Howe returned to Spithead on 14 November. He had relieved Gibraltar in the face of an overwhelmingly superior force. His great skill and superior equipment had enabled him to overcome the numerical superiority of his opponent. Gibraltar was safe for the foreseeable future.[24]

Captain Curtis travelled home on board Howe's flagship, HMS *Victory*, as he had been sent home by Eliott to give an account of the Grand Attack and the destruction of the floating batteries. On reaching England Curtis was knighted for his services. The naval command at Gibraltar now passed to the captain of HMS *Porcupine*, Sir Charles

Knowles, who flew his pennant from the captured *Saint Michael*, formerly the *San Miguel*.[25]

The siege still went on. The French forces were withdrawn but the bombardment continued, and the Spanish gunners tried very hard to destroy the *St Michael* which was moored at the New Mole. On 19 December twenty-nine Spanish gun and mortar boats made a determined attack, but Knowles saved his ship from blowing up by landing some of the ship's gunpowder and dropping the rest overboard.[26]

Peace negotiations were now under way and the preliminaries were signed in January 1783. The Great Siege officially came to an end on 5 February 1783. It remained to divide the prize money for the captured enemy ships. This amounted to £16,000 for the floating batteries and £14,000 for the *St Michael*, making a total of £30,000; £3,187 10s 0d of this was allocated to the Naval Brigade.[27]

Under the Treaty of Versailles the American colonies became independent, but much more important to Gibraltar was the return of Minorca to Spain. Gibraltar was now the Royal Navy's only base in the Mediterranean.

Notes and References

(1) Clowes 4:25.
(2) *Authentic Journal* 11; Colledge 1:231; Drinkwater 52; McGuffie 44.
(3) Duro 7:271; Luna 430; McGuffie 73.
(4) *Authentic Journal* 4, 10.
(5) *Authentic Journal* 13-17; Drinkwater 65, 68-82; McGuffie 49.
(6) Spinney 304-305.
(7) Drinkwater 95.
(8) Spinney 306-312; Clowes 3:449.
(9) Spinney 315; Clowes 3:451.
(10) Clowes 3:451.
(11) Spinney 313; CO.91:26 - Secretary of State's letter of 11 March, and Eliott's letters - No 4 of 28 January and No 6 of 13 February.
(12) Spinney 305; Clowes 3:450; Drinkwater 107, 110.
(13) *Authentic Journal* 29-30; Drinkwater 110-112.
(14) *Authentic Journal* 32; Drinkwater 114.
(15) *Authentic Journal* 65, 68; Drinkwater 132.
(16) McGuffie 91-92.

(17)   Clowes 3:502-503; Drinkwater 147-158.

(18)   Drinkwater 160, 175, 179, 200, 274; *Authentic Journal* 88.

(19)   Clowes 4:66-69.

(20)   McGuffie 108; *Authentic Journal* 124; Drinkwater 230-231, 246; Spilsbury 39, 71.

(21)   *Authentic Journal* 125.

(22)   McGuffie 157-160; Russell 228-250; Duro 7:313-322; Drinkwater 295-301.

(23)   *Authentic Journal* 161; Drinkwater 321-323.

(24)   Clowes 3:540-543; *Authentic Journal* 162-164; Drinkwater 323 et seq.

(25)   McGuffie 174, 188.

(26)   Russell 270.

(27)   Russell 286.

CHAPTER V

FRENCH REVOLUTIONARY WARS.

The Great Siege left Gibraltar completely devastated and all naval installations, apart from the Hospital and the New Mole, in ruins. With the loss of Minorca, Gibraltar was now the only base in the Mediterranean and it was necessary to repair and replace everything that had been destroyed. Masons were brought in from Genoa, Portugal and Britain for the work, and building materials from wherever they could be obtained, including Morocco - which had reopened its ports to British vessels with the coming of peace. The first priority was, of course, to rebuild the fortifications that had been severely mauled in the long bombardment and particularly the Grand Attack; and barracks and storehouses came second. They all had priority over the civilian buildings in the town, and the inhabitants continued living in Hardy Town (above the Naval Hospital) where they had taken refuge from the bombardment, or returned to town and camped among the ruins of their dwellings.

Relations between the naval and military authorities were not always easy. Rear-Admiral Joseph Peyton, who commanded the Mediterranean fleet from 1787 to 1791, got involved in a long and acrimonious argument concerning jurisdiction over the New Mole, with Major-General Charles O'Hara who was the CinC at Gibraltar in the absence of the Governor. Peyton accepted the jurisdiction of the military on shore but in August 1789 he claimed that no supply ships could tie up at the New Mole without his permission. This resulted in a bitter correspondence between the Admiral and the General which continued for almost a year. The Secretary of State weighed in with an appeal to both parties to be sensible and cooperate and avoid exercising their authority when it was not necessary. However, O'Hara received support for his stand from Governor Eliott in England and won the day.[1]

The Admiral should have concentrated on the problems presented by Morocco, for the authorities there veered between making difficulties in supplying the Navy and the garrison and begging for favours. These ranged from having their warships rigged in the Dockyard (which was done) and requesting that ships be hired to them to cruise against the Knights of Malta (which was refused).[2]

The War of American Independence had left France bankrupt, and the state of the public finances required the convening of the States General to deal with the problem. This was the first step in the process that was to lead to the French Revolution in 1789. Public opinion in Britain at first welcomed the events in France, but, as the revolutionaries became more radical, most of the kingdoms of Europe declared war on them. When news was received of the execution of Louis XVI in January 1793, the French minister was expelled from London and within a few days both countries were at war. Spain joined the coalition against France shortly after and, for a while, Spain and Britain were allies.

While Lord Howe cruised in the Atlantic with the Channel Fleet, Lord Hood was sent to blockade Toulon, where 30 ships of the line were fitting out. Hood's force was only 21 strong but on the way out he called at Cadiz. Nelson, who was then in command of HMS *Agamemnon* 74, described in a letter to his wife how he was shown round the dockyard there by Admiral Langara (the veteran of the Moonlight Battle of 1780) and how impressed he was with the Spanish ships - though he did not think that their system produced good fighting seamen. Hood was joined by Langara with 17 ships, and when they arrived at Toulon he issued a proclamation to the Royalists, which was so well received that he was able to occupy the town with a mixed Anglo-Spanish force of soldiers and sailors, without much difficulty. The occupation lasted a few months and came to an end when a young artillery officer called Napoleon Bonaparte was sent to bombard and retake the place.

Hood had been in communication with anti-French patriots in Corsica for some time and he sent a force to capture it. When he returned to Britain in October 1794 and handed over the command to Vice-Admiral Hotham, Corsica had become the Navy's main base for the blockade of Toulon, though Leghorn in Italy was also used extensively. The following March, Hotham was lying with his fleet in Leghorn Roads

65

when he received news that the French Admiral Martin had sailed from Toulon to attack Corsica. When the fleets met they were equal in numbers, and after a long drawn-out battle, two French ships of the line were captured. Martin returned to Toulon where he was reinforced by ships sent from Brest, but Hotham also received reinforcements that gave him superiority over the enemy. During the time Hotham was in command two groups of French ships evaded him and broke out into the Atlantic, but the blockade was made more effective when Admiral Sir John Jervis took over the command in December 1795.

The Mediterranean is abandoned

Napoleon was appointed commander of the French forces in Italy in 1796, and in a series of brilliant battles he subdued the north and centre of the country in a few months. The year before, the French army had entered Spain and threatened Madrid, forcing the Spaniards to make peace. The victorious French were able to bring pressure to bear to make Spain re-enter the war on their side, and she declared war on Britain in September 1796. Jervis was now in a difficult position. His fleet was decidedly outnumbered by the French. His bases in Corsica, Elba and Italy were badly positioned to control the entrance into the Mediterranean, and he was not able to stop the Franco-Hispanic fleet from concentrating in the Channel and threatening an invasion of Britain in conjunction with the Dutch. Jervis was therefore ordered to evacuate Corsica and concentrate his fleet in the Strait from where he could watch the Spanish fleet in Cadiz and prevent the Toulon ships from breaking out into the Atlantic.

In the changed circumstances Gibraltar assumed greater importance. Efforts had been made to improve the naval base there, and in 1793 Captain Harry Harmwood RN was appointed the first of a number of Commissioners of the Gibraltar Dockyard and accommodation had to be found for him. The Mount was rented from General Sir William Green for him. The building and its extensive grounds were bought outright for £1,500 in 1799 and it has been the residence of successive SNOs at Gibraltar ever since. But Gibraltar still had many deficiencies as a base for a large fleet and Lisbon had to be organised once again as a base for the supply and repair of ships of the

66

Royal Navy; in September 1797, Captain Isaac Coffin RN (who had been commissioner of the dockyard at Ajaccio in Corsica) was sent as Commissioner of the British base there.[3]

The Mediterranean was now abandoned and Jervis anchored his fleet off Rosia Bay on 1 December 1796. The progress from Corsica had been slow because each sail of the line had towed a ship of the valuable Smyrna convoy, all the way. Langara had been cruising in the Mediterranean in company with a French squadron under Villeneuve and on 10 December his fleet was seen from the Rock making its passage from east to west. There was a gale blowing from the ESE and Jervis was unable to sail out of the Bay in pursuit, so Langara reached Cadiz unhindered. The gale increased in violence and HMS *Courageux* 74 dragged her anchor and was driven from her mooring towards the north-west side of the Bay. After managing to set some sails her crew beat out into the open sea and they were just beginning to relax, thinking she was safe, when she was driven onto the rocks near Mount Abyla. She sank with the loss of 464 lives. Other ships were damaged in the storm. HMS *Gibraltar* hit the Pearl Rock but her strong mahogany hull saved her and she was able to return to the fleet. After sending Nelson (on the 15th) with a force of frigates to evacuate the Island of Elba, Jervis sailed for Lisbon the next day. He left the frigate HMS *Terpsichore* behind 'to cover supplies of the Rock, and protect the convoys between that port and Barbary.'[4]

Whilst entering the Tagus without pilots, HMS *Bombay Castle* 74 went aground on a sandbank and became a total loss. After the *Gibraltar* and other ships which had been damaged in the storm and subsequent mishaps were sent to England or were put under repair at Lisbon, Jervis was left with ten ships of the line. He stayed in port for several weeks as Don José de Cordoba, who had succeeded Langara, had moved his fleet to Cartagena. On 18 January Jervis set sail with a Brazil convoy and after seeing it safely on its way across the Atlantic he made for Cape St Vincent where he rendezvoused with his reinforcements from Britain on 6 February.

Battle of St Vincent

Cordoba had been ordered to take his fleet to Brest and he set sail from Cartagena on 1 February 1797. He intended to call in at Cadiz to

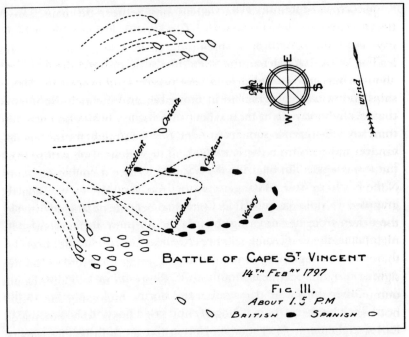

BATTLE OF CAPE S.ᵀ VINCENT
14ᵀᴴ FEBᴿʸ 1797
FIG. III.
ABOUT 1.5 P.M
BRITISH ● SPANISH ○

Plan taken from Clowes' *History of the Royal Navy* showing how Nelson in HMS *Captain* broke the line at St Vincent to stop the enemy getting away.

replenish his ships before sailing into the Atlantic. On the way he fell in with the frigate HMS *Minerve* flying the broad pennant of Commodore Nelson, but she was able to get away and carry the news to Jervis that the Spanish fleet was on its way. Nelson met Jervis off St Vincent and transferred to HMS *Captain* 74. In the meantime Cordoba had not been able to enter Cadiz harbour, because a Levanter storm swept him towards Cape St Vincent. In the early hours of the morning of St Valentine's Day, when the wind had just changed to the south-west, Jervis was notified by a Portuguese frigate that had been scouting ahead that Cordoba was five leagues ahead. Jervis led his ships south though he realised he was outnumbered by 27 to 15. But the Spanish squadron was undermanned and this was to have important consequences when the engagement, at close quarters, took place.

Jervis formed line ahead and led his ships between the main Spanish fleet to starboard and a few stragglers to port, and closing the main body, gave them the benefit of his broadsides as he sailed past. When his leading ships had reached the Spanish rear he ordered them to wear about in succession. This would have been a long process for fifteen ships and would have resulted in the stately and inconclusive minuet that was the outcome of most sailing ship battles, but Nelson who was third from the rear, drew out of line and headed straight for the Spanish van, throwing it into confusion. This unprecedented departure from the formal rules led to a ferocious melee. After a couple of hours, Nelson, seeing that HMS *Captain* was too disabled to manoeuvre, grappled with the *San Nicolas* 80 which had become entangled with the three-decker *San Josef* 112 and boarded and captured them both. By nightfall two more Spanish ships had struck. That night both fleets lay to, repairing damage, and the following morning they were still within sight of each other, sailing in line ahead on opposite tacks. Cordoba still outnumbered Jervis by 21 to 15 and had the weather gauge but he did not engage again and made his way to Cadiz. Jervis, who was created Earl St Vincent for this victory, took his ships back to Lisbon for repairs. This port was better situated than Gibraltar for intercepting Cordoba if he decided to continue to Brest, and the repair facilities were also superior.[5]

On 31 March, after refitting and receiving reinforcements St Vincent left with 21 ships of the line to blockade Cadiz, where Cordoba had been deprived of his command for incompetence, and had been replaced by Admiral Mazarredo. A blockade was now started which continued without interruption for almost three years. Gibraltar became vital for supplies and for essential refitting, though the condition of the ships deteriorated because of the long period they spent at sea. As they could not be spared they were kept on station, until many were in such a terrible state, that, had they gone into a British dockyard, they would not have been allowed to go to sea. During this time, the mutinies at Spithead and the Nore began to spread to the Mediterranean fleet, but St Vincent a strict disciplinarian, put them down with a firm hand.

The naval base at Gibraltar

Whilst blockading Cadiz in his flagship *Ville de Paris* 104 (a French ship captured by Rodney in the previous war), St Vincent worried about the shortcomings of Gibraltar as a base, and he wrote to the Admiralty about the problems faced in watering a fleet there,

> The sheets of water that pour down the rock during the rainy season, used formerly to deposit in the red sand [Alameda], and form a perpetual source; since parades and military roads have been made over the sand, it rushes down (on the north side) to the parapet of the Ragged Staff, and carries with it large quantities of loose sand, which have in a great degree choked up that little useful mole, insomuch that boats can only enter at high water. The revenues of the garrison are ample, and cannot, I conceive, be so well employed as in clearing this and the Old Mole also, much filled up;

He went on to suggest that tanks and watering facilities be provided at Rosia as 'labour is only wanting to effect everything' but owing to the number of workmen absent in privateers, he felt that this work should be deferred until peacetime when it could be carried out at a fraction of the cost. He was to be instrumental in getting the work started a few years later.[6]

The British fleet had established a moral superiority at the Battle of St Vincent, and in spite of its greater numbers the Spanish fleet did not emerge. The following year, after receiving reinforcements, St Vincent sent Nelson, now a rear-admiral, to show the flag in the Mediterranean, and this led to the Battle of the Nile on 1 August 1798, during which the Toulon fleet was almost totally destroyed. Four French ships were burnt or sunk, six were taken and only two of the line and two frigates escaped. The Royal Navy now had the upper hand in the Mediterranean.

In October St Vincent was able to detach a small squadron under Commodore Duckworth to occupy Minorca, which once again became available as a Mediterranean base and Coffin was transferred there, from Lisbon, to organise the facilities for the Navy. Minorca was not held for long as it was returned to Spain at the Peace of Amiens in 1801, but

Malta, which had been liberated from the French the year before, was retained as a British possession at the request of its inhabitants.

Lord St Vincent was now 64 years old and infirm, and he was worn out with the labour of blockading the enemy coasts, at Toulon and Cadiz, for almost three years, so in October 1798 he moved ashore to Gibraltar and raised his flag on HMS *Guerrier*. This was the former French *Peuple Souverain* 74 which had been captured by Nelson at the Nile. She had been renamed and hulked and fitted with sheer-legs to step the masts of warships being refitted, and was moored at the New Mole to serve as a depot and guardship at Gibraltar. She was broken up eight years later. The old Admiral found himself modest living quarters in Rosia House leaving Captain Inglefield in possession of the more imposing Commissioner's residence at the Mount.

St Vincent was now in a position to reorganise the dockyard facilities at Gibraltar where he had always found 'a great want of vigour and exertion'. Commissioner Inglefield he found to be

an honest man, and sufficiently intelligent but pompous, flowery, indolent, and wrapt up in official forms - stay-tape and buckram. He has however corrected many gross and abominable abuses and peculations practised under his predecessors. There is still much to do; and, to prevent the artificers from employing their time in working upon masts, boats &c upon the beach, between the north boundary of the yard and the tanks, it will be necessary to continue the wharf so as to join the pier projecting from them, and I have the governor's permission so to do. This will naturally check, if not entirely put an end to, the shipwrights slipping through the wickets, prevent thefts, and give great space for the operation of a fleet. In short much more may be made of this arsenal than I was aware of until a three months' residence and unremitted attention to it, showed me the means. Five or six ships of the line may be moored safely in the Mole; and while we maintain our naval superiority in the Mediterranean ... it will prove a very great resource, especially if the governors think as I do, that the only use of Gibraltar is to furnish the navy of Great

Britain with supplies, and thereby enable it to maintain the empire of the adjacent seas.[7]

The strain that supporting a large fleet put on the Dockyard meant that it was constantly out of essential materials. 'We are literally without a fathom of rope, yard of canvas, foot of oak or elm plank, board or log to saw them from; have not a bit of iron but what we draw out of condemned masts and yards,' wrote St Vincent to the Admiralty in January 1799. This was serious because some of the ships with which Lord Keith was trying to maintain the blockade of Cadiz were 'in so crazy a state, they are obliged to come occasionally to the Mole to be patched up.'[8] He also had to bring pressure to bear on the army to vacate the Naval Hospital as it was needed for the Navy's sick. The army transferred theirs to South Barracks.[9]

St Vincent thought that the warehouses were inconveniently situated and needed reorganising. He wanted to move them from the town to Rosia, where they would be more accessible. Several plans were put forward and he favoured those prepared by a local builder Giovanni Maria Boschetti, which included a mole in Rosia Bay for the loading and unloading of supplies. He was confident that these projects could be paid for with the proceeds from the sale of the properties in town, for he was 'sanguine enough to expect twenty thousand for the buildings and ground at Waterport, exclusive of the White Convent and the residence of the agent, which will probably bring in five thousand.' He had an argument with O'Hara about the Navy's right to the proceeds from the sale of the properties it held and the right to demand land for new building at the same time. The governor also insisted that the new stores should be bomb-proof, which St Vincent felt would make them prohibitively expensive. However, the negotiations reached a satisfactory conclusion and on 8 February 1799, St. Vincent was able to report that 'General O'Hara has consented to spare a sufficient quantity of ground in the Rosier [sic] quarter to erect the reservoir and victualling stores and offices.'

Work began on the water reservoir at Rosia in 1799 and by 1804 it was ready for use and could store 6,000 tons of water. The million bricks needed to line it were probably shipped from Britain. In July 1807 the

Navy Board authorised the construction of the new Victualling Yard. Construction started the following year and was completed in 1812, as was the wharf. The result was a massive building, 190 by 160 feet, built on the lines of contemporary magazines, with eleven vaulted rooms in each of the two floors. The walls are of stone and the vaults of brick. The walls and ceilings are so thick that they not only provide a dry temperature-controlled environment for provisions but must also be considered bomb-proof in terms of shot fired from unrifled muzzle loaders. The total cost was over £60,000.

Over the main gate of the Yard Boschetti set up the inscription G.III D G M B & H R &. which signifies *Georgius III Deo Gratia Maiestate Britanniae et Hibernias Rex &c.* and means: 'George III Monarch of Britain and King of Ireland etc'. He obviously chose this archaic formula because it carried his own initials - GMB - in the centre. This gate leads to a small enclosed courtyard with a two-storey office for the Agent Victualler to the right and a range of store sheds at the back, while the entrance to the main building is on the left.[10]

There was another matter on which St Vincent had to take up cudgels with O'Hara. The Governor had been in Gibraltar for ten years and had cultivated good relations with the Spanish military on the frontier. When he first arrived he had seen the destruction that had been wreaked during the Great Siege, even ten years later it had not been completely made good, and he was determined to avoid it happening again. He had therefore negotiated a local truce. He undertook not to engage in any hostilities on the frontier as long as the Spaniards left Gibraltar well alone. This meant that the Spanish gunboats were free to roam the Strait and attack shipping, but would not cannonade Gibraltar and they would not be fired on by the Rock's batteries.

Trade between Gibraltar and Spain continued without hindrance. Spain supplied fresh food and in return received manufactured goods and tobacco which she could not otherwise obtain through the Royal Navy's blockade. The British Government approved of these arrangements, not only because they were beneficial to Gibraltar, but also because these exports were paid for in bullion which Britain needed to meet the expenses of the war. This trade was legally endorsed by two Orders in Council. One, on 4 April 1798 expressly allowed leaf tobacco to be exported from Gibraltar. This Order was necessary because a previous one in 1751 had prohibited the trade. The second one dated 4 December 1799 allowed imports from Spain to continue in time of war, so that the garrison should not have to rely entirely on supplies from Morocco.[11]

St Vincent complained that an army officer had been put under arrest for firing on the Spanish gunboats, and that the captains of the enemy vessels visited Gibraltar regularly and were even entertained by the governor. He related the story of a naval officer dining at the Convent who found the commander of one of the gunboats with which he had been closely and warmly engaged a few hours before, standing behind his chair. 'The gallant Englishman handed his antagonist a very liberal allowance of plum-pudding, and a glass of wine, which the Spaniard took with perfect nonchalance.'[12]

All this should not have shocked St Vincent unduly, for he himself had maintained cordial relations with the Spaniards while blockading Cadiz. A young officer of engineers who visited his flagship with a group of sightseers, including ladies, recorded in his diary,

There was much on board the *Ville de Paris* to amuse us. The bumboats which came off by stealth every night from the Spanish shore emptied their cargoes of fruits and retailed them between the guns on our quarter deck while the boats from the fleet came at a certain hour to make their purchases. If these cargoes were not disposed of before nightfall they were placed under charge of a sentinel till the next day, the vendors sleeping in their own boats. ... tho' every night the armed boats of the squadron were sent off to bombard and harass the city, a sort of civil reciprocity of feeling was maintained between the contending parties. The Governor of Cadiz not unfrequently sent off presents to the Admiral and his guests of game, fruit and flowers and singing birds in decorated cages for the ladies.[13]

In the archives there is an amusing letter written by O'Hara on 30 September 1798, explaining that when news was received of Nelson's victory at the Nile the garrison greeted the glorious news with a royal salute, but he first advised the Spanish General Escalante of the occasion for the discharge as he did not wish him to be alarmed. This must stand as the best reason ever given for not firing at an enemy. O'Hara added that the inhabitants manifested their zeal and loyalty on this occasion by 'Illuminating & every demonstration of Joy.'[14]

In March 1798 the French fleet broke out from Brest under the command of the Minister of Marine, Vice-Admiral Bruix, and made its way to the Mediterranean. The plan was to establish command of that sea by assembling an overwhelming force. Bruix was supposed to be joined by the Spanish fleet from Cadiz, but when he reached that port, Mazarredo was unable to come out in the teeth of a strong south-westerly gale, nor was Bruix able to approach or wait because of Keith's blockading squadron. St Vincent learnt of the approach of the French when the enemy fleet was seen passing the Strait on 6 May. That night the hired cutter Penelope was sent out to reconnoitre and got in close enough to hear orders being given in French, she was discovered but was able to make her getaway and return to Gibraltar with information on the composition of the enemy force. It was important to recall Keith from Cadiz at once, but because of the Spanish gunboats and the bad weather a small boat would be unable to get through and St Vincent had no major units with him. But Captain Sir Isaac Coffin, who was on his way from Minorca to Canada, volunteered to obtain a passport from the Spanish governor of San Roque to go through Spain to Lisbon, and when he reached Faro, hire a boat and carry the orders to Keith.

It was quite normal in the 18th century for enemy nationals to be given permission to go about their peaceful business, whether it was trade or tourism, but if found carrying orders or military dispatches they might be executed as spies.

Nevertheless Coffin's good humour was so infectious that a smiling St. Vincent took his hand and bade him 'Good b'ye Coffin, you'll be hanged tomorrow!' But nothing could dampen the irrepressible captain's high spirits and he set off for the frontier singing a bolero. His hidden orders were not discovered and Coffin got through to Keith as he had planned. St Vincent commented afterwards, 'I never imagined a Spaniard of our days a match for an American, which Sir Isaac is, an Indian hunter, every inch of him.'[15]

When Keith had reached Gibraltar and the other scattered ships had been collected, St Vincent set off after Bruix, flying his flag on the *Ville de Paris* once more. But Bruix realised that his projected combination had failed and that he was inferior to the forces being concentrated against him. He therefore took refuge in Toulon. Thereafter there were a number of sorties and local operations but the strain of the blockade was too much for St Vincent's health and in June he hauled down his flag and returned to Britain leaving Keith in command. Later in the year Bruix broke out from Toulon and made his way to Brest joining up with Mazarredo who sortied from Cartagena. Keith followed in hot pursuit, but the combined fleet, 40 sail strong, reached Brest one day ahead of him.

Keith returned to the Mediterranean, and with no sizable Spanish or French forces to oppose him, he devoted his efforts to the blockade of Malta and the Italian coast. In October he embarked a considerable landing force at Gibraltar, under General Sir Ralph Abercromby, in order to attack Cadiz. But when they arrived off that city they found it in the grip of a serious yellow fever epidemic and it would have been imprudent to land the army. So after holding a council of war the fleet set sail for Egypt and the expeditionary force was employed in driving the French out of that country.

The Battle of Algeciras

In June 1801 Rear-Admiral Durand-Linois left Toulon for Cadiz with four ships that had returned from Brest - *Formidable* and *Indomptable* 80s, *Desaix* 74 and the frigate *Muiron*. He reached the Strait on 1 July. The only naval vessel at Gibraltar was the polacre *San Josef* 16 which had been captured off Malaga the previous October and had been renamed HMS *Calpe* after the old Greek name for the Rock. She could not venture out in full view of the powerful French squadron, and Janvrin, her lieutenant, was sent in a small boat to alert Rear-Admiral Sir James Saumarez who was blockading Cadiz with six ships of the line. In the meantime, Linois beating against strong WNW winds had decided not to confront Saumarez's superior force and had taken his ships into Algeciras. He anchored off the town on the evening of the 4th. When Saumarez arrived two days later flying his flag in HMS *Caesar* 80 with

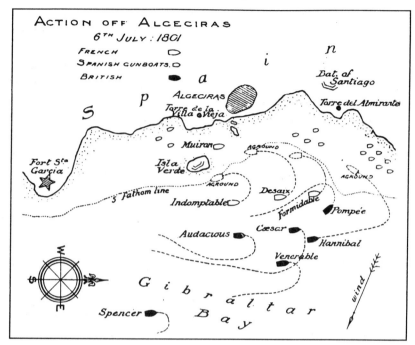

Plan from Clowes' *History of the Royal Navy.*

HMS *Pompée, Spencer, Venerable, Hannibal* and *Audacious* 74s, he found Linois' ships anchored in a line, 500 yards from each other, in 9 to 12 fathoms. The strong batteries on the Isla Verde and the fort of Santiago were manned by sailors from the *Muiron,* as were other guns in Fort Santa Garcia and the towers of Villa Vieja and Almirante. There were also 14 Spanish gunboats with their long-range guns for additional protection.

The British squadron started rounding Punta Carnero in light winds at 7 am and were soon in action. For three hours the cannonading was heavy on both sides, but Saumarez noticed that HMS *Pompée,* which had anchored close to the *Formidable,* was in trouble as she could only bring her forward guns to bear, he therefore ordered the *Hannibal* which had not been heavily engaged hitherto, to go to her assistance by raking 'the French admiral'. Captain Ferris instantly cut his cable and using the light winds to best advantage sailed to the north to get between the *Formidable* and the shore, but he sailed too far in and ran aground. Afraid that the other British ships might follow her example with more success, Linois ordered his ships to cut their cables and run themselves ashore. The combination of a light breeze, a strong current and the rocks and shoals to leeward, meant that the rest of Saumarez's ships were now too far away to inflict damage on the enemy and could get no closer. At 1.35 pm Saumarez ordered his squadron to withdraw but the *Hannibal* was left fast aground within range of the enemy's batteries and Captain Ferris was obliged to haul down his colours and surrender. When the French took possession they followed their usual custom and raised the Union Flag upside down. This rather confused the *Calpe* who took it as a signal for assistance and sent a boat to the *Hannibal* and the crew was made prisoner. The first round had been won by the enemy though five of their gunboats had been sunk.[16]

Saumarez's ships had been badly battered but the reorganised Gibraltar Dockyard proved equal to the occasion and in two days all the ships except the *Pompée* were seaworthy and ready for action again. In the meantime Linois had sent to Cadiz for assistance and Don Juan Moreno arrived in the Bay on the 10th with five ships of the line, one of which was French. He was followed by HMS *Superb* 74 which had been left behind to keep a watch.

Moreno anchored off Algeciras, and at noon on the 12th the combined squadron got under way leaving the captured *Hannibal* behind; by 1 pm their leading ships were off Punta Carnero and HMS *Caesar* was warping out of the New Mole. Her band was playing 'Come cheer up my lads,' and the garrison band played them out with 'Britons, strike home.' By 8 pm the enemy had cleared the Bay and Saumarez was chasing the eight enemy liners with his five. At 8.40 he ordered the *Superb*, which was his fastest ship, to sail ahead and attack the enemy's rear which was disappearing into the sunset. Captain Keats pressed on and at 11.30 overtook the three-decker *Real Carlos* 112. Disregarding the difference in size and power he shortened sail and gave her three broadsides from a distance of 300 yards, which set her on fire. He then set sail again and caught up with the *St Antoine* 74. After an engagement lasting half an hour he forced the French ship to surrender.

Whilst the *Superb* was thus engaged the *Real Carlos* started firing on other Spanish ships in error. The fire started by the *Superb* was spreading fast and she blew up suddenly. At the time she was foul of the *San Hermenegildo*, another Spanish three-decker, and the explosion set her on fire and she also blew up. The wind freshened and the chase continued and there were sporadic engagements in which the *Venerable* lost her masts and was in danger of going aground on Cape Trafalgar, but her crew managed to save her by putting up a jury rig. The rest of the Franco-Spanish squadron entered Cadiz harbour safely.[17]

Saumarez was made a Knight of the Bath for this successful battle and he was invested with his insignia' by O'Hara, in a ceremony held in the Grand Parade.[18]

This was the last important naval engagement in the Mediterranean before the cessation of hostilities was proclaimed on 10 October 1801.

Notes and References

(1)   Correspondence in CO.91:35.
(2)   CO.91:34 - Eliott's letter No 37 of 7 December 1786. The request was made because the Knights of St John had refused to allow the Emperor of Morocco to ransom the Moslems they held as slaves.
(3)   Clowes 4:152; Coad *Historic Architecture* 101, 103.
(4)   Brenton 1:220-221; Clowes 4:289-290; Jackson 185.
(5)   Clowes 4:305-320; Sherrard 104-107.
(6)   Tucker 1:425-426.
(7)   Brenton 1:471.
(8)   Brenton 1:475, 480.
(9)   CO.91:40, O'Hara to Portland, 6 August 1798.
(10) Brenton 1:470-471; Coad *Historic Architecture* 126-127; Coad *Dockyards* 324; *Gibraltar Directory 1939* 240; CO.94:44, Otway to Trigge, 14 March 1804.
(11) CO.91:45 Fox Memorandum, dated 11 January 1805.
(12) Brenton 1:469; CO.91:40, O'Hara to Portland, 16 February 1798, O'Hara to St Vincent, 8 March 1798.
(13) Whitmore 11.
(14) CO.91:40, O'Hara to Portland.
(15) Tucker 1:339-403. Coffin was born in Boston, Massachusetts.
(16) Clowes 4:459-464; Jenkins 237-238.
(17) Clowes 4:465-470.
(18) CO.91:42, O'Hara to Secretary of State, 18 November 1801.

CHAPTER VI

NELSON.

The peace did not last long, as Napoleon, enshrined as First Consul of France and soon to become emperor, was still thirsting for glory. The immediate cause of the war was Britain's refusal to give up Malta, whose strategic position and fine harbour and facilities were to prove of great value to the Navy. Napoleon insulted the British ambassador and this led to the breaking off of relations. On 16 May 1803 the British Government authorised the issue of letters of marque and general reprisal against French ships. Two days later war was declared and Nelson, newly appointed CinC Mediterranean, raised his flag at Portsmouth and made his way to join his squadron.

Nelson arrived in Gibraltar on board the frigate HMS *Amphion* 32 on 3 June and issued a number of orders to place the establishment in a high state of preparedness. He ordered the Naval Store Keeper to pay strict attention to the care and issuing of stores and to make sure that he only did so against the regulation orders from the captains of ships. He also ordered the gunboats and flat-bottomed boats to be fitted out and HMS *Guerrier* 'Sheer-hulk' to be altered to accommodate 40 officers and 300 men. Above all he wanted to ensure that supplies to Gibraltar were not interrupted and he detailed the sloop HMS *Bittern* 18 to cruise off Gibraltar and afford every assistance to Lieutenant-General Trigge, the lieutenant-governor. Nelson was very conscious of the importance of Gibraltar both as a base for the supply of his fleet and as occupying a vital position in the Strait from which the entrance to the Mediterranean could be watched.[1]

The following day he left for Malta and arrived there on the 15 June. After a couple of days he left to join the fleet that was already on station outside Toulon. During the two years that Nelson was involved in the blockade of the French Mediterranean coast his correspondence shows his concern for Gibraltar and the importance he attached to it. He did his best to ensure that there was an adequate naval guard there, and he regulated the ships that were to use the dockyard facilities for refitting and repairs. But of course Gibraltar was very far from Toulon and Nelson used the Maddalena Islands to the north of Sardinia as an advanced anchorage and base for the fleet.

Nelson was very concerned when he heard that a yellow fever epidemic had broken out in Gibraltar in September 1804, and as the fleet used Spanish ports regularly he wrote an explanatory letter to the Captain General of Barcelona. He informed him that a fever had broken out in Gibraltar similar to the one in Malaga, but the troops were healthy and there was no disease in the fleet. The last ship had left Gibraltar on 26 September and the only communication with the fortress since had been through the lazaretto. In the circumstances Gibraltar could not be used by the Navy and other arrangements had to be made for the frigate HMS *Medusa* which was due to go there for a refit.[2]

But the peace with Spain was not to last much longer as her royal family had fallen under the thumb of Napoleon and was providing him with funds for the war. They were warned that this was a *casus belli* but they were not in a position to stop the payments. In October four Royal Navy frigates intercepted the South American treasure fleet outside Cadiz. In the fighting one of the treasure ships was sunk but the other three were captured and yielded over £1,000,000 in silver. Spain declared war on England in December.

The Trafalgar Campaign 1805

Once again it was necessary to blockade Cadiz and at the beginning of 1805, Vice-Admiral Sir John Orde was sent with a fleet for the purpose. As Orde was senior to Nelson, the CinC, he in effect constituted an independent command. Fox, the lieutenant-governor, found that Spanish ships were blockading Gibraltar and intercepting the boats that brought the garrison's beef from North Africa. He applied to Orde for assistance but was referred to Nelson, who was unable to assist him as he was short of the small vessels needed for trade protection. On 30 March he wrote to Commissioner Otway at Gibraltar asking him to explain matters to Fox.

> I have not the pleasure of being known to General Fox. I wish you would tell [him] of the absolute want of Small Craft at Malta, and that I have them not under my command or Gibraltar should not have been neglected by me. If Sir John Orde was junior to me, I should instruct him...

Nelson felt that Orde was responsible for the protection of Gibraltar as he commanded the ships in the area, but he could not instruct him to do so because of his seniority. On the other hand, Gibraltar was still his main supply base and he wanted to maintain his control over it - as otherwise an independent admiral could take 'all the stores he chooses or fancies he wants, for the service of his fleet; thereby placing the fleet in the Gulf of Lyons in great distress for many articles.'[3]

But Nelson's problems now changed, for Vice-Admiral Pierre Villeneuve left Toulon with his fleet on 30 March. The shadowing frigates lost touch and when the information reached Nelson, four days later, he had no idea of Villeneuve's destination. For some days he cruised round Sicily in the hope of intercepting the French should they be heading for Egypt once more. 'Broken hearted as I am, at the escape of the Toulon fleet' he wrote to Fox, 'yet it cannot prevent my thinking of all the points intrusted to my care, amongst which Gibraltar stands prominent: I wish you to consider me particularly desirous to give every comfort to the good old Rock.' On the 19th he received definite information that Villeneuve had reached Cadiz and had driven off Orde's blockading ships ten days before, but the winds were unfavourable and it took him two weeks to reach the Strait. 'I cannot get a fair wind,' he wrote, 'or even a side wind. Dead foul! Dead foul!'[4]

Nelson sailed to Tetuan on 4 May to take on board water and fresh beef; he anchored his ships in Mazri Bay which for many years had been the Navy's favourite watering place in these parts. There is a note in his diary which explains why. Ships could anchor in Mazri Bay in ten to twenty fathoms as close as half a mile to the Martin River which 'runs inside a beach and parallel to it, so the Boats may come alongside the beach the whole extent of the Bay, and roll their casks over to the River, and fill them.' The wind blew from the south the following day and he immediately stopped loading supplies and set off for Gibraltar. The wind was still basically westerly but Nelson anticipated that it was about to turn into a Levanter. The fleet had only been anchored at Gibraltar for five hours when, at the first sign of an easterly breeze, Nelson gave the order to sail and they left towing their supply ships.[5]

Nelson was convinced that Villeneuve was bound for the West Indies and he was determined to follow him there, but as he had no definite information this was a gamble. 'If they are not gone to the West Indies, I shall be blamed;' he told his secretary, 'to be burnt in effigy or Westminster Abbey is my alternative.' Once outside the Strait and out of danger of being boxed in by contrary winds, the fleet anchored in Lagos Bay to complete their stores from the supply ships they had towed from Gibraltar. On the 11th he received confirmation of Villeneuve's destination and he set sail across the Atlantic.[6]

Villeneuve had arrived at Martinique on 14 May after a slow crossing, with eighteen sail of the line, six of which were Spanish - under General of the Navy Federico Gravina. Nelson made a much faster crossing and arrived at Barbados with his eleven liners on 4 June. Now began a game of hide and seek among the islands and Nelson was unable to catch up with his opponent. Working on the information that he had garnered he came to the conclusion that Villeneuve intended to return to the Strait. On the 13th he set sail in pursuit. Villeneuve had a five day start, but he did not make his way to Cadiz but to Ferrol, where he expected to be met by reinforcements.

On the way across the Atlantic, Nelson sent two vessels with warnings of the approach of the allied fleet, one to Sir Robert Calder who was blockading Ferrol, and another to Rear-Admiral John Knight at Gibraltar and Vice-Admiral Cuthbert Collingwood who had taken over the blockade of Cadiz from Orde. When the fleet reached the Azores on 10 June he sent another dispatch to Knight and Commissioner Otway. He informed them that he was not certain whether the fleet would anchor at Gibraltar. It all depended on the enemy's movements, but the dispatch boat carried no private letters for he wished the approach of the fleet to remain a secret, 'for everything which is known on the

Rock gets into Spain.' Otway was, however, to prepare a fore-yard for HMS *Canopus* one of his 'crazy-ships' that had been on blockade for over two years, as hers was rotten through.[7]

On the 19th June, Nelson's fleet anchored off Rosia Bay, and the admiral went ashore for the first time in two years; the last time he had set foot on dry land had been at Malta on 16 June 1803. He was appalled at the state of the town, which was still recovering from the effects of the yellow fever which had carried off half the civilian population, though the army had got off more lightly. When he met Aaron Cardozo, the leading local merchant and a supplier of beef to the Navy, he told him grimly, 'If I survive Cardozo you shall no longer remain in this dark corner of the world.' A few months later when Nelson was blockading Cadiz and was concerned about the supply of fresh beef, essential for keeping his crews free from scurvy, he sent Cardozo in the sloop HMS *Termagant* to Oran, to negotiate a treaty with the Bey. After Nelson's death, Rear-Admiral Lord Northesk, who had fought at Trafalgar, and was charged by Nelson's trustees with distributing personal mementos among the dead Admiral's friends and associates, sent Cardozo 'a gold medal commemorative of the Battle of the Nile.' Cardozo is remembered today for the handsome mansion he built himself in John Mackintosh Square, which is now the City Hall.[8]

Nelson was concerned about the lack of maritime defences at Gibraltar and wrote to Barham, the First Lord, suggesting a resurrection of Curtis' Naval Brigade which had been of great service during the Great Siege. If the town and garrison were 'to be saved from the harassing and distress occasioned by the Gun-boats,' he recommended that between ten and twenty gunboats 'of the Praam kind' should be built and manned.[9]

It was vital for the fleet to replenish its supplies, as during the mad rush round the West Indies they had received 'not the smallest refreshment, or even a cup of water.' At Gibraltar they took in a four months, supply, 'except bread of which there was not sufficient quantity;' and on the 22nd they sailed to Mazri Bay to water and take 'on board a fortnight's fresh provisions, of which, and refreshments,' the fleet was 'much in want, every ship having much of the scurvy, but, thank God not the smallest symptom of any other complaint.' Many of the ships took on board 200 tons of water in one day, but no onions were to be had 'for the people's broth'. Fortunately, Hardy, his flag captain, remembered seeing a Spanish boat with a cargo of onions at the Old Mole. Nelson asked the naval victualler at Gibraltar to purchase 300 lbs, even though they might cost as much as 2d or 2 1/2d a lb, and send them over in HMS *Gun-brig*.[10]

Before sailing for the west Nelson ordered Knight to take under his command 'His majesty's Sloops and Gun-Brigs *Guerrier, Phoebe, Decade, Martin, Termagant, Halcyon, Dexterous, Gun-Brig* and *Fervent* Gun-Brig and employ them ... for ... the protection of commerce' to guard British merchant ships from capture by the numerous Spanish gunboats in the Strait. The *Guerrier* was of course a captured ship of the line but as a harbour hulk she had the complement of a sloop and was rated as such.[11]

On the evening of the 24th the fleet took advantage of a brisk Levanter and set sail in pursuit of Villeneuve. Whilst off Tarifa HMS *Victory* was approached by the *Termagant* with mail. Nelson thought that she came from Lisbon and as he did not wish to be delayed he ordered her to Gibraltar, not realising that she had just come from there with his clean laundry. As a result she carried back all his things down to his last spare shirt. When he reached the Bay of Biscay, Nelson learnt that the enemy fleet had had an encounter with a squadron under Calder and had taken shelter in Ferrol and Corunna. As there was now no enemy fleet in the Mediterranean, he felt justified in returning to England for a well earned rest.[12]

Villeneuve had been ordered to go to Brest to raise the blockade, and he set off on 18 August, but on meeting the Channel Fleet he despaired of his ability to achieve this, and he turned round for Cadiz which he reached with 29 sail on 28 August. He brushed aside Collingwood's four ships, which were blockading the port, and entered. There were now 33 sail of the line in Cadiz harbour, of which 18 were French and 15 Spanish. Collingwood's squadron was therefore quickly reinforced and on 28 September Nelson arrived in the *Victory* and assumed command. Once again he had started on what could turn out to be a long and tedious blockade.

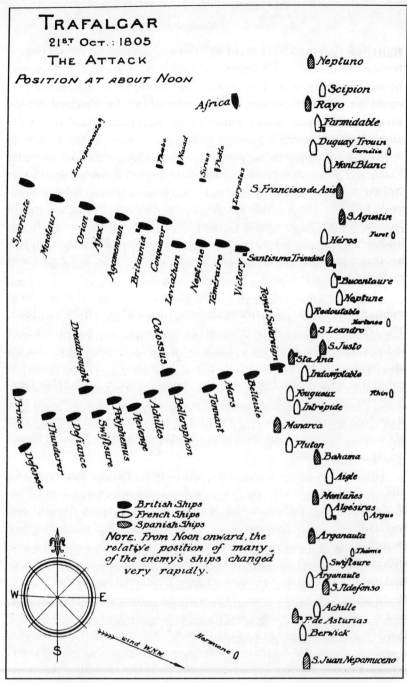

Plan from Clowes' *History of the Royal Navy* showing the position of the opposing fleets at the beginning of the Battle of Trafalgar.

Battle of Trafalgar

Nelson occupied his time in instructing his commanders on the tactics he would employ if the allied fleet came out to fight, and, as his fleet could not stay on blockade without replenishing, he arranged to send small numbers of ships in rotation to take in supplies at Gibraltar. He also followed his usual practice of staying out of sight of land so that his opponent should have no accurate information about his strength. Villeneuve knew that his own fleet was superior, but he thought that Nelson only had 21 ships with him. However when he sailed out of Cadiz on 19 October with his full strength of 33 ships of the line he was to find Nelson waiting for him with 27. But Villeneuve was a man in a hurry, his successor Admiral Rosily was on his way to Cadiz, and the only way he could redeem his reputation was to win a battle before he was replaced.

The two fleets did not catch sight of each other until the following evening (the 20th). The next morning the wind was WNW and light. The allies were sailing towards the south but on sighting the British fleet in the west they turned north. Nelson formed his ships into two columns and he sailed towards the enemy at 2 or 3 knots. He led the northern column in HMS *Victory* 100 and Collingwood the southern in HMS *Royal Sovereign* 100. The wind was light and the approach was slow. At this stage Nelson made his famous signal 'England expects every man to do his duty'. This irritated Collingwood who exclaimed 'I wish Nelson would stop signalling!'

The *Victory* was within firing range at 12.20 pm but Collingwood had already broken through the enemy's line some minutes before. The *Victory's* slow approach made her a target for the enemy's fire and she was badly mauled before she crossed the wake of Villeneuve's flagship *Bucentaure* 90 at 1 pm. She then ground against the *Redoutable* 74 and within a few minutes a marksman perched on the latter's fighting top had mortally wounded Nelson who had to be taken down below. Before he died at 4.30 Nelson knew that he had won a great victory. The steady and rapid firing of his ships and the discipline of their crews, had won the day, and 18 of the enemy were taken. Nelson sensed that there was a westerly storm brewing, and because so many of his ships and their captures were disabled he asked Hardy to make sure that the fleet anchored at nightfall, for he knew the damage that could be wreaked by a storm on a lee shore, in the condition the ships were in.

By 5 in the evening the battle was over. Out of the enemy line of battle of 33, 18 had been taken, four French vessels had broken away for Brest, and eleven had returned to Cadiz - five French and six Spanish. Collingwood left his disabled flagship and raised his flag in HMS *Queen* 98 to take over command of the fleet and resume the blockade. The captured *Achille* blew up and the other 17 prizes were disabled as were half his own ships, but Collingwood did not comply with Nelson's deathbed instructions to anchor. The following day it blew a south-westerly gale and a small French squadron came out from Cadiz and recaptured two of the captured ships. Others were retaken by their crews or went aground and were wrecked, so in the end only four of the prizes reached Gibraltar.[13]

On the 23rd the cutter HMS *Flying Fish* arrived in Gibraltar with news of the victory and Collingwood's dispatches. The following day the Gibraltar Chronicle had a worldwide scoop as it was the first newspaper to publish the news of Trafalgar. The damaged ships were brought to Gibraltar to be repaired, including the four captured vessels, and one of them the *San Juan Nepomuceno* 74 was retained to be used as a hulk in replacement for the *Guerrier*. She was listed under the shortened name of HMS *San Juan*. The cabin in which her commander, Commodore Cosmé Damian Churruca, had died was always kept locked out of respect for this brave officer, who at one stage during the battle had gallantly engaged five of Collingwood's ships.[14]

The dismasted *Victory* with the body of Nelson preserved in a barrel of spirits was towed to Gibraltar by HMS *Neptune*. She arrived on the 28th and anchored in Rosia Bay where she was repaired and her masts and rigging refitted. Although some writers have claimed that Nelson's body was brought ashore at Rosia, there is no evidence of this. On 3 November after being repaired, *Victory* sailed for England carrying Nelson's body and still flying his Vice-Admiral's flag at half-mast. She anchored at St. Helens on 4 December.

After Trafalgar

The blockade of Cadiz was continued under Collingwood's command until the middle of 1808. In May of that year the population of Madrid rose against Joseph Bonaparte, Napoleon's brother, who had been imposed on the Spaniards as their king. In June a Junta met at Seville and declared war on France. Rear-Admiral Purvis who was blockading Cadiz with ten of the line, offered his help to the Spanish patriots in capturing the five French ships of the line and one frigate that still lay in their harbour, but his offer was refused by General Morla, who commanded at Cadiz. The French ships were anchored in the narrow channel of La Carraca, so the Spaniards prepared a force of 45 gunboats and mortar-boats, and built batteries to overlook the ships; they started their attack on 9 June. A number of the gunboats were sunk by the French gunfire but they were replaced by others which had arrived from Malaga. After several days of hard fighting Rosily surrendered on the 14th and the French ships were incorporated into the Spanish Navy. The long blockades had at last come to an end.[15]

This was the last of the major naval operations in the vicinity of Gibraltar although the war lasted for another six years and the French built many new ships which had to be countered by the Royal Navy retaining squadrons at sea.

In 1810 the French sent their army to operate against Cadiz, which had become the seat of the Spanish Government and the patriot forces were supported from the sea. At this time the frontier fortifications of La Linea were razed with the consent of the Spaniards in order to prevent Marshall Soult, who was operating in the area, from seizing them and using them against the British. In October, two British and one Spanish regiment were landed at Fuengirola, in an attempt to seize Malaga, but were counter-attacked whilst besieging Fuengirola Fort. Lord Blayney the British commander proved incompetent and he was captured with part of his force. The rest were rescued through the intervention of Captain Burton in HMS *Rodney* 74 assisted by a Spanish battleship *El Vencedor*.[16] The following year, General Graham was landed with a large force at Tarifa in order to try and raise the siege of Cadiz. He reached Chiclana, but after a spirited action on Barrosa Beach he gave up the attempt to relieve Cadiz and returned to Gibraltar.

The war against merchant shipping continued and both the Navy's cruisers and the privateers from Gibraltar continued to bring in rich prizes. But trade with occupied Europe became increasingly more important in the face of Napoleon's Continental System. Napoleon knew that if he destroyed her trade Britain would not find it possible to raise the finance to continue the war. As he was in political control of most of Europe he thought he could achieve this by banning trade with his enemy, but he did not allow for the desire in the occupied countries for colonial and manufactured goods which could only be obtained from Britain.

Much of this illicit, but highly advantageous trade for Britain, was conducted through Gibraltar and it brought in a substantial amount of Spanish and European silver coins which were badly needed to defray the expenses of Wellington's Peninsular Campaign. William Mark, the purser of HMS *San Juan* described the situation during the later years of the war,

> Amongst other things, during this important period, was the collecting money for the use of Lord Wellington's Army. We generally had a ship of war in Gibraltar Bay, taking on board money for Lisbon, and every month we sent from a million to a million and a half hard dollars to carry on the war, while, for this purpose, not a dollar was to be procured anywhere else; there was no coin in England that would answer the purpose. All this is public and notorious. Lord Wellington was often reduced to the greatest difficulties for the want of money, on which his supplies so principally depended, and he has often declared the great importance of Gibraltar from that very circumstance.[17]

Mark felt that this more than justified maintaining Gibraltar as a free port which could trade without restriction with all parts of the world.

Although there were a number of brilliant single ship encounters there were no more big naval battles after Trafalgar. But France built herself an imposing new navy and it was necessary to blockade Toulon again. Minorca had been returned to Spain in 1802 but Malta was now found eminently suitable as a base, though Gibraltar was still used.

Malta's small shipyard in the Grand Harbour of Valetta, which had serviced the warships maintained by the Knights of St. John, was quickly developed; and by the end of the war in 1814 it was twice as big as the Dockyard at Gibraltar, employing 378 artificers and labourers as compared to 170.[18]

Notes and References

(1)   Nicolas 5:78, 80, 81.

(2)   Nicolas 6:237.

(3)   Nicolas 6:386-387, 415; Mahan 626.

(4)   Mahan 653; Clarke & M'cArthur 3:93.

(5)   Mahan 654; Nicolas 6:486.

(6)   Mahan 655, 657.

(7)   Nicolas 6:469; Mahan 664.

(8)   Nicolas 6:475; *Cardozo* 21-24; Ellicott 15-35. In later years, Cardozo received letters inscribed 'Your sincere friend' from both Lord St Vincent and Admiral Sir Sidney Smith (Cardozo 2, 20)

(9)   Nicolas 6:476.

(10)   Nicolas 6:480, 485, 490; Clarke & M'cArthur 3:111.

(11)   Nicolas 6:492; Mark 196.

(12)   Mahan 11.

(13)   Clowes 5:126-162; Mahan 713-742; Barbudo 9-11.

(14)   Gibraltar Chronicle passim; Gonzalez 27.

(15)   Barbudo 14-18.

(16)   Mark 216-218.

(17)   Mark 215-216.

(18)   Morris 224.

CHAPTER VII

VICTORIAN DAYS.

With the coming of peace the number of ships in service was dramatically reduced. By 1816 the Mediterranean fleet consisted of only one first rate and six smaller vessels; although there were temporary increases in times of crisis, such as during the confrontation with Turkey over Greece in 1828 and the Crimean War of 1854-1856. But the main base was now Malta, with its excellent harbour and central position which made it more suitable for protecting Britain's expanding political interests in the eastern basin.[1]

The facilities in Gibraltar were therefore drastically cut. In 1817 the hulk *San Juan* was struck off the list and the following year Captain Isaac Wolley RN, who was Commissioner of the Dockyard, moved to Malta. Henceforth the official at Gibraltar held the less exalted title of SNO, while Malta with its expanding dockyard warranted the only Commissioner of HM Dockyards in the Mediterranean. It is little wonder then, that by the middle of the century, the cost of the dockyard at Gibraltar was only £400 a year of which £41 was for 'postage and regulating the dockyard clock'![2]

There was no call for the Naval Hospital at Gibraltar and in 1816 it was handed over to the Army which had been sharing the facilities for some years. It was handed over subject to accommodation continuing to be provided for a number of commissioned and warrant officers who had their quarters in the Hospital. The building could be reclaimed by the Navy at any time but this was not done until the end of the century. In 1892 the Navy took back half the building and the hospital was re-established. After the completion of the Military Hospital in 1904, the RN once again controlled the whole of the building.[3]

Apart from visiting ships there was normally a gunboat of some description stationed at Gibraltar which would give assistance to British shipping whenever required, and in which, the SNO, who resided at the Mount, flew his pennant. In addition, the old wooden frigate HMS *Samarang* 36 was made guardship in 1847 and it also housed the offices of the Captain of the Port. The *Samarang* was sold for breaking up in 1883, and the Captain of the Port then set up his office on land, but even today the Port Office is still referred to as 'the *Samarang*' by many of the older inhabitants.[4]

Smugglers and pirates

During the course of the century the Gibraltar guardships were involved in a number of confrontations with Spanish *guardacostas* (coast guard cutters) which intercepted boats suspected of smuggling sailing from Gibraltar. The peace of 1815 had left a considerable number of men, who had settled in Gibraltar to crew the privateers fitted out by the local merchants, without any means of earning a living. There was no large merchant or fishing fleet or any manufacturing activity which could offer them alternative employment. Inevitably the unemployed men and boats turned to smuggling. At first the goods smuggled were textiles and tobacco, but as Spain's industrial revolution got under way the market for smuggled textiles was eroded and by the second half of the 19th century the smuggling by the Gibraltar boats was mostly tobacco.[5]

These Gibraltar registered boats were 'fair traders' in the high seas and within the territorial waters of Gibraltar and therefore entitled to the Royal Navy's protection. But it was too much to expect a Spanish coast guard vessel to restrain itself, when a known smuggler sailed out of harbour, from trying to capture the suspicious craft before it disappeared into the darkness even if it was not yet within Spanish territorial waters. The Royal Navy was usually alerted of untoward incidents by special signals from the station at the top of the Rock. A red triangular pennant over a black ball hoisted on the north yardarm meant 'Guarda Costa in pursuit of trader of unknown nationality'. And a red flag hoisted on the staff with two red pennants on the south yardarm meant 'Guarda Costa in possession of a British trader'. At night a gun would be fired to draw attention to the lights which would be hoisted on the staff. A red over a white light signalled 'vessel in distress east' and a red light over a white and a red, 'vessel in distress west'.

There were therefore frequent confrontations between the RN gunboats and the Spanish customs boats. But the latter did not have it all their own way for the habits of the ex-privateers died hard. In 1816, three Gibraltar smuggling boats, boarded and captured the Spanish customs cutter *El Feroz* which was inhibiting their activities on the coast near Malaga and brought her captive to Gibraltar Bay.[6] A quarter of a century later, a clerical visitor to Gibraltar described 'the Gibraltar trader' as

> a most suspicious looking craft she is. She lies rather low in the water, sharp in the bows, and carries enormous lateen sails. Her cargo looks peaceable enough, but not so her crew, who are far too numerous to be required for the management of such a vessel if she were honest, and have a desperado look about them which seems to intimate some other employment besides peaceable navigation - a suspicion which is more than confirmed by the no-way equivocal appearance of two large swivel-guns poking out their wide black muzzles from under a tarpawling amidship. In short, she is a smuggler - a lawless freetrader - and her numerous and daring crew require the guarda-costa to be well armed and manned before she presumes to ask any questions.[7]

Attempts to stop this trade was objected to (on both sides of the frontier) as bearing too hard on the poor who could no find no other means of scraping a living for themselves and their families. It was not until after the construction of the Dockyard offered other employment to the indigent on both sides of the border that the Tobacco Ordinance of 1896 put an end to this trade.

The depredations of the Salé Corsairs were put an end to before the end of the 18th century, but, at times, the Gibraltar gunboats were called out to deal with the Riffian pirates who infested the northern coast of Morocco. In 1846 the trading brig *Ruth* that had sailed from Gibraltar was captured near Melilla, and HMS *Fantome* 16 was sent to recover the captured vessel. She was found aground on Cape Tres Forcas, and a landing party managed to bring her away before her valuable cargo could be stolen.[8]

The Navy was less successful two years later when the brig *Three Sisters*, on passage from Gibraltar to Malta, was captured by pirates near the same place. The crew of the *Three Sisters* were unable to put up any resistance but managed to get away in the ship's boat. A week later the vessel was sighted by the paddle sloop HMS *Polyphemus* fast aground under some high cliffs and surrounded by at least 500 armed looters who brought up a 6 or 9 pounder gun. Afraid of incurring heavy casualties if he landed his seamen in the face of such strong opposition, the captain of the *Polyphemus* decided to leave the captured vessel in the hands of the pirates.[9]

In 1851 the brigantine *Violet* was also captured but by the time the wooden paddle sloop *Janus* 4 reached her, she had been completely stripped and only the ribs of the vessel could be seen on the beach.[10] But in 1854 when the *Cuthbert Young* was captured, the crew of the paddle sloop HMS *Prometheus* managed to tow her back to Gibraltar in the face of heavy resistance.[11]

The pirates of the Riff were active until the end of the 19th century and Captain Joshua Slocum, on his single-handed trip round the world, had an encounter with them in the Strait in 1895, but managed to outsail his pursuers.[12]

Spanish and American rebels

The Royal Navy also had to deal with mutinies in the Spanish Navy. Early in 1873, King Amadeo, a prince of the Italian House of Savoy, resigned the crown of Spain after a short and troubled reign, and the country was declared a republic. Not all Spaniards accepted the new constitution and the bulk of the Spanish fleet including four ironclads declared itself for the *Intransigentes* who were opposed to the republic. Four Royal Navy ironclads were dispatched from Malta to keep an eye on the mutinous ships, helped by a small German squadron, as the loyal fleet commanded by Admiral Lobo was much weaker and could not stand up to the mutineers.

After some weeks of confrontation HMS *Swiftsure* in the company of the German battleship *Friedrich Karl* met two of the rebel ships flying no flags and declining to hoist any, until a shot from the *Friedrich Karl* across the bows of the frigate *Almansa* brought a Spanish flag to the peak and

The Confederate sloop-of-war *Sumter* capturing two Federal
merchantmen off Gibraltar. The *Sumter* later became SS *Gibraltar.*

a flag of truce to the truck. The German ship then boarded and captured her opponent while the *Swiftsure* did the same with the ironclad *Vitoria*. The two Spanish ships were taken to Escombreras Bay and anchored there. On 1 September the *Vitoria* and *Almansa*, under a strong escort, steamed past the rebel fleet, with Royal Navy crews aboard, on their way to Gibraltar, which they reached the following day and on the 26th they were handed over to Admiral Lobo.[13]

At the beginning of the 19th century the US Navy maintained a squadron in the Mediterranean to protect American shipping from the Barbary pirates, and having no home port, the ships spent a lot of time at Gibraltar. In later years Gibraltar was a favourite port of call when US Navy ships visited European waters. On the evening of 26 August 1843, the whole of the town was 'as light as day' when the paddle-steam frigate *Missouri*, which had arrived at Gibraltar on her maiden voyage and was anchored by the Line Wall, burst into flames. After seven hours, during which the crew fought the flames without success, the *Missouri* exploded at 3 am and was a total loss. Fortunately, both magazines had been flooded by then, and there was only a muted explosion which did not endanger the town or the other ships at anchor. The officers and crew were all saved by boats sent by the port authority.[14]

The only casualty was the ship's pet, a brown bear called Bess. She wall an amiable creature very popular with the crew. She normally slept high up on one of the masts and in the confusion caused by the fire had been forgotten when the ship was abandoned. She took refuge from the flames at the end of the spanker boom and the unfortunate animal was killed when the ship exploded.[15]

During the American Civil War, the Confederate steamer *Sumter*, which had been fitted out as a commerce raider by the famous Captain Raphael Semmes, arrived in Cadiz after capturing fifteen Union ships in the West Indies. Spain did not recognise the Confederate States and the *Sumter* was ordered out, though she was first allowed to dock to repair damage to her bottom and her propeller. On Saturday 18 January 1862, she arrived in the Strait and stopped two US brigs. One was freighted with a British owned cargo for Newport and was allowed to proceed under a ransom bond. The other was on passage from Messina to Boston with sulphur, which was considered contraband of war, and Semmes had her burnt. That evening the *Sumter* anchored at Gibraltar.

The following day she was given pratique and Semmes called on the governor, Sir William Codrington. The authorities received Semmes courteously, but it was a different matter when he tried to buy stores. Horatio Sprague, the popular US Consul, whose family had lived in Gibraltar for many years made sure that the rebel ship was boycotted by the local merchants. Semmes had great difficulty buying an anchor and chain which he required. He tried to buy coal from the hulks, which were anchored to the north of the town and supplied passing steamers, without success, so he applied to the SNO for permission to buy coal from the Dockyard and this request was referred to the Admiralty.

Whilst Semmes awaited the reply from London, the US steam frigate *Tuscarora* anchored in the harbour on 12 February, and shortly after was joined by the *Kearsarge* and the *Ino.* The Sumter was now blockaded by a greatly superior force. The crews of the hostile vessels fraternised in the local wine shops but there were no incidents.

At this stage HMS *Warrior* arrived in the harbour. She had been sent to make sure that no hostilities were committed in British waters. The *Warrior* was a brand new iron frigate and carried heavy armour and a strong broadside battery of forty 110 and 68 pounder muzzle loaders. The first of her kind, she marked a great advance in warship design. Semmes was shown round her and thought her 'a marvel of modern architecture. She is monstrous' he wrote, 'an impregnable floating fortress and will work a revolution in shipbuilding. Wooden ships, as battleships, must go out of use. With this single ship I could destroy the entire Yankee fleet blockading our coast.' In fact the design of the newly completed *Warrior* was already obsolescent.

While Semmes was in Gibraltar, the Confederate Navy was completing the conversion of the frigate *Merrimac* into an armoured ship carrying ten large guns. On 8 March the *Merrimac* got in among the wooden U S warships at Hampton Roads, Virginia, and caused havoc. But the following day the new U S armoured ship *Monitor* arrived and the contestants fought an inconclusive duel. The *Monitor* was the much smaller ship but she carried two 11-inch guns in a swivel turret which were considerably larger than the guns of her opponent; and she demonstrated the superiority of her armament. The two duelists did not meet again, as the following month the Confederates had to abandon the Virginia coast, and the *Merrimac,* with her unreliable engines, had to be scuttled. The *Monitor,* not a very seaworthy vessel, foundered at sea. But the superiority of the little *Monitor* meant that the days of warships with broadside batteries like the *Warrior,* were numbered, and within three years the Royal Navy was laying down battleships with swivel turrets.

Eventually, Semmes was informed that the Foreign Office had decided that in keeping with Britain's neutrality in the conflict, the Royal Navy could not supply him with coal, but he managed to make arrangements with a newly arrived collier. When the *Sumter* went alongside the collier to coal, her boilers started leaking so badly that her furnaces were extinguished. A survey showed that the boilers needed replacing and as this could not be done in Gibraltar, she was paid off on 11 April. Semmes was on his way home when he received instructions to take command of the new frigate *Alabama,* built in Liverpool. In an astonishing cruise of 22 months, during which he ranged the Atlantic and Indian Oceans, the *Alabama* captured 82 enemy vessels before she was sunk off Cherbourg.

The little *Sumter* had also done well for her owners. For an outlay of $28,000 she had inflicted losses totalling $1,000,000, a very considerable sum in those days. In December she was sold by public auction for $19,500 and was renamed SS *Gibraltar* under the British flag. The following February she made her escape under cover of a Levanter gale, and managed to evade the sole US gunboat that was blockading the Bay. She made her way to Britain where she was fitted out as a blockade runner, but after making one voyage to Charleston she was lost in the North Sea.[16]

The Convict Establishment
From 1787 onwards, prisoners who escaped the death penalty (which in those days was applied to a whole range of what today would be considered minor crimes, including some categories of burglary) were transported to Australia. In 1837 all transportation to Australia (except Tasmania) was terminated at the request of the colonies. But within a

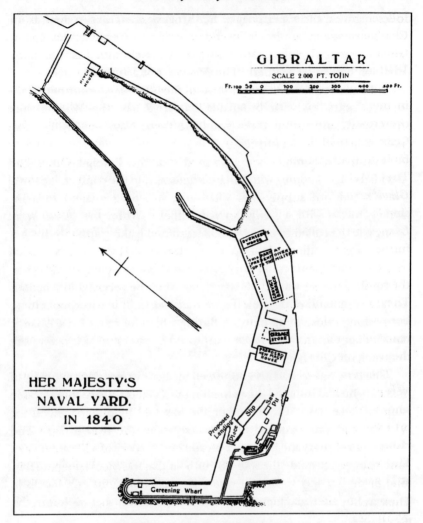

GIBRALTAR

SCALE 2 000 FT. TO 1 IN

HER MAJESTY'S
NAVAL YARD.
IN 1840

The Dockyard in 1840 from A Gonzalez

few years Tasmania had become so over-crowded that alternatives had
to be found. Prisons which could accommodate long-term convicts were
planned in Britain but while they were being built other alternatives had
to be found. An Order in Council of 1 April 1841, provided for the
setting up of a convict establishment at Gibraltar, and in October of the

following year, the old frigate HMS *Owen Glendower* arrived from Chatham with 200 convicts on board to start a penal settlement in Gibraltar harbour. This was set up under the Home Secretary but in 1840 control was transferred to the Governor of Gibraltar.

The number of convicts increased until it reached a maximum of 889 in the years 1847 to 1849 but at these levels the establishment was overcrowded and numbers were subsequently reduced to about 750. Cells were built in the Dockyard to house them. Some were of stone, built flush against the Line Wall, and others were free-standing sheds. They could accommodate up to some 500 prisoners. The *Owen Glendower* had room for 150 more but it was used mainly as a hospital ship for the convicts and normally only held 70 men. The prison hulk *Euryalus* (a former frigate built in 1803) arrived in 1847 and housed a further 230.

The convicts worked in stone quarries which provided material for the construction of military and naval installations, and in building work. They were marched to and from work under armed guard. Those whose behaviour could not be trusted were kept in hand-cuffs until they reached their destination. About 130 men worked for the dockyard and the rest under the military engineers.

Their pay was 2d a day, of which 1d was reserved for them until they were released. The other 1d was normally spent on tobacco, although smoking was not allowed in English prisons and it was expressly prohibited by the written rules of the Gibraltar convict establishment. However, they were allowed half an hour for smoking in the evenings. They were also given half a pint of grog a day which was normally served at 11 am and received an extra ration if they had to work under water. Their weekly rations included $8\frac{3}{4}$ lbs of bread, $2\frac{1}{4}$ lbs of fresh meat, 2 lbs of salt pork, 2 pints of dried peas, $1\frac{1}{2}$ lbs of vegetables, $10\frac{1}{2}$ ozs of butter, 7 ozs of cocoa and $1\frac{1}{2}$ ozs of tea.

The establishment was run by an overseer with three mates, and there were 40 guards who were assisted by trustee convicts who were termed monitors while others acted as cooks. In addition there was a surgeon with an assistant, a chaplain, a clerk and a steward. There were regular visits from the Methodist clergyman. The Home Office limited the convicts' working day to eight hours, as compared to the ten hours usual at the time. They returned to their quarters at 3 in the afternoon and dined at 3.15. Wash and mend was from 5 to 7 after which they were locked away for the night.

On the whole, conditions were reasonably good for the period and labourers in England had to work harder and fared worse. A number of projects were carried out by the convicts, including the building of slips for boats, and the repair and extension of mast houses, stores and barracks. It was also decided to lengthen the Mew Mole, and 700,000 tons of rock were quarried for this purpose. By the time the Convict Establishment was terminated in 1875, the Mole was 1,400 feet long with a width of about 130 feet. It was four times longer than before and provided much better shelter in bad weather.

The convicts were sent from England and Gibraltarian prisoners were normally confined in the prison in the Moorish Castle, but at least one Spaniard, who was convicted in the Gibraltar court of receiving stolen property, served six months before he was expelled from Gibraltar.

An enquiry in 1860 established that convict labour (half the cost of £24,000 a year of the establishment, was paid by the Navy) was more expensive than free labour imported from Spain and the days of convicts in Gibraltar were therefore numbered. On 15 May 1875 the last 127 convicts were embarked for their return journey to England and the establishment was closed down.

The *Euryalus*, which had been renamed *Africa*, had been sold in 1860 to a Mr Recaño for scrap, but the *Owen Glendower* was retained as a receiving ship until 1883, when she was sold to F Danino and also broken up.[17]

The end of O'Hara's Folly

Perhaps the most unique piece of demolition on record was that carried out by HMS *Wasp* in 1887. General O'Hara had built a tall tower on the Rock's southern peak, which was then known as Sugar Loaf Hill (now O'Hara's Battery) in the fond hope that he would be able to make out the movements of the Spanish fleet in Cadiz Bay from the top. This wishful thinking was not fulfilled, but the tower was kept on as a lookout post and a couple of guns were mounted on it. In 1887 it was decided to demolish it in order that it should not obstruct the field of fire of the 6-inch gun that was to be placed close by. The commander of the composite gunboat *Wasp* happened to dine at the gunners' mess and there was a lively discussion on whether the tower, some 1,400 feet above sea-level, could be destroyed by gunfire.

The next morning the *Wasp* was sailing for the China station. Before leaving she anchored in calm water in the west of the Bay and to everyone's surprise opened fire with one of her 4-inch guns. The first round thudded into the Rock 100 feet below the tower. So, to get the extra elevation required, the gun was removed from its carriage and lashed on top of timber and spars, and then fired again. The sixth shot smashed into the centre of the tower. Honour satisfied, the *Wasp* sailed off, never to return, because she foundered with all hands after leaving Singapore, in October of that year.[18]

The need for a dry dock

The opening of the Suez Canal in 1869 made the Mediterranean route to the east a lot busier and many more ships called at Gibraltar for coaling. This was done from the hulks anchored to the north of Waterport, and their numbers increased greatly. The coaling industry was in competition with Algiers, which was an area of low wages. As price was an essential element in commercial competition a large, poorly paid labour force grew up in Gibraltar, part of which lived over the border, in Spain, and crossed over to work every day. The condition of these workers was abject as the cost of living in Gibraltar was higher than in Algiers, and a number of benevolent institutions had to be founded to alleviate their dire poverty.

On 1 July 1871, the Channel Fleet, consisting of six battleships, set sail from Gibraltar to Halifax, and while manoeuvring in the Strait, HMS *Agincourt* ran aground on the Pearl Rock off Punta Carnero. Three gunboats were immediately sent from Gibraltar with lighters and pontoons in tow, to give assistance. Guns, carriages, spars, anchors, provisions and all other movable and heavy items were unloaded and the coal thrown overboard, to lighten the ship. Another battleship, HMS *Hercules*, then placed herself stern to stern with the *Agincourt* and made fast with a chain five fathoms long, from each of her hawse pipes. The rise of the tide moved the stranded ship and with the assistance of smaller vessels the *Hercules* was able to tow her off. The *Agincourt* came off the rock with a lurch and damaged the *Hercules*, which, however, was able to tow her to the Bay of Getares where an inspection showed that her hull was sound. She was therefore taken to Gibraltar and repaired. It was lucky that there was no serious damage below the waterline as there were no facilities for drydocking, and this incident highlighted the deficiency. The following year, Captain Phillimore the SNO, proposed that a dry dock should be constructed at Gibraltar, and this was followed by proposals for a floating dock. Nothing came of this until Lord Brassey, a former Civil Lord of the Admiralty, founded his influential 'Naval Annual'. In the first edition that appeared in 1886 he wrote,

> At Gibraltar the want of any docking accommodation is a grave deficiency. The greatest battles of the past have been fought near the entrance to the Mediterranean, and the battles of the future may probably be fought in the same waters. The new weapon, the torpedo, will deal its blow below the water-line, and inflict injuries which can only be repaired in dock. Our requirements at Gibraltar might be met, as at Hong Kong and the Cape, by cooperation between the admiralty and private enterprise.[19]

The building of a dock at Gibraltar would be an expensive venture and the participation of local civilian capital had its attractions. M A Serfaty, a local merchant, proposed the formation of a company with local capital, but a Committee of Enquiry chaired by the Civil Lord, recommended that the Government should construct a dock, a further extension to the New Mole, and provide a commercial coaling pier to replace the numerous coaling hulks in the Bay. The Committee came down heavily against the suggestion of a commercial dry dock.[20]

The deficiencies of the port of Gibraltar were highlighted in March 1891 when the SS *Utopia* was coming to anchor off Ragged Staff, one stormy night. She struck the ram of the battleship *Anson* and sank within a few minutes. Half an hour later only her funnel and masts were out of the water. The *Utopia* was on her way to New York with 879 Italian emigrants on board and the death toll was heavy. Rescue work was started immediately, the fleet switched on its searchlights so that the rescuers could see what they were doing and all available boats were launched. The propeller of the steam pinnace of HMS *Immortalité* was fouled by a rope and she was in danger of drifting onto the rocks. A small boat was launched to assist her by William Seed, the Chief Inspector of the Gibraltar Police, and the pinnace's crew was saved, though two of the sailors were drowned. In all, 566 people were drowned that night within a few hundred yards of the town walls. There were many acts of bravery performed and among those who were decorated for gallantry were Seed, and William Undery and others of the Port Department.[21]

Notes and References

(1)   Elliott 51.
(2)   Clowes 6:188; Padfield 84; Colledge 1:482.
(3)   *Report of the Barracks etc* 1:57; *Gibraltar Directory 1939.* 231; Bill Cumming in *Gibraltar Chronicle*, 23 October 1984.
(4)   Colledge 1:487; Fremantle 307; Cavilla 40.
(5)   See page 73 for the encouragement given to these activities during the previous war by the authorities on both sides of the frontier.
(6)   CO.91:61, 4 December 1916.
(7)   William Robertson 202.
(8)   Clowes 6:360-361.
(9)   Clowes 6:361.
(10) Clowes 6:362.
(11) Clowes 6:391.
(12) Slocum 50-52.
(13) Clowes 7:242; *Gibraltar Directory 1916* 156.
(14) *Gibraltar Directory 1916* 129.
(15) Beach 151-152.
(16) *Gibraltar Directory 1916* 142; Semmes *Cruise* 184-346; Semmes *Memoirs* 307-345.
(17) CO.91:219, report of Dr William Baly; McConville 201-203, 393-396; Gonzalez 24-30; Colledge 1:197, 401.
(18) Hire Ms 66-67; Preston & Major 228.
(19) *Brassey's Annual 1886* 100.
(20) Gonzalez 32-35.
(21) Benady *Police* 17; Gonzalez 35; Palao 96-101.

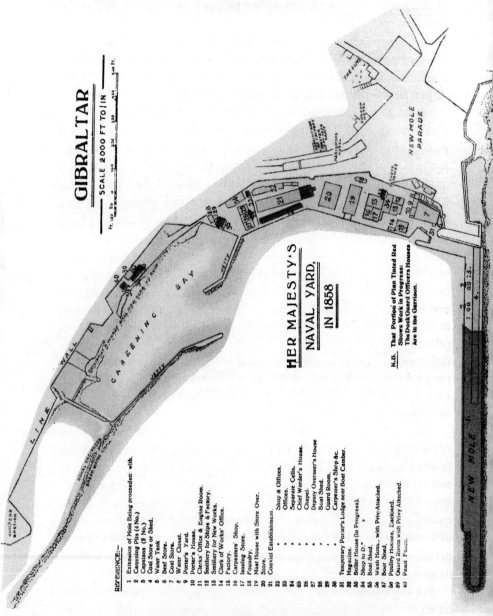

The Dockyard in 1858 from A Gonzalez

CHAPTER VIII

THE BUILDING OF THE DOCKYARD.

Events were afoot on the international scene that were to give the construction of a proper base at Gibraltar great importance and urgency. The 1880s brought a period of increased colonial expansion by the European powers as the scramble for Africa entered its final phase. Britain used her naval and commercial might to secure a large part of the spoils, but other countries shared her ambition. France in particular, recovering from the humiliation of the Franco-Prussian War of 1870, was anxious to restore her national dignity by extending her overseas empire. This led inevitably to confrontation between France and Britain. The rivalry was exacerbated by French memories of defeat at Waterloo and Trafalgar, and there was an important school of naval officers, the *Jeune Ecole* who were convinced that Britain could be defeated at sea with the use of modern weapons. French torpedo boats presented a threat to Britain's preponderance in heavy ships, and French fast cruisers could decimate the ships employed in overseas trade on which Britain's economy depended.

France had started rebuilding her fleet in 1878 and Britain did not really respond until 1885, by which time she no longer retained the two power standard under which the Royal Navy was as strong as the next two strongest navies. The Naval Defence Act of 1889 tried to remedy the situation but with Russia and Italy also increasing the size of their fleets, catching-up was slow. After the opening of the Suez Canal, almost a third of British trade went through the Strait of Gibraltar, and the threat presented by France was a worrying one. The Admiralty had to rethink its strategy.

For three quarters of a century, the Mediterranean Fleet had been based on Malta, but that island was not the right place from which to guard the entrance to the Mediterranean, nor was it well situated to stop

France's main fleet based at Toulon from reaching the North Sea to attack the United Kingdom. The mine and torpedo had made impossible the close blockade of enemy coasts of the wars of sailing ship days.

The new plans provided for the Channel Squadron to make for Gibraltar to guard the Strait and bottle up the French fleet, as soon as a crisis occurred. The Mediterranean Fleet was also to concentrate with it there. The DNI noted that 'Gibraltar owes all its importance to the fact that it is a narrow strait interposed between two divisions of a foreign fleet which cannot concentrate without passing through it.' As Professor Marder has pointed out, Gibraltar now became Britain's key position in the Mediterranean, but though strongly fortified it could hardly be called a naval base. 'It had an insecure anchorage, inferior coaling facilities, and was almost lacking in dockyard accommodation.'[1]

Clearly something had to be done. When he presented the 1894/95 Estimates, the First Lord announced the expenditure of £801,000 at Gibraltar: £405,000 for the extension of the New Mole from 1,400 to 3,500 feet; £366,000 for the building of a dry dock within the angle between the New Mole and the shore; and £30,000 for new magazines. In addition, it was intended to build a commercial and coaling mole to the north, running west, which could be situated either at King's Bastion or Waterport. If the latter site were chosen there would be need for an additional mole so that the entrance to the harbour could be closed with a boom, to make the anchorage secure from attack by French torpedo boats.

The following year the option for the commercial mole at Waterport was selected and the cost of the additional work required was estimated at £700,000, of which £400,000 would be contributed by the colony of Gibraltar at the rate of £14,000 a year for 57 years; this figure included interest. Lord Brassey commented, 'The decision of the Admiralty to make a harbour ... at the important strategic position of Gibraltar cannot be too highly commended.'[2]

The works were started in 1895. The following year the new Conservative Government decided to build three dry docks instead of one. The total estimated cost had now increased more than sixfold to £4,613,300: £1,939,000 for the moles and £2,674,300 for the three docks and the extension to the dockyard. The work entailed considerable reduction in the height of the New Mole Parade which had an area of $3\frac{1}{4}$ acres, and was to become part of the dockyard. The rubble from the excavation was used for reclaiming land outside the Line Wall.

As more filling was required, quarries were opened at Europa (between Camp and Little Bays), North Front (under the shadow of the Rock), Puente Basura (opposite the Ice Box), Catalan Bay (above the village) and Monkey Alameda (where the Naval Oil storage tanks are now situated). A temporary railway line was laid to transport the stone and rubble to the areas being reclaimed. It ran from Catalan Bay to Bayside and Waterport, and from there on a temporary timber viaduct to the Commercial Mole and Dockyard. (All the area outside the Line Wall from Rosia to Waterport is reclaimed ground, apart from the area of the New Mole Parade, though much of the reclamation dates from World War II or later.) The railway from the North Mole along Reclamation Road to the Dockyard, was retained for 50 years for the transport of coal and other heavy materials.[3]

A yard was constructed in Devil's Tower Road with shops for repairing quarry tools and plants, and for making concrete blocks for the new moles. The machinery employed in the works included 30 cranes, 13 locomotives, 10 pontoons, two large steam dredgers and two tugs, and specialised equipment for making and moving the massive concrete blocks.[4]

The machinery and equipment came from Britain, as did the technical and supervisory staff, many of who came straight from working on the recently completed Manchester Ship Canal. But the bulk of the labour was Spanish. The number of labourers employed during the first few years of construction was 2,200 at an average wage of 11.25 pesetas a day. As this worked out at 2s 3d it may not seem unduly generous, but by the standard of the agricultural wages current in Andalusia at the time, it was attractive, and men flocked to La Linea and Algeciras from all over the province. In the final years of construction the numbers employed rose to 4,400 in winter and 5,000 in summer. These figures included 400 employed in quarries in Spain - at Teba, Peña Rubia and elsewhere. This influx brought a big increase in the population of La Linea and Algeciras and a boom in local trade.[5]

In April 1898 the USA and Spain went to war over Cuba, and although this did not affect Gibraltar directly it had important side effects. The official currency in Gibraltar was the Spanish peseta, which within a few weeks was devalued from about 20 to the pound sterling to over 50. This brought tremendous problems to the Gibraltarian and Spanish labourers as the cost of living doubled and there was a great deal of industrial unrest. The coal heavers went on strike in May for the right to be paid in sterling. The coal merchants refused and brought in Spanish blackleg labour which led to violence by the strikers.

Eventually, after mediation by the governor, General Sir Ralph Biddulph, it was agreed that half the wages should be indexed at the rate of exchange of the day, and the strike was settled. The labourers in the dock installations were new to the area and not organised, but unrest was prevalent. The problem was solved by changing the legal currency in Gibraltar to sterling on 1 October 1898.

The great increase in the scope of the works and the problems of dealing with a large, and mostly foreign labour force, appear to have been too much for the Admiralty and a contract was signed on 3 December 1898, with Topham, Jones and Railton (who already had the contract for lengthening the New Mole) to take over full responsibility for the works. The contractors bought all the equipment that the Admiralty had on site and work continued smoothly enough, although the following July, 3,000 workmen went on strike for an increase in wages, but after sixteen days they returned to work and their leaders were sacked.

The contract with Topham, Jones and Railton provided for the completion of the following works:

1 The New Mole (henceforwards known as the South Mole) was to be extended to a total length of 3,560 feet, with head and lighthouse, wharf wall, paving and railway, and two thousand feet of coaling sheds.

2 The Commercial Mole (afterwards known as the North Mole) and Viaduct, with coaling sheds on the mole and bonded shed on Waterport Wharf.

3 The completion of the Navy Yard to include three docks, slipways (some to hold vessels up to 400 tons), gun wharf, torpedo boat camber, engine house, stores and offices, with roadways and railway.

4   The enclosed area of water including the approaches to the docks and wharf walls to be deepened to a minimum depth of 21 to 38 1/2 feet.

5   The construction of a detached mole with heads and lighthouses.

The work on the latter had already been started. Fleming and Ferguson had built a steel caisson shaped like the base of a pyramid, with a length at the bottom of 100 feet and at the top of 74 feet. It was 33 feet broad with a depth of 37 feet, and weighed 350 tons. The caisson was partially erected at the site of the slipways and launched on 23 March 1898. It was then towed further out for completion, as there was not sufficient depth of water near the shore. On 11 June it was sunk on a bed prepared for it on the site of the Detached Mole and it was then filled with concrete to form the support for the two Titan cranes, which, working in opposite directions, lowered the concrete blocks that made up the mole. These blocks were laid in a sloping position and had joggles which wedded them together; they were made in different sizes and weighed from 18 to 36 tons. They had to be allowed to stand for two months to dry out before they were placed in position. The last block was set in the north head by the Duke of York (later King George V) on 20 March 1901. The Detached Mole has a length of 2,720 feet.

In order to indicate where the underwater work was taking place, old hulks were painted green or red according to their position, and moored at the extremities of the intended moles. At night they showed red lights. Some of the divers working on the placing of the blocks took to underwater-fishing while they waited for the blocks to arrive, and on more than one occasion they had to come to the surface because an octopus was obstructing their air valve.[6]

The work took longer than originally anticipated and the Naval Works Act of 1899 fixed the completion of the moles for 1904, and the docks for 1905. But, Topham, Jones and Railton needed a dock in which to repair their floating plant without having to send it to Cadiz, and Dock No 4, which was 251 feet long, was built on Reclamation Road (now Queensway) opposite King's Bastion. The first vessel docked there was the dredger *St Martin* in August 1900.

Additional works were also contracted, including the construction of Coaling Island and the building of new Naval stores at Ragged Staff. But the most spectacular of these works was undoubtedly the tunnel under the Rock between the Dockyard and the Monkey Alameda on the east side. This tunnel is 1,053 yards long and work on it was started from both ends simultaneously. Starting from the Dockyard end the strata through which it was driven consists of 170 yards of sandy clay, 80 yards of shale, 692 yards of solid limestone, and another 111 yards of sandy clay.[7]

All the buildings constructed on reclaimed land were built on piles of 12" x 12" pitch pine, with cast iron shoes, driven deep into the 'made ground'. But the massive foundations for the 100-ton sheer-legs, by the Admiral's Tower, gave a great deal of trouble and many attempts were made before the concrete set satisfactorily. As the Rock's limestone is hard and brittle it cannot be worked easily, so most of the limestone ashlars used in constructing the dock walls and as dressings to buildings came from Spanish quarries, while the granite copings were imported mainly from Norway, but some came from Cornwall and Italy.

In April 1903, King Edward VII, while on a visit to Gibraltar in the Royal yacht *Victoria and Albert*, set the coping stone on the 460-foot long No 3 Dock which was named 'King Edward VII's Dock'. It was a happy coincidence that the first ship to use it in March 1905 was the flagship of the Atlantic Fleet, the battleship *King Edward VII*, which, as it had an overall length of 454 feet must have been a tight squeeze. In 1904 Queen Alexandra named No 2 Dock, which was 550 feet long, after herself. The first warship to be docked here was the cruiser *Berwick* which had escorted the Queen's yacht on her visit to Gibraltar.

In 1906, the Prince and Princess of Wales (later George V and Queen Mary) visited Gibraltar on their way back from India and No.1 Dock was named the Prince and Princess of Wales Dock. This was appropriate since it was built as a double dock designed to hold two ships at a time. The inside dock had to be approached through the outer one and both docks had to be emptied and filled at the same time. They could, however, be divided in two by a sliding steel caisson, and they had an overall length of 850 feet. The steel sliding caissons for all the docks were made by Thames Ironwork and Shipbuilding Company, and the penstocks by Stothert and Pitt. Most of the North Mole which had originally been planned as a commercial mole, was ultimately taken over

Above: Relief of Gibraltar by Lord Howe's fleet in 1782, from the painting by
Richard Paton. *(Courtesy Gibraltar Museum)*
Below: Miniature stamp sheet issued by Gibraltar Post Office of Stanfield's
painting of HMS *Victory* being towed to Rosia Bay for repairs
after the Battle of Trafalgar.

The Channel Fleet anchored off King's Bastion in 1877 *(Photo courtesy Garrison Library)*

View of the harbour from King's Bastion 1877. The breakwater was built by the Royal Engineers to protect the town's walls. *(Photo courtesy Garrison Library)*

Above: The 10,600 ton broadside battleship HMS *Agincourt* at the New Mole in 1879. Her armament consisted of 17 9-inch MLRs.
(Photo courtesy John Martinez)
Below: The two Titan Cranes used to construct the Detached Mole in position, July 1899. *(Photo courtesy Gibraltar Museum)*

Above: The Building of the Dockyard 1903. *(Photo courtesy Gibraltar Museum)*
Below: The construction of No 3 Dock in 1903.
(Photo courtesy Gibraltar Museum)

Above: Rosia Bay and South Mole circa 1905. *(Photo courtesy A Garcia)*
Below: HMS *King Edward VII* being floated out of No 3 Dock
on 11 March 1903. *(Photo V B Cumbo)*

Above: A *King Edward VII* class battleship in No 2 Dock with a *Diadem* class cruiser in No 1. *(Photo courtesy A Garcia)*

Below: The US Navy's 'Great White Fleet' in the harbour in 1909 after their round-the-world voyage. *(Photo courtesy A Garcia)*

HMS *Hood* and *Renown* at the South Mole circa 1936. (Photo courtesy A Garcia)

Above: The Republican destroyer *Jose Luis Diez* aground off Catalan Bay on
New Year's Day 1939. Sir Thomas Allin's fleet came to grief near here in
1662. The Dockyard tug *Rollicker* is in attendance. *(Photo Bertie Curton)*
Below: HMS *Cormorant* moored at Coaling Island between the wars with HMS
Hart astern and a D class cruiser behind.

Above: Home Fleet at Gibraltar - Spring Cruise 1939.

	Newcastle		*Revenge*	
Sussex		*Shropshire*		*Ramilies*
Nelson		*Warspite*	*Malaya*	*Royal Oak*

Maine

RFA Viscol

Below: The combined fleets at Gibraltar in 1935. The hospital
ship *Maine* in the foreground. *(Photo A L Pizarro)*

Above: Home Fleet at Gibraltar - Spring Cruise 1939.

Glorious   Repulse   Guardian
Glasgow
London   Hood   Devonshire   Rodney   RFA Delphinium
                                                RFA Reliant
    Southampton   Sheffield   Aurora
       Galatea
    Cormorant   Hart

Below: The combined Fleets at Gibraltar in 1935. The depot ship *Woolwich* with submarines in the foreground and a good view of the old sheer-legs.
(Photo A L Pizarro)

Warship Rains Shells On Spanish Rebel Town

First pictures of the bombardment of Algeciras by Spanish Government warship *Jaime I*—taken by *Daily Express* Cameraman Tovey. Women refugees from Spain were among those watching battle from roof-tops in Gibraltar saw columns of smoke and fire rising as twelve-inch shells thundered into their home-town. On right British sailors watch *Jaime I*, in action. Picture taken under extreme difficulty. Spanish warship was five and a half miles away.

On 11 August 1936 *The Daily Express* published photographs taken from Gibraltar of the Government battleship *Jaime I* bombarding Algeciras on the 6th. The photograph shows a Royal Navy destroyer anchored in the harbour in the foreground with the Detached Mole behind.

Above: Naval parade in Reclamation Road 1935. The black building to the left is the old World War I RNAS hangar turned into a cinema between the wars. *(Photo A L Pizarro)*

Below: Sailors and Royal Marines take part in the Ceremony of the Keys at Casemates on 8 January 1942. *(Photo Imperial War Museum)*

Above: HMS *Ark Royal* entering harbour 1940.
(Photo Imperial War Museum)
Below: A 6-inch coast defence gun from Devil's Gap Battery overlooks Force
H in the harbour in 1941. HMS *Argus* is tied up at the South Mole with
either the *Rodney* or *Nelson*. The cruiser at anchor to give her AA battery a
wide arc of fire was probably HMS *Hermione*.
(Photo Imperial War Museum)

Above: Force H, HMS *Renown*, *Malaya* and *Ark Royal* sail past the east side of the Rock in 1940. *(Photo Imperial War Museum)*
Below: Force H at sea in November 1940 whilst engaged in Operation White to fly off Hurricanes to Malta. Photograph taken from *Sheffield* of *Argus*, *Renown* and *Ark Royal*. *(Photo Imperial War Museum)*

Below: Sailors join the Army and civilians in the VE Day celebrations in the Grand Parade. *(Photo Imperial War Museum)*
Below: U-541 is brought into the harbourafter surrendering on 12 May 1945. *(Photo Imperial War Museum)*

by the Admiralty (westward from the Viaduct) and five piers were built to accommodate destroyer flotillas. The colony later built its own commercial wharf at Waterport.[9]

The area enclosed by the moles was 448 acres, of which it was necessary to reclaim some 64 acres of land for the dockyard extension and other works, including Coaling Island and Reclamation Road (now Queensway). David Beatty (later Admiral of the Fleet Earl Beatty) saw the works when he visited Gibraltar as the captain of the cruiser HMS *Juno* at the end of 1902 and was suitably impressed,

> I walked over the Gibraltar Dockyard which is truly a remarkable achievement - or will be when complete. They have moved away hills mostly of solid rocks, by hundreds of square yards and pushed the sea back 1/2 a mile in which to cut and make the Dockyard and what was originally a bare coast line they have turned into a mighty harbour. It certainly makes one stop and think, when one realises that the greater part has been accomplished in 6 years, that there is no end to the might of science and brains nowadays.

However, he had reservations about how safe these works would be in the face of Spanish gunfire.[10]

During the Spanish-American War four emplacements for heavy guns had been made at Algeciras, one on the north side and the others to the south of the town, and a number of 9 and 10-inch guns were brought, but the war ended and they were not mounted. In 1899-1900 Major Garcia Roure (Rovira?), a Spanish engineer officer, published a number of reports recommending the erection of 12 forts and batteries from which the fire of 70 guns would command Gibraltar harbour. Nothing came of these proposals, but distrust of France aroused fears of a possible combination which would enable mobile heavy artillery to be brought by rail and used to make the harbour untenable.[11]

In 1901, Thomas Bowles MP, the publisher of *Vanity Fair* brought out a pamphlet *Gibraltar a National Danger* which advocated the abandonment of the construction of the dockyard, and its replacement by works on the east side, which would be more sheltered from gunfire

COMMERCIAL MOLE

DETACHED MOLE

SECTION A A

NEW MOLE EXTENSION

SECTION B B

SCALE TO SECTIONS 100 FEET TO 1 INCH

CONCRETE BLOCK YARD

QUARRY

QUARRY

QUARRY

QUARRY

DIMENSIONS OF DOCKS

	LENGTH	WIDTH OF ENTRANCE	DEPTH ON SILL AT L.W.O.S.T.
Dock N.º 1	850 Ft.	95 Ft.	35 Ft. 6 ins.
" 2	550 Ft.	95 Ft.	35 Ft. 6 ins.
" 3	450 Ft.	95 Ft.	35 Ft. 6 ins.

DOCK Nº 1 IS SUBDIVIDED TO FORM AN INNER DOCK OF 450 FEET. AND AN OUTER DOCK OF 380 FEET LONG.

GIBRALTAR

PLAN SHEWING NEW HARBOUR
——— AND ———
DOCKYARD EXTENSION.

Scale of Feet

The new protected harbour from *Brassey's 1903*

from Spain. As this would have meant an expenditure of some £6,000,000 in addition to the £5,000,000 already spent, the proposal was a non-starter. Nevertheless, Bowles was correct in his conclusions, and if Gibraltar has proved a valuable naval base in two world wars it has only been because Spain has not intervened actively. Bowles obviously tempered his anti-Spanish stance in later years, as it is recorded that he died in Algeciras in 1922 and was buried at North Front.

While the expansion of the dockyard was being studied and carried out, the modernisation of the defensive armament of the Rock was also taken in hand. William Armstrong had introduced the first breech loading rifled guns (BLs) in 1855, but after some accidents caused by the weakness of the breech mechanism, British ordnance reverted to muzzle loading (rifled muzzle loaders or RMLS). This was a retrograde step at a time when France, Germany, Spain and the USA, were experimenting successfully with BLs. But for the next twenty years all British ordnance consisted of RMLs and it was not until 1881 that BLs came into general use.

The most impressive of the RMLs were undoubtedly the 100-ton guns. In the 1870s two were sent to Malta and two to Gibraltar, where they were mounted at Victoria Battery (in the Alameda behind the Fire Station) and Napier Battery (at Rosia behind FHQ). This last gun can still be seen in place. The reason why these monsters, which had a calibre of 17.7 inches and fired a 2,000-pound solid shell, were sent to the Mediterranean bases was that the Italian Navy had ordered eight from Armstrong to mount on the two battleships of the Duilio class. It was feared therefore that the existing coast defence batteries at Gibraltar and Malta would be outranged.

In 1888 all the defensive guns in Gibraltar were RMLs and it was not until 1889 that the first 6-inch BLs were placed at O'Hara's, Lord Airey's and Genista Batteries. The first 9.2-inch BL was in place in Jews' Cemetery Battery by 1891. Although the work of modernising the batteries went ahead, by the beginning of the 20th century many of the batteries still mounted RMLs. The 100-ton gun at Napier's was still counted as part of the Rock's armament in 1902, when it misfired during a practice shoot. By 1914 the Rock's batteries had all been modernised and they mounted the not inconsiderable total armament of 13 9.2s and

20 6-inch - some of them having a very wide field of fire and long range from the top of the Rock. There were also a score of 12-pounder and 4 and 4.7-inch QFs to protect the harbour from attack by torpedo craft. In 1905, in the light of the experience gained in the Boer War, an armoured train was prepared with two 12-pounders and a searchlight mounted on trucks, for the defence of the North Mole. But the improvements in the fixed batteries made this innovation superfluous and the experiment was suspended after a couple of years. This very heavy gun armament was designed not only to protect the Rock and the naval base, but also to command the passage of the Strait and deny it to the enemy, but it was never required to do so, perhaps the threat it presented was sufficient.[12]

HMS *Cormorant*

A prominent feature of the naval base for many years was HMS *Cormorant*. She was built as a composite sloop which meant that her keel, ribs and beams were of iron planked with teak. She was 170 feet long and displaced 1,130 tons. Her armament consisted of 2 7-inch and 4 64-pounder MLs, and she was a barque-rigged three-master with a single screw driven by a compound reciprocating engine, which, if pushed, could develop as much as 1,100 hp and drive the ship along at 12 knots. She sailed well but the design of her machinery was described as mediocre.

Cormorant was commissioned at Chatham in July 1878 and sent to the Australian station for six years. She returned to Britain in 1885 and paid-off at Portsmouth for refitting where her guns were altered to BLs (2 6-inch and 6 5-inch). She then served for four years on the Pacific coast of Canada and in 1889 was ordered to Gibraltar to become an accommodation ship. Although only eleven years old her faulty machinery had done for her, though her stout teak hull was to ensure her survival for another 60 years. She arrived on 4 November, and the following day was commissioned as tender to HMS *Goshawk* the duty guardship. In 1894 she recommissioned as Gibraltar Depot Ship and the SNO flew his flag in her for the next 52 years. Her armament was reduced to a saluting battery of 6 3-pounders, later reduced to 4, but during World War II she was fitted with automatic 20mm AA guns. At first *Cormorant* was anchored within the New Mole, but in 1912 she moved to Coaling Island on which the stacks of coal had been replaced by oil tanks, and she and her tender Hart presented a proud picture with their snow-white canvas covers, coal-black hulls and white boot-topping and red water line.[13]

The *Cormorant's* tender and companion at Coaling Island for 35 years was HMS *Hart*. Originally she was called HMS *Rapid*, a composite built corvette launched at Devonport in 1883. She was larger than her companion (200 feet long, displacement 1,420 tons) and as she had a partially armoured deck she was later rated as a 3rd class cruiser. Her armament consisted of 2 6-inch and 10 5-inch BLs. After serving in the African and Australian stations she returned to Devonport and was laid up in 1902. The following year she was sent to Gibraltar to provide accommodation for workmen in the Dockyard. In 1911 she was acting as depot for the submarine flotilla at Gibraltar and the following year she became a coaling hulk. In 1916 she was renamed *Hart* and became tender to the *Cormorant*.[14]

Notes and References

(1) See Marder *Anatomy* chapter 1, also pages 120, 123, 143, 144, 146, 183-184, 212-216.
(2) Marder ibid 209; Gonzalez 35; *Brassey's 1895* 13.
(3) Bowles 7; Gonzalez 36, 38, 39; *Brassey's 1903* 103.
(4) Gonzalez 39, 44.
(5) Gonzalez 38-41.
(6) Gonzalez 39-40.
(7) Bowles 8; Gonzalez 41-42, 44.
(8) Gonzalez 42, 43, 44.
(9) Gonzalez 43, 47; *Gibraltar Directory 1939* 305-306; *Brassey's 1903* 107.
(10) Ranft 10; *Brassey's 1903* 107.
(11) Bowles 10.
(12) Hire Ms.
(13) Colledge 1:137; Preston & Major 220-22; *Gibraltar Illustrated* (magazine).
(14) Colledge 1:452; Palao 81-82.

CHAPTER IX

THE NEW BASE AND WORLD WAR I.

After the moles had been completed and Gibraltar had an enclosed and defensible harbour, 30 moorings were laid down in September 1903 to accommodate the battleships of the combined Mediterranean and Channel Squadrons. The following year, when Sir John Fisher became First Lord of the Admiralty he reorganised the disposition of the ships of the Royal Navy. Many of the obsolete gunboats stationed round the globe were withdrawn and the battle squadrons were concentrated in European waters. Fisher was of the opinion that foreign stations could be rapidly reinforced if necessary and he saw no virtue in dividing his fleets into penny packets. The Mediterranean battle squadron was reduced to six ships of the Duncan class and the Channel Fleet was renamed the Atlantic Fleet and reorganised, its main strength was to be the eight battleships of the King Edward VII class, the famous 'Wobbly Eight', which were allocated to it as they came into service. These, the best and newest battleships of the Royal Navy were to be based at Gibraltar, from where they could control the entrance to the Mediterranean, and quickly reinforce the Mediterranean Fleet or the Channel (formerly Home) Fleet, as circumstances required.[1]

By now the international situation had changed very considerably. The confrontation between Britain and France had come to a head in the clash at Fashoda in the Sudan in 1898, and even though France concluded an alliance with Russia, a rapprochement was in the offing. The three decades of acrimonious rivalry in the scramble for imperial possessions were terminated through an alliance between the two countries enshrined in the Entente Cordiale of 1904. They united in the face of the growing military power of Germany, on land and at sea. In 1897, Admiral von Tirpitz, had become minister of marine and he at once began to plan the expansion of the German Navy. The new

German High Seas Fleet was designed to provide a serious challenge to the Royal Navy's mastery of the seas. From the first years of the 20th century all new construction and developments in the Royal Navy were made with the German threat in mind.

This was a time of rapid changes in the design of ships and their armament. The torpedo was developed to become a more potent weapon, with a longer range and heavier warhead, and large flotillas of destroyers were built to carry them. The submarine was improved to become a viable threat to surface ships. But the queen of the seas was still the battleship, which became increasingly bigger, more heavily armoured and more formidable. The, by now traditional, armament of RN battleships of 4 12-inch guns, was supplemented by increasing numbers of smaller guns. The King Edward VII class, for example, carried 4 12-inch, 4 9.2-inch, and 10 6-inch, as well as numerous 12 and 3-pounders. Forward looking tacticians realised that with the new heavy long range guns, battles at sea would be fought at greater ranges than had hitherto been thought likely. No longer would fleets be expected to slog it out at ranges of between one and three miles, but fighting could be expected to take place when battleships were anything between five and ten miles apart. This highlighted the problem of controlling the big guns to ensure that shells should find their target at this distance. It was realised that the multiplicity of sizes of guns in one ship made the ranging and control of shots very difficult, and naval writers started to advocate 'the all big-gun battleship'. This was an innovation close to Fisher's heart and the *Dreadnought*, which was bigger than any previous battleship and carried an armament of 10 12-inch guns, and 27 12-pounders to deal with destroyers and torpedo boats, was laid down in October 1905 and completed in 15 months.

The *Dreadnought* outclassed all previous battleships and made them obsolete. For not only did it carry a heavier main battery, but the thickness of its armour was increased from 9" to 11", and it had turbine engines which gave it a speed of 21 knots, an advantage of 3 knots over older ships with reciprocating machinery. In addition, turbines were smoother in operation, gave a steadier gun-platform and made it easier to maintain speed. She was followed by similar ships, all of which were termed Dreadnoughts; their anti-torpedo boat armament was increased from 12-pounders to 4-inch guns, and eventually to 6-inch.

The new Dreadnoughts were all allocated to the Channel Fleet, to face the German High Seas Fleet which was also being equipped with numbers of these vessels. This armament race was bound to lead to war and the Admiralty began seriously to prepare for the coming conflict. After the Coronation Review by Edward VII in 1902, the hitherto colourful ships began to be painted in grey. By the spring of 1904 'the black battlefleet' with its black hulls, white upperworks and buff funnels and ventilators, had given way to a uniform grey.[2]

In 1912 there were further alterations in the disposition of Britain's battleships. The Atlantic Fleet was redesignated the 3rd Battle Squadron and returned to the United Kingdom, and the Duncans from Malta became the 4th Battle Squadron and moved to Gibraltar. The ships were really required in home waters, but it was felt necessary to find some use for the newly completed dockyard at Gibraltar for the time being. However, when the threat of war became more evident they were moved to Dover. This meant that while Britain took on the full burden of facing the German High Seas Fleet, the defence of the Mediterranean against potential enemies (Austria and probably Italy) was left to the French Navy. But in order to show the flag and counter Germany's Mittelmeer Squadron, the main unit of which was the new battle-cruiser *Goeben*, the 2nd Battle-Cruiser Squadron was stationed at Malta.[3]

The *Goeben*

At the outbreak of war in 1914, the *Goeben* was in dock in the Austrian port of Pola on the Adriatic coast, having her boilers overhauled, but she soon cleared harbour and on 3 August bombarded the Algerian Port of Philippeville. At the time she was being shadowed by Admiral Milne with his battle-cruisers, but Britain's ultimatum to Germany had not expired and she had not yet joined France in the war. When she did the following day, the German squadron was coaling at Messina. Milne kept his squadron cruising between Bizerta and Sardinia. He wanted to prevent the Germans from breaking out to the west to attack the convoys carrying troops from North Africa to France, or steam past Gibraltar into the Atlantic to attack Britain's ocean trade.[4]

At the time, there was no force at Gibraltar that could stop the German squadron. The old cruiser HMS *Edgar* and the scouts HMS *Active* and *Attentive* were out patrolling the trade routes, so apart from the batteries of the fortress there were only the local torpedo flotillas. These consisted of three small harbour-defence submarines of 280 tons, *B6*, *B7* and *B8* powered by petrol engines and armed with two 18" torpedo tubes each. Although they later served in the Dardanelles campaign they only had a limited range and were not very satisfactory, and in 1917 they were converted into surface patrol vessels at Malta. They retained their original numbers but the identification letter was altered to S.[5]

There were also eleven, twenty-year-old torpedo boats, of just over 100 tons; *Nos 83* and *87-96* were rated as tenders to the *Cormorant*, and were moored at the Torpedo Boat Camber. They could scarcely maintain 20 knots in a running sea, and it was doubtful whether they would ever be able to get within the 600 yards of the fast German ships, which was the maximum range of the 14" torpedoes that they carried. Nevertheless, they were out patrolling the Strait from the outset of war and captured a number of German merchant ships that tried to slip through the Strait. They continued their patrol in all weathers right through the war. On 1 November 1915, *No 96* sank after a collision with the troopship *Tringa* and 11 out of her crew of 25 were lost. A memorial tablet to those who died was erected on the wall of the Police Post at the North Gate of the Dockyard. On 25 April 1918 *No 90* capsized in rough seas and 13 of her crew were drowned.[6]

However, when the German squadron left Messina it headed east, not west, pursued half-heartedly by Milne, who did not seem to realise that the main reason for his presence in the Mediterranean was the destruction of the *Goeben* and her escort. The *Goeben* and *Breslau* passed the 1st Cruiser Squadron which was stationed at the entrance to the Adriatic to watch for the emergence of the Austrian fleet. But Rear-Admiral Troubridge was sadly lacking in the Nelson spirit and refused to engage, pleading instructions forbidding him to engage a superior force. These had been given to stop him getting involved with the main Austrian fleet, not a detached squadron. Troubridge commanded four cruisers, well-armoured with a 6-inch belt, which had a main armament of 22 9.2-inch guns that were a match for the 10 11-inch of the *Goeben*. The British cruisers could fire a total broadside of 8,500 lbs, which was 1,100 lbs more than the Germans. The Goeben and her consort therefore got away and reached Constantinople unscathed; they lived to fight another day.[7]

The Gibraltar Dockyard was kept busy from the earliest days of the war and proved its worth. In September 1914 the AMC *Carmania* came into dock to repair damage she had received in the encounter in which she had sunk the raider *Cap Trafalgar* off the coast of Brazil; and the battle-cruiser HMS *Inflexible* came for a refit the following month, after taking part in the Battle of the Falklands. The naval war in the Mediterranean moved to the eastern basin with the Dardanelles Campaign, but a number of ships damaged in action were brought to Gibraltar to be repaired and *Inflexible* had to be towed back and docked after being mined. Many of the wounded were brought from the Dardanelles to both the Military and Naval Hospitals.[8]

The U-boat threat

The German U-boat campaign in the Mediterranean was to highlight the importance of Gibraltar as a base. The parts for a number of small 130-ton U-boats were transferred overland to the Adriatic coast of Austria, where they were assembled and launched. The German Navy also decided to send out a number of large boats, which could travel round the British Isles and through the Strait of Gibraltar into the Mediterranean. The 650 ton *U-21* left for the Mediterranean in April 1915. Arrangements were made for her to be refuelled by a ship hired in Spain, but when they met, the Spanish supply ship was found to be carrying fuel oil instead of diesel. But *U-21* managed to complete the voyage to Cattaro without refuelling. She was commanded by Lieutenant-Commander Hersing, one of the leading German submarine aces, who soon made his presence felt. On 25 May he sank HMS *Triumph*, a pre-Dreadnought battleship, off the entrance to the Dardanelles, and two days later sank another old battleship HMS *Majestic*. Hersing was followed a few months later by *U-33, 34, 35, 38* and *39*, all of which negotiated the Strait without difficulty; and which, once based inside the Mediterranean, not only posed a serious threat to the naval superiority of the allies, but also presented a serious threat to Britain's vital trade route. Virtually all the jute and rice imported into Britain at the time came through the Mediterranean, as did three-quarters of the petrol, wool and hemp, and half of the manganese and rubber.[9]

Naval Intelligence was aware of these German movements and efforts were made to strengthen the Gibraltar patrols. Two 150 ton steam trawlers were hired and armed under the names of *Cormorant II* and *IV*, and a drifter was engaged and renamed *Cormorant III*. A mine barrage was later proposed to bar the passage to U-boats, but the great depth of the Strait, strong currents and the need to respect Spanish territorial waters on both the European and African sides made the barrage impractical.[10]

The RNAS established a base in order to improve observation of traffic in the Strait. The Army had had facilities for captive balloons for some years and the Bland salvage tug *Rescue* had been fitted out as a balloon tender for service in the Dardanelles. (This vessel saw many years of service after returning to civilian service in 1919 and became very popular when it was used for the Tangier ferry service from 1940 to 1950.) It was also decided to operate RNAS aeroplanes from the Rock.[11]

The first machines sent to Gibraltar were half a dozen two seater Gnome Cauldrons and BE 2Cs, which operated from the race course for several months. But four of the machines were wrecked and when one of the BEs crashlanded on the Spanish side and was retrieved without permission, it caused problems with the Spanish authorities and the experiment was ended. A seaplane base was started and a large hangar was built on Reclamation Road, which then bordered on the sea. This housed a Short two-seater, three White tractors, and a couple of Porte 2-ton Flying Boats. These machines had problems when they tried to take off in strong Levanters as the gusts tumbling down from the top of the Rock onto the harbour would impede their take-off, and they were not sufficiently sea-worthy to taxi out into the Bay before taking off. However, the base was operated right through the war and was taken over by the RAF on April Fool's Day 1918.[12] When RNAS Flights 265, 266 and 364 were formed into Gibraltar's first RAF squadron No 265, which flew anti-submarine patrols until it was disbanded in 1919.[13]

The success of Naval Intelligence

With everything that took place in the harbour visible to watchers in Spain there were undoubtedly a number of German agents stationed in Algeciras; but Naval Intelligence conducted from Gibraltar also had its successes. This was directed by a member of the Admiral's staff, Lieutenant-Colonel Charles Thoroton RMLI, known to his friends as 'Charles the Bold', who eventually controlled an extensive organisation which covered not only Spain, but also North Africa and Greece. There is not much known of Thoroton's activities as in later years he burned all his papers, except, he informed his superiors, those he would need to defend himself if he was attacked for some of his 'more questionable activities'. Thoroton ran a very efficient and successful organisation and when the war ended the Spanish Government asked the Admiralty to allow him to continue operating as he supplied them with more reliable information about disaffection and strikes within Spain than their own police force.[14]

Amongst the agents recruited by Thoroton, was Juan March, a young tobacco smuggler from Mallorca who used Gibraltar mainly for registering the small ships he used in his smuggling activities. March entered into an arrangement with Thoroton to supply details of German activities, in return for the Royal Navy and French authorities not interfering with his smuggling into Spain of tobacco from Algiers and Gibraltar. He provided very accurate information of U-boat movements, which he was very conversant with as he used his Gibraltar registered ships to supply them. In later years he became the richest financier in Spain and he financed the airlift of Franco's army from Morocco in 1936. When he escaped from prison in Alcalá de Henares (where he was held on a charge of conspiracy to murder his wife's lover) and made his way to Gibraltar in 1933, his break out was supposed to have been organised by his friends in NI. In spite of his strong Axis connections, March again offered his services to NI in World War II.[15]

The most striking coup by NI in Spain was undoubtedly the waylaying of a shipment of wolfram (tungsten ore) meant for Germany, in 1918. At the end of 1917 it became known that a Spanish brigantine *Erri Berro* was sailing from Bilbao with a clandestine cargo of 80 tons of wolfram to rendezvous with two U-cruisers off the Canaries. The *Erri Berro* sailed on the last day of the year and the following day was stopped by the ABS *Duke of Clarence*, which unfortunately struck her a glancing blow while taking her in tow and the brigantine sank with her valuable cargo. It now remained to intercept the U-boats. Four E class submarines had been sent to Gibraltar so that two should be on patrol in the area of the Canaries at any one time. On 17 January 1918, while *E.35* was out of sight of land recharging her batteries, *E.48* discovered *U-156* on the surface and fired three torpedoes at her, two missed and the one that hit did not explode. *U-156* crash dived and got away, but the men on deck had to save themselves by swimming to the shore.[16]

This was a very disappointing outcome but *E.35* was to make up for it some weeks later. On 2 May information was recovered from a U-boat sunk in the Straits of Dover, that two other U-cruisers were to rendezvous off Cape St Vincent on the 11th. *E.35*, which was still at Gibraltar, was sent to patrol the area and on the evening of the 10th found *U-154* cruising on the surface. After stalking her for over two hours, *E.35* fired a torpedo which ran below the target but fortunately went unnoticed. She then approached nearer and fired two more from a distance of 500 yards, which hit, and *U-154* sank leaving a large oil slick. *E.35* surfaced but a periscope was sighted and she crash dived in time to escape being hit by a torpedo fired at her by *U-153*. *E.35* returned to Gibraltar in triumph, and D'Oyly-Hughes, her commander was awarded a bar to his DSO.[17]

U-boat attacks and false alarms

In the early morning of 3 November 1915, *U-38* on passage through the Strait, entered Gibraltar Bay and was fired at by the two 4-inch QFs of Prince George's Battery. The alarm having been given, the U-boat submerged and continued its journey. Some hours later, when she was 40 miles to the east of Ceuta, she came across the SS *Woodfield* carrying a cargo of mechanical vehicles for the army and a detachment of soldiers. Approaching her quarry on the surface she started firing at her with her guns. The *Woodfield* put up a plucky resistance with her 3-pounder, but she eventually had to be abandoned and was sunk by torpedo. Most of her crew and the soldiers managed to make their way in the ship's boats to the Spanish *presidios* of Alhucemas and Peñón de la Gomera on the Moroccan coast, but a lifeboat carrying two sailors and ten soldiers fell into the hands of Riff tribesmen and were held captive until the Spanish military negotiated their release. The soldiers were, however, interned in Spain for the rest of the war.[18]

On the last night of the year, other batteries joined Prince George's in firing at a submarine suspected to be in the Bay, a total of 16 guns taking part, including three 9.2-inch; but they must have been firing at shadows, as there was no submarine activity in the vicinity, though the gunners claimed to have sunk one. A similar event took place on 2 June 1917, and again there were claims of the sinking of a U-boat which were not substantiated later; but 6-inch shells from the Devil's Gap Battery did score hits on the Algeciras cemetery.[19]

The increasing submarine activity and the need to protect the hundred merchant ships that sailed past the Rock every day led to the strengthening of the flotillas which were allocated to Gibraltar. By March 1916 they consisted of 33 vessels in all. Eight armed yachts, four ABS, two sloops, nine trawlers bought from Portugal, and the ten torpedo boats that survived after the sinking of TB.96. The U-boats based at Cattaro concentrated on the nearer hunting grounds in the central and eastern Mediterranean, but long-range U-cruisers based on Germany and the Belgian coast, operated off the Atlantic coasts of the Iberian peninsula and Morocco. On 6 November 1917 *U-63* sank the Q-ship *Peveril* off Gibraltar.[20]

Convoys and the US Navy

The mounting shipping losses became even more serious after the German Government announced unrestricted submarine warfare in January 1917. Merchant shipping losses began to exceed 500,000 ton a month and something, obviously, needed to be done. The obvious solution was to revive the system of ocean convoys that had proved so successful in the days of sail. But the Admiralty was of the opinion that convoys could not be operated with modern steam ships and thrashed about for alternatives without success. Eventually they gave in to political pressure, and the first trial convoy of sixteen ships sailed from Gibraltar on 10 May 1917. It was escorted by the Q-ship *Rule* and yacht *Mavis* and had an additional escort for the first three hundred miles of three of the armed Gibraltar yachts. The convoy was met by flying boats and destroyers as it entered the Channel and it arrived at its destination without suffering any losses. It had obviously been a great success but the Admiralty still prevaricated. As Lloyd George, the Prime Minister, caustically put it, 'The Gibraltar convoy was ... successful. But these disappointing successes simply irritated the Admirals into sullen recalcitrance.' But they could not fly in the face of logic forever and a system of regular convoys which left Gibraltar for Britain every four days was instituted the following July. The first one left on the 26th of the month.[21]

At this stage only ships sailing to Britain were convoyed. Ships sailing outwards had to take their chance independently and often fell prey to submarines before reaching Gibraltar, though once they arrived they could join convoys to Oran or else be escorted along the Spanish coast to French waters, and from there to Marseilles or Genoa. This arrangement and the heavy losses suffered by their colliers, upset the Italians as they were dependent on British coal and their industry and railways were virtually brought to a stop by the sinkings on the Britain to Gibraltar run. So the first outward convoy OE1, left Liverpool for Port Said on 3 October. Ships for other destinations would leave the OE convoys at Gibraltar and join other convoys.[22]

The great shortage of escort vessels was eased by the entry of the USA into the war. An American battle squadron was sent to join the Grand Fleet at Scapa Flow, and some of their best and most recent destroyers were based at Queenstown (Cobh) to escort the Atlantic convoys, but Gibraltar also obtained substantial reinforcements.

On 6 August 1917, the new gunboat USS *Sacramento* reached Gibraltar as the advance ship for the squadron that was to be based there. She was followed a few days later by the light cruiser *Birmingham* flying the flag of Rear-Admiral H B Wilson who handed over the command to Rear-Admiral A P Niblack in November. The relations between the RN and USN were excellent and Niblack had the greatest respect for Rear-Admiral H S Grant who was SNO at Gibraltar. The American squadron continued growing until it included three light cruisers (the only ones the US Navy possessed at the time), seven gunboats, five old destroyers, coast guard cutters and armed yachts, a total of some 33 ships with crews that numbered 5,000 in all.

The ships that formed the 15th Destroyer Squadron were among the oldest in the US Navy, coal-fired antique vessels of 420 tons, carrying two 3-inch guns and two torpedo tubes. They were stationed in the Philippines at the beginning of the war, where they were considered so decrepit that they were not allowed out of the sight of land. Nevertheless they made the voyage through Suez to Gibraltar without incident, although they were so rusty that when a block of cement ballast was lifted out of USS *Barry* some of the plates came up with it and she had to be docked. They did good service, but on 19 November 1917, the USS *Chauncey* was run down by one of the merchant ships that formed part of a convoy she was escorting in the Strait, and sank with the loss of 21 lives including the captain. The members of the Squadron subscribed for a memorial tablet which was erected on the wall of the Armament Building near Gun Wharf and may still be seen.[23] During this period there was a tremendous number of ships calling at Gibraltar. In December 1917, for example, 751 merchant ships arrived, 252 coaled, 47 discharged coal or cargo and 107 were repaired in the Dockyard. Supplying fresh food for such a large number of ships became a difficult matter, and though as much as possible was imported from Spain and Morocco, there was never quite enough and the civil Police was charged with rationing it out. The US sailors were lavishly fed by RN standards, and in the Police files there is a letter written by the Commissioner of Police to Saccone and Speed, who were the victualling agents for the US Navy, that he regretted that stocks would not admit an increase in the 1,000 Moorish eggs supplied to the US Navy daily.[24]

Although the American expeditionary force to France had travelled direct to Britain and the Atlantic ports, by 1918 much of their supplies were routed to Marseilles and other Mediterranean ports, and two (later four) modern destroyers were added to the detachment at Gibraltar to escort the supply ships. The Dockyard was so overworked that the US Navy sent a very efficient 7,000 ton repair ship, the *Buffalo* to repair and refit their own ships and she proved a great asset.[25]

The Gibraltar patrol was a truly international affair. Every morning there would be a conference of Admirals Grant and Niblack, representing the Royal and US Navies, and the French and Italian naval representatives. At sea it was even more polyglot with Canadian trawlers and the occasional Japanese destroyer from Malta, added to the escorts. Brazil decided to add a contribution to this international array. Two light cruisers and four destroyers left for Europe in May 1918, but they were delayed for a long time at Freetown, because of sickness among the crews, and did not get to Gibraltar until the closing days of the war. Their only taste of action was when on 10 November they fired on a submarine chaser, mistaking it for the conning tower of a submarine in the heavy swell.[26]

The Gibraltar patrol was not able to stop U-boats from traversing the Strait, but it had its successes. The first was when *UB-70* was sunk in the Strait by the destroyer HMS *Basilisk* and the armed yacht USS *Lydonia*. On 8 September 1917, *UB-49* was so seriously damaged in an encounter with H M Yacht *Narcissus* that she had to go into Cadiz for repairs and was subsequently interned for the rest of the war. The following 21 April, one of the Gibraltar motor launches *ML.413* commanded by Lieutenant J S Bell was keeping hydrophone watch 4½ miles east of Punta Almina when she picked up sounds of an engine being run at high speed and observed a large bow wave approaching from the west. *UB-71* crossed the ML's bows at a distance of thirty feet and then dived. Bell dropped his four depth charges and afterwards heard nothing. He waited till morning, when, with *TB.92* which had been standing by all night, they were able to pick up debris from the sunken submarine. Bell was awarded the DSC. Three weeks later the gunboat USS *Wheeling* and the US armed yacht *Venetia* had an encounter with a U-boat while escorting a convoy from Bizerta to Gibraltar. One of the merchants ships was sunk and the *Venetia* hunted the U-boat for some time and dropped depth charges, to good effect. This was *U-39*, which was heading for Cartagena for repairs when she suffered a further attack by French seaplanes on 15 May. The bombs damaged her pressure hull and she therefore went into that port to be interned and surrendered to France after the war.[27]

By October 1918, the Austrian army had been defeated and could no longer guarantee the safety of the naval base of Cattaro, so the U-boats had to evacuate the Mediterranean. Ten were scuttled because they were not in a fit state to make the long journey back to Germany, and on 28 October fifteen set off to break through the Strait of Gibraltar. Thirteen got through. *U-35* was damaged and interned herself in Barcelona. *U-34* tried to slip through the neutral waters of Spanish Morocco but on the evening of 8 November, she was depth-charged by *ML.155* and the Q-ship *Privet* and sunk. *UB-50* which was in company got through the Strait that night and the following day she torpedoed and sank the battleship *Britannia* off Cape Spartel with a heavy loss of life. The survivors were taken to Gibraltar and the funeral of some who died after they were rescued took place on the 11th, which rather subdued the rejoicings on Armistice Day, as the *Britannia* was one of the 'Wobbly Eight' and well known in Gibraltar.[28]

The departure on 11 December of the US Navy ships stationed in Gibraltar, to rousing cheers from the crews of the ships of the Royal Navy, marked the return to peacetime routine.

Notes and references

(1)   Marder *Anatomy* 491-492.
(2)   Marder ibid 420.
(3)   Marder *Dreadnought* 1:287; Lumby 72.
(4)   Bassett *Battle-Cruisers* 42.
(5)   *Navy List* August 1914; *Jane's 1914* 92; Ackermann 125; Le Fleming 115.
(6)   *Navy List* August 1914; *Jane's 1914* 90; *Gibraltar Chronicle* August/October 1914.
(7)   Bassett *Battle-Cruisers* 42.
(8)   Chatterton *Sea Raiders* 162, 273; Basett *Battle-Cruisers* 274; *Gibraltar Chronicle* passim.
(9)   Halpern *Naval War* 51, 107-116.
(10)   Colledge 2:88; Halpern *Royal Navy in Mediterranean* 245, 248.
(11)   Elliott Ms 5; Somner 45.
(12)   Elliott Ms 6.
(13)   Fairbairn 70.
(14)   Beesley 190-191.
(15)   Benavides 78-79, 186; Beesley 190; Jato 198.
(16)   Beesley 191-200.
(17)   Winton *Glorious* 80; Taylor 149.
(18)   Chatterton *Seas of Adventure* 152-155; Hire Ms 72.
(19)   Hire Ms 37, 46, 50, 51, 72, 75, 90, 91.
(20)   Colledge 2:276; Chatterton *Seas of Adventure* 195; Winton *Convoy* 93.
(21)   Winton *Convoy* 48, 65-66, 72, 77.
(22)   Halpern *Naval War* 346, 376; Winton *Convoy* 93.
(23)   Sims 160-161; *Gibraltar Directory 1939* 247; Halpern ibid 446.
(24)   Halpern ibid 446; Benady *Police* 23.

(25) Halpern ibid 514, 515.

(26) Halpern ibid 444-446.

(27) Taylor 162; Chatterton *Seas of Adventure* 278, 301-302; Sims 162-163; Layman 66.

(28) Chatterton ibid 311-312; *Gibraltar Directory 1939* 314.

CHAPTER X

BETWEEN THE WARS.

After the end of the war ships no longer had to call at Gibraltar to await their convoys and the congestion in the harbour disappeared. The patrol flotillas were dispersed, but some destroyers were maintained in reserve with reduced crews and rated as tenders to *Cormorant*. The Portuguese trawlers were sold to Cruz Brothers and most of them rejoined the Portuguese fishing fleet;[1] and the TBs were sold to Bland Line for breaking up. However, *No. 94*, the most serviceable, was converted for civilian use and renamed *Brack*. She was employed in chasing ships in trouble in the Strait and negotiating terms with them on behalf of Bland's salvage vessels. In 1920 she replaced the little wood-built 32-ton *Rocket* (ex TB 4), which had been employed in this work since 1906 and was almost 40 years old. But, after two years, the Brack too was retired as the increasing use of radio by merchant ships made her services unnecessary.[2]

Under the terms of the Washington Naval Treaty of 1922, the number of capital ships in the Royal Navy was reduced to 22, and was to be reduced further to 20 when the two powerful new battleships, *Rodney* and *Nelson* were completed. After the London Treaty of 1930 there was a further reduction to 15. But the Mediterranean Fleet was still an elite force and it was reconstituted with the 4th Battle Squadron of six battleships of the Iron Duke class, six light cruisers, 16 destroyers and a flotilla of submarines. In later years there were changes in the ships that composed the fleet but until the outbreak of war in 1939 there were normally at least five battleships on station. Malta became the main base and the naval establishment in Gibraltar was considerably reduced although the Mediterranean station at the time included the western approaches of the Strait as far as a line from Cape St Vincent to the Moroccan coast.[3]

The Naval Hospital, the oldest such establishment run by the Royal Navy was closed down in 1922 and later converted into living quarters for officers of the Navy and the Dockyard. Greenwich Hospital was of course older, but it was not really a hospital in the modern sense but an alms house for old and needy sailors, and the hospital at Haslar was only completed five years after the one at Gibraltar. The Navy in the Mediterranean was now catered for by the hospital at Malta, in addition to which, the fleet was usually accompanied by a hospital ship, the RFA *Maine*, a passenger ship converted during the war. The conversion had been paid for by voluntary contributions from the citizens of the State of Maine. Urgent cases at Gibraltar were treated at the modern 200 bed hospital built by the Army in Europa Road. When this hospital was transferred from the Army in 1962 and renamed the Naval Hospital, the previous building became known as the Old Naval Hospital.

The RAF had no further use for the seaplane hangar and it was returned to the Navy, as all reclaimed land was RN property. But in February 1920 the Navy handed over Reclamation Road (Queensway) to the civilian authorities and it became city property. In 1921 the hangar was handed over to HMS *Cormorant* to be turned into a cinema for serving officers and men. It was run as a trust and all profits went to naval charities. Equipment was bought with a grant of £250 from the Naval Canteen Fund. In 1931 the advent of 'talkies', made the equipment obsolete and the cinema was closed. The Base Supply Officer however, arranged to install modern equipment and it was reopened later the same year under its old name and was now also open to civilians. It was a great success under the management of successive BSOs. The 1940 incumbent was surprised to find that technically he owned it and arrangements were made to form a charitable trust to run it. The three trustees are the FO Gibraltar, the captain of *Cormorant* and the BSO. In 1944 the name was changed to the Naval Trust Cinema Gibraltar. The old building burnt down in August 1948, when a fire started in the projection room which soon spread to the heavy coatings of tar on the outside of the corrugated iron edifice. Although it was a total loss, another shed building was put up in its place and the cinema was reopened in July 1950. By 1960 competition from new civilian cinemas brought financial problems. The cinema was therefore sold to

Bassadone Brothers and renamed 'Regal'. It was closed down in 1984 and has since been demolished and Regal House built on the site. The Naval Trust continues in existence and has assets of £190,000. It is a registered charity and makes grants to local civilian charities and for naval welfare in Gibraltar.

The limestone archway of the American War Memorial at Orange Bastion was constructed during the years 1932 and 1933 by the American Battle Monuments Commission, to commemorate the achievements and comradeship of the American and Royal Navies in the Strait during World War I. It was designed by Dr Paul Cret of Philadelphia. An American contingent arrived on the cruiser USS *Raleigh* in October 1937 for the formal dedication and handing over although it had been completed four years earlier.

During the war the cost of living had risen very considerably and this bore heavily on the working classes in Gibraltar, who had great difficulty in making ends meet even though the price of bread was subsidised by the Government. Spanish coal heavers had gone on strike in 1918 for higher wages, but Gibraltarian workers felt that their patriotism precluded them from striking in time of war. Rear-Admiral Sir Reginald Tyrwhitt, who took over as SNO Gibraltar in 1919, after the Harwich Force had been disbanded, found a great deal of labour unrest at the Dockyard. In a letter to Sir Roger Keyes he wrote, 'I am not in love with Gibraltar and I hate the sight of the Dockyard and everybody in it. We are constantly having strike troubles ...' But the strikers were on a hiding to nothing, for the size of the labour force was soon drastically reduced. There were no increases in pay but the cost of living dropped through the 1920s and 30s.[4]

In 1922 the Eastern Telegraph Co (later part of Cable and Wireless) began to use No 5 Jetty at the North Mole for their cable ships, and No 1 Jetty and the coal sheds on the western arm were rented to the local coal merchants for some years. In 1932 a consortium of the Gibraltar coal merchants formed Gibraltar Transporters Ltd to offer coaling facilities at the North Mole, and the latest bulk coal handling equipment made by the Tyne engineering firm of Clarke and Chapman was installed. Ships could now tie up for coaling inside or the outside of the Mole. The coal hulks gradually disappeared and with them the hundreds of heavers who laboriously coaled passing ships carrying baskets on their backs. This improvement encouraged more merchant ships to call at Gibraltar and a cartel was organised with the ports of Oran, Bonne, Algiers and Ceuta, which fixed prices and quotas, and became known as GOBAC after the initials of the ports involved. The coal bunkering trade reached its peak in 1937 when an average of 80,000 tons a month was handled. Soon after sales started to decline as more oil burning ships came into service and 20 years later only the memory of the 20-foot stacks of coal on the North Mole remained.[5]

The number of people employed in the Dockyard had increased to 4,300 during the war, but after the war many men were laid off. In 1922 it was announced that there would be strict economies at Gibraltar to save £58,000 a year. By 1923 the labour force had reduced to 1,200, one-third less than in 1914. Malta on the hand, though its labour force had been reduced from a war-time peak of more than 10,000, still employed more than 61,000, 50% more than in 1914. It appears that during the first few years after the Gibraltar Dockyard had been completed every effort had been made to keep the docks and repair facilities fully employed in order to justify the heavy expenditure on the works. But now the Admiralty was prepared to admit that Gibraltar was not essential and Malta with its large labour pool which consisted entirely of British subjects was given preference. The labour force at Gibraltar was only a fraction of that of the big home dockyards at Portsmouth, Devonport and Chatham, and half of Hong Kong's.[6]

The docks themselves had also become completely inadequate. At the time they were completed, the latest of the Royal Navy's battleships could fit even into No 3 Dock, and Nos 1 and 2 were considerably longer, but all the docks were only 95 feet wide. By 1914 battleships with a beam of 90 feet were coming into service. During the war it had been discovered that these ships were too narrow to resist damage by mine and torpedo, to which they were extremely vulnerable. It therefore became necessary to fit them with external bulges - large underwater blisters, compartmented and filled with sealed metal tubes, which it was hoped would cause the underwater weapons to explode further from the hull proper and therefore cause less damage. All the battleships retained post-war were fitted with bulges and their beam increased to over 100 feet, so they were no longer able to use the docks at Gibraltar. Later battleships also had a beam of over 100 feet as they had internal bulges filled with fuel oil or water and with empty compartments designed to absorb the expansion of underwater explosions.

It was not until the late 1930s that No 1 Dock was altered from a double to a single dock and widened to 118 feet. It could now take any RN ship; No 2 Dock was also lengthened to 584 feet so that it could accommodate all the latest cruisers apart from the County and Town classes. This work was completed in 1938, just in time for the outbreak of war.

On 23 March 1922, the destroyer HMS *Versatile* accidentally rammed HMS *H-42* off Europa Point and the submarine sank in 500 fathoms with all hands. The 26 members of the crew were all lost.

On 1 April 1931, the aircraft carrier *Glorious*, whilst engaged in an exercise 60 miles east of Gibraltar, ran into one of those impenetrable fogs that occur in the area at a time of a change of winds from the moisture-laden Levanters to the warmer, drier westerlies; being unable to manoeuvre (as she had to recover the aircraft she had in the air) she collided with the French liner *Florida* and returned to Gibraltar with considerable damage to her bows. But the facilities at Gibraltar were not up to permanent repairs so a temporary wooden bow with a coffer-dam erected over the forward bulkheads was fitted, so that she could reach Malta.[7]

In 1922 the Atlantic Fleet made the first of the Spring Cruises during which it joined up with the Mediterranean Fleet for exercises which took place either in the Mediterranean or in the western approaches. These exercises normally examined some problem of naval tactics or convoy protection, but sometimes, as in 1931, they also involved the land defences of the garrison, and in 1932 the Atlantic Fleet tried a night raid on Gibraltar. After the exercises were over, both fleets would enter the harbour so that the officers could discuss the lessons of the exercise. These became an annual event, and every year the harbour was filled with over fifty warships, the light grey of the Mediterranean ships mingling with the dark grey of the Atlantic Fleet, which was renamed the Home Fleet in 1932.

Normally the occasion was enlivened with a parade of some sort: the massed bands of the fleet beating retreat at the Alameda Parade Ground or Naval Sports Ground. Some years there would be a march past of the crews, when as many as 6,000 sailors and marines would march from Ragged Staff, past the Convent, where the Governor would take the salute, and then down Main Street and return along Reclamation Road. Sometimes there was a parade on the racecourse at North Front.

In addition Jack would have a run ashore. The Governor closed down the brothels in New Passage in 1922 and encouraged more wholesome activities by rescinding the Ordinance which prohibited sports on Sundays. The playing fields in the Reclamation Road were in constant use when the fleet was in harbour, there were also tugs of war and pulling races between boats representing the various ships. In the evenings they could drink beer in the garden of the Garrison Recreation Rooms (now Ince's Hall). They could also buy cooked Mediterranean prawns, assorted nuts and massive strawberries from street vendors. The sailors would also patronise the souvenir shops, and the crews of the larger warships could obtain scarves for their wives and girl friends on which were printed a picture of their ship with the Rock in the background.

The more adventurous would visit one of the cafes in main Street - Universal, Trocadero, Royal or Suizo - which featured female bands and English and Spanish dancers. One matelot described the girls,

The Spanish señoritas stamped and clattered their castanets, whirled to float their ankle-length red dresses high to reveal shapely slender legs, shapely hips, flat stomachs. We whistled encores, drank more beer, whistled louder. The London girls bounced in semi-rhythm and were applauded just as loudly, for Jack ashore is generous; they were overweight, blowsy, rocked the stage dangerously. They knew; they appreciated our applause and kicked higher.[8]

The inexperienced and unwary would try out the locally distilled *anis* in one of the backstreet bars, and finding it deceptively sweet and smooth would imbibe too much. This would produce the most horrible hangover the following day and many a matelot left Gibraltar convinced that the locals had tried to poison him. The drunk and disorderly were dealt with by the naval pickets who operated from the Naval Picket House situated at the end of Main Street, by the Charles V Wall. The Picket House was demolished to allow for the building of the Referendum Arch in 1969.

The portent of war

The Italian invasion of Abyssinia in July 1935 heralded a period of international crisis. Attempts were made to stop Italian aggression by endeavouring to get the League of Nations to impose economic sanctions. These did not work, but relations between Britain and Mussolini's government deteriorated. Because of fears of an Italian air attack on Malta, which had very little AA defence and no fighter aircraft, the fleet moved to Alexandria in October; and though it was reinforced from other stations, the western Mediterranean was left uncovered. Detachments of the Home Fleet were therefore sent to Gibraltar, consisting of the Battle-Cruiser Squadron - *Hood* and *Renown*, accompanied by the 6th Destroyer Flotilla; but the combined exercise did not take place that year.

After the fall of Addis Ababa the following May, Britain decided to accept the *fait accompli*. The Emperor Haile Selassie, who had to flee his country, arrived at Gibraltar with his suite on board the cruiser *Capetown* on the 29th, stayed overnight at the Rock Hotel and left for England on board the Orient liner *Orford* the following day.[9] Naval units were beginning to leave the Mediterranean for their proper stations when the Spanish Civil War broke out.

The Spanish Civil War

The political situation in Spain was chaotic and had led to a breakdown in law and order. Afraid of a left-wing take over, a number of senior officers organised an uprising in July 1936. Their main strength was in the Army of Morocco, where General Franco, one of the leaders of the insurrection, had flown to take command. It was crucial for the Nationalists to transport this force across to Spain.

The Spanish Fleet was therefore ordered to the Strait on 17 July to stop this proposed invasion; but the two first vessels that arrived, the destroyer *Churruca* and gunboat *Dato* joined the uprising and escorted the first ships with troops from Ceuta to Cadiz. Franco's call to the Navy was not transmitted, instead a message went out from the Ministry of Marine to all the crews of Spanish naval vessels to watch their officers and stop them from joining the rebellion. This led to sailors' committees taking over control of the ships as soon as the officers tried to join the uprising, and most of them were arrested and imprisoned. The first 'official mutiny' took place on board *Churruca* which was reincorporated into the Government Navy. The *Dato* and a number of other ships, including those in dock and being built at Ferrol, were taken over by the insurgents, but the bulk of the Navy's ships remained loyal to the Madrid Government.[10]

Gibraltar became aware of the uprising because of events at the frontier and many residents were caught attending the La Linea Fair when the fighting broke out. Algeciras was taken over quietly with the help of the troops newly landed from Morocco but there was fighting in La Linea on 18 and 19 July. On the 21st the paddle-wheel dockyard tug *Energetic* was sent to Algeciras to bring away 130 British and Spanish refugees, and the following day the destroyer HMS *Shamrock*, which was rated as tender to *Cormorant* brought in 40 more from Malaga. The 4th Destroyer Flotilla was sent to Gibraltar from Malta to assist in protecting shipping and helping in the evacuation of refugees. Within a few days there was a Royal Navy guardship in virtually every major Spanish port to try and save lives and protect British property. Over 1,200 refugees were brought to Gibraltar and the RN had to arrange accommodation and food for many of them when they first arrived. The Battle-Cruiser squadron was sent to join the Mediterranean Fleet and while the *Hood* stayed off the north coast, HMS *Repulse* which had just completed a major refit and had replaced her sister-ship *Renown* which had been docked for reconstruction, arrived in Gibraltar on the 25th.[11]

In the meantime a Spanish Republican squadron concentrated at Tangier to bar the passage of the Strait to Franco's forces. Some troops were transported across by an airlift organised by Juan March. An international naval force of one British, two Italian and two French cruisers, and two French and three Portuguese destroyers gathered in Tangier to protect the neutrality of that international harbour. The port was kept under observation by Nationalist planes and bombs were dropped near the Bland steamer *Gibel Dris* while it was entering the harbour. Fortunately she was not hit. The destroyers HMS *Whitehall* and *Wild Swan* were also bombed in the Strait.

On 22 July the Government squadron, consisting of the battleship *Jaime I*, two cruisers, seven destroyers and smaller vessels, anchored outside Gibraltar harbour. They asked for oil, coal, water and fresh provisions, and this request was passed on to London. The reply was that nothing could be supplied from naval stocks but that commercial purchases could be made. Torpedo boat *14* was running short of fuel but the Republic had no credit with Gibraltar Transporters Ltd and two petty officers had to go ashore to buy sterling to pay cash for 15 tons. The ships were then asked to move out of territorial waters as it was feared that if they were attacked, bombs might fall on Gibraltar, and the following day they moved to the north of the Bay. That afternoon the warships were bombed and some of the AA shells they fired landed on Gibraltar, fortunately without causing casualties. The cruisers *Libertad* and *Cervantes* then shelled La Linea but caused no damage.[12]

The officers of the Royal Navy were unable to communicate with their opposite numbers, who were mostly imprisoned on board their own ships, and they did not have much sympathy for the sailors' committees which had taken over.

With so many combatant ships in the area mistakes were bound to occur, and after February 1937 all British and French warships in the area had white, red and blue bands painted on their B turrets, and tarpaulins with stripes in the same colours placed on their torpedo tube mountings to aid identification from the air. Aircraft carriers had stripes painted on their flight decks. The Germans used red, white and black stripes and the Italians, red, white and green. Photographs of naval ships taken during the period of the Spanish Civil War can be dated through what became later known as the 'Nyons' colours.[13]

On 5 August one of the destroyers loyal to the Spanish Government which was on patrol in the Strait was driven off by aerial bombing and that evening an insurgent troop convoy of three ships escorted by the

Dato successfully crossed from Ceuta to Algeciras. The other destroyer was driven off by the gunboat in an encounter two miles from Europa Point. The following day the *Jaime I* and the *Libertad* sailed from Malaga and shelled Algeciras harbour causing much damage and sinking the *Dato*, but the troops had already dispersed. This lunch-time bombardment was clearly seen and photographed from Gibraltar.[14]

On the morning of Sunday 23 August, while the Admiral and his staff were in church, a distress signal was received from Bland's SS *Gibel Zerjon* which had been stopped outside Melilla by the Republican cruiser *Miguel de Cervantes* and ordered to Malaga. HMS *Repulse* and the destroyer leader HMS *Codrington*, which were in harbour at four hours' notice for steam, were ordered to sea immediately. Both ships were clear of the harbour in two hours. The *Codrington* reached the *Gibel Zerjon* first and the captain boarded the Spanish cruiser to protest. The Spanish captain apologised and the *Gibel Zerjon* returned to Gibraltar and left again for Melilla a few days later.[15]

Although the great powers concluded a non-intervention agreement at the Nyons Conference in September 1937, Italy and Germany continued to assist the Nationalists with armaments and men and Russia and France supported the Loyalists. This fuelled the conflict which became one of the bloodiest on record and assassinations were rampant. In August the naval officers under arrest were killed or drowned by order of the sailors' committees in retaliation for atrocities committed by the Nationalists. But the killings were not one-sided, and the Admiral Superintendent of the Ferrol base and the captain of the cruiser *Cervera* which was in dry dock there were shot, for refusing to join Franco's forces.[16]

There was a varied international gathering in Gibraltar in August 1936, which included the German pocket battleship *Admiral Scheer* and the Italian cruiser *Gorizia* which had suffered a petrol explosion in her bows while at Tangier, and had been towed over stern first to be repaired in No 1 Dock. Measurements taken while she was in dock showed that she exceeded the limit of 10,000 tons stipulated by the Washington Treaty.

In September the bulk of the Loyalist fleet moved to the Bay of Biscay to aid the Republican forces in the north, and at the end of the month a Nationalist squadron consisting of the *Cervera* and the newly completed 10,000 ton cruiser *Canarias* entered the Strait and after sinking the Loyalist destroyer *Ferrandiz* established control over the southern waters of the Peninsula. Although, after the loss of the whole of the northern coast, the powerful Government fleet concentrated in the south, it was not properly led and was unable to re-establish its ascendancy.[17]

The Royal Navy continued to patrol the seas round Gibraltar to protect British shipping from molestation, but not without suffering losses. On 13 May 1937, the destroyer HMS *Hunter*, while on patrol off the south east coast of Spain, struck a mine which had been laid by a fast launch operating from Malaga which was held by the Nationalists, and one of the boilers exploded. The *Hunter* was almost broken in two and lay dead in the water until she was towed by a Spanish fishing boat into Almeria which was still in Republican hands. As she was in danger of sinking her crew camped on the dockside until that night the hospital ship *Maine* arrived, all lit up in accordance with the Geneva Convention. The 24 wounded were taken on board but the rest of crew had to stay on the quayside. The bodies of three of the eight men killed were recovered and given burial in Almeria. The next morning the flotilla leader *Hardy* arrived to take them off. The *Hunter* was towed to Gibraltar by the cruiser *Arethusa* and docked, and the *Maine* brought the wounded to the Miltary Hospital. Three other dead bodies were taken from the wreckage and there was a solemn ceremony at Gibraltar in which the bodies were carried on gun-carriages through the streets and buried at North Front. Two others were never found and must have been blown into the water by the force of the explosion.[18]

As the Nationalist fleet was small, Franco bought two modern submarines from his Italian allies and in addition a number of 'Legionary submarines' with Italian crews operated against ships in Republican waters. The new destroyers of the Royal Navy were particularly at risk because they had similar silhouettes to those built in Spain which were of British design. On 31 August 1937, the destroyer HMS *Havoc* was near-missed by a torpedo whilst on patrol off Cape San Antonio (south of Valencia) and sighted a submarine which crash-dived. The *Havoc* hunted the submarine for three hours and after making an asdic contact carried out a depth-charge attack. The cruiser HMS

Galatea, with Rear-Admiral (D) James Somerville on board, and the destroyers HMS *Hasty*, *Hereward* and *Hyperion* later joined in the hunt, but the Italian submarine managed to elude them after being hunted for twelve hours. This was the *Iride* one of the Legionary submarines which was commanded by Prince Junio Valerio Borghese, whose further adventures are described in chapter 11. This incident led to the withdrawal of the Legionary submarines, but Franco protested vehemently and in September four submarines were seconded to the Spanish navy for five months, and given Spanish names while retaining their Italian crews. The *Iride* was one of these and became the *González López*, she survived the Civil War but on 22 August 1940 was sunk by torpedo-carrying Swordfish in the Gulf of Bomba.[19]

The Royal Navy's ships were not the only ones attacked by mistake. On 28 May 1937, two Republican aircraft dropped four bombs on the pocket battleship *Deutschland* in Ibiza harbour. Two bombs hit, one destroyed the aft starboard 5.9-inch battery and the other penetrated the deck forward of the bridge and hit a paint store by the crew's mess deck. There were 22 dead and 83 wounded of which nine more died. After tidying up much of the damage she entered Gibraltar harbour on the 30th and tied up by the Admiralty Tower to transfer her wounded to the military Hospital. The Hospital did not have the staff to deal with so many serious cases so four additional sisters were flown out in RAF flying boats. The following day 24 sailors were buried at North Front in a ceremony attended by the Governor. The Germans retaliated with a two hour bombardment of Almeria by the squadron flagship *Admiral Scheer* and four destroyers. The German admiral later called at Gibraltar to thank the Army and the Navy in Hitler's name for looking after the wounded and presented the staff of the Military Hospital with German decorations.[20]

On 5 March 1938 occurred the most important naval battle of the Civil War. Two Republican cruisers and five destroyers attacked three Nationalist cruisers protecting a small convoy off Cape Palos near Cartagena. There was a confused melee in the dark during which the Nationalist cruiser *Baleares* was hit by three torpedoes from the destroyer *Lepanto* which produced a tremendous explosion and the whole of the bows section burst into flames. The other two cruisers shepherded their convoy away and the Republicans returned to harbour satisfied with their victory. The destroyers HMS *Kempenfelt* and *Boreas* saw the explosion from 40 miles away and hastened to the scene. When they arrived the bows of the cruiser were awash and she had a heavy list to starboard. The *Kempenfelt* tied up on the port side abaft the propeller, which was out of the water, and started taking off survivors, but the cruiser sank shortly after and the destroyer had to cast off. The destroyers then continued rescuing sailors from the sea with the assistance of HMS *Blanche* and *Brilliant* and 470 survivors were picked up, 743 died.

After dawn the two other Nationalist cruisers returned and the destroyers were transferring the wounded to them by boat, when they were bombed by Republican aircraft from Cartagena. A British seaman in a whaler was killed and others injured. The two cruisers then proceeded to Palma followed by the *Kempenfelt* with a heavy load of survivors, while the *Boreas* steamed to Gibraltar at full speed with the British wounded.[21]

The last naval encounter of the Civil War took place in Catalan Bay. It came about like this. The Republican destroyer *Jose Luis Diez*, which had gone north with the fleet in 1936, was left behind at Gijon to protect the Asturian coast. She was not very active and earned the sobriquet of 'Pepe el del puerto' or 'Joe the harbour boat' and the British tabloids called her 'HMS Non-Intervention'. In October 1937 the *Diez* went to Falmouth and after spending some time there left for Le Havre for lengthy repairs. On 20 August 1938 she left to rejoin the main fleet at Cartagena, and after sinking some fishing vessels entered the Strait on the 26th where virtually the whole of the Nationalist fleet - three cruisers, two destroyers and two minelayers - was waiting for her. That night, after an encounter with the destroyer *Ceuta* she was hit by an 8" shell from the cruiser *Canarias* which holed her side and destroyed her Y gun turret. She took refuge in Gibraltar harbour, where she was transferred to a mooring buoy close to Coaling Island. Here, over a period of months, the crew, with the assistance of a French engineering firm, repaired the gap on the side, working behind a tarpaulin which hid the repairs from view.

When the worst of the damage had been repaired, the captain bravely decided to face the heavy odds outside, although part of the main armament was still out of action. At 1am on the evening of 31 December the *Diez* slipped her mooring, leaving a man on the buoy holding a light, in order to fool the Nationalist ships waiting outside into thinking that this was her anchor-light and she was still at her mooring. But her departure was noticed by a pro-Franco sympathiser and he let off a rocket at Europa Point in order to alert the Nationalist ships. Presumably this was a prearranged signal. Whilst rounding Europa Point the *Jose Luis Diez* was attacked by the ships waiting for her. She was faster than her four opponents but as she rounded Europa Point the minelayer *Vulcano* got so close that a torpedo fired by the destroyer went over the minelayer's quarter deck and entered the water on the other side. The two ships collided. A shell from the gunboat *Calvo Sotelo* entered the engine-room and severed the main steam pipe and the *Diez* ended aground at Catalan Bay. A number of shells fell on the village, and the local bobby, Joseph Baglietto, did his best to get the inhabitants under cover, although he himself was wounded. He was awarded the King's Police Medal.

In the early hours of the morning the *Diez* was boarded by a party of soldiers from the garrison and her ensign lowered. The crew were removed to Windmill Hill and then sent to Britain for internment until the end of hostilities. The *Jose Luis Diez* was refloated by the boom defence vessel *Moorhill*, and the harbour tugs *Rollicker* and *Rambler* towed her into harbour, while the destroyer HMS *Vanoc* stood by to make sure that the Nationalist warships did not interfere. After the war was over she was returned to the Spanish Navy and towed to Algeciras on 25 March 1939.[22]

The airfield
As the combined fleets were always accompanied by one or more aircraft carriers when they met at Gibraltar during the Spring cruises, the need became apparent for an airfield for use as an emergency landing ground as well as for air defence. In 1925 the Committee of Imperial Defence came to the conclusion that Gibraltar did not require fighter defence because the weather conditions in a Levanter would prevent flying on

many days of the year. Beatty, who was First Sea Lord, thought this was nonsense. And when he was informed that Major Barnby RM had commanded the seaplane base during the war, asked for him to be found. Barnby was stationed at Chatham at the time, and when contacted was playing tennis, but answered the phone and eventually remembered a photo in his family album showing a flying boat in the air with the characteristic Levanter cloud over the Rock. When Beatty was informed of this he ordered, 'Tell him to come to the Admiralty at once, and bring his book with him.' 'He is playing tennis, sir, and is in flannels.' he was informed. 'I don't care if he is in his bath. Tell him to come as he is.' The photo was produced for the Committee and the objections were quashed.[23]

Whilst fighter defence was now authorised progress was slow. There were a number of problems: money was one, and in addition the only place where an airfield could be constructed was the racecourse at North Front. This was the only open flat area in Gibraltar and was not only needed by the town for recreation and the garrison for training but there were difficulties connected with its possession. Unlike the rest of the Rock it had not been ceded under the Treaty of Utrecht, but had taken over later and this was justified as common use of neutral ground. Possession was later claimed under prescription rights (ie rights of ownership through occupation) the validity of which depended on the interpretation of tricky points of Spanish Law. When the Foreign Office were consulted, they tried to avoid controversy with Spain and advised against the building of an airfield. In 1935 legal opinion was taken about the sovereignty of the neutral ground and the result was so discouraging that it has never been made public. Normally government files are opened after 30 years, but in this case it was decided that the contents of the file were so sensitive that they should remain closed for 50 years. The files at the Public Records Office were therefore due to be opened in 1986 but they continue closed without any explanation being given.[24]

Nevertheless, the request of the Committee of Imperial Defence was studied in 1932 and the inevitable conclusion was arrived at, that the only practicable place for an airfield in Gibraltar was at North Front. In May 1933 the Admiralty wrote to the commanders of the Home and Mediterranean Fleets and the SNO Gibraltar, informing them that limited work would be carried out for a landing ground for the FAA which was restricted for use in emergencies only. The work was to consist of placing the rail posts and gates of the racecourse in sockets which did not protrude above ground level, so that they could be removed leaving a clear landing strip; and provisions were also made for the rifle butts to be bridged over.[25]

In March 1935 the Governor wrote to the SNO Gibraltar, that as the isthmus was also required for other things, the emergency landing field could only be used by prior arrangement with Fortress Headquarters. This was not entirely satisfactory, but as the aircraft carriers were only in the area for a few weeks every year, it had to do. Two RAF officers from HMS *Furious* studied the proposed arrangements and were of the opinion that aircraft could land without the rails being removed, provided the butts were boarded over and some unnecessary posts were removed. The required preparations were made and the emergency landing ground was declared usable on 10 March 1936. It was operated under naval control in consultation with FHQ. Pilots were, however, warned that they might find men working, or in the firing trenches, and that cattle might be grazing or people exercising horses.[26] From September 1935 to August 1936, Short Rangoon and Singapore flyingboats of RAF Squadron No 210 were temporarily based at Gun Wharf.[27]

During the Munich crisis in September 1938, concern was felt about the activities of the *Deutschland*, which was in a Spanish port. HMS *Hood* was sent from Gibraltar and sighted her fuelling off Cape Finisterre and shadowed her until the crisis was over.[28] With the Spanish Civil War virtually over, the combined exercise of the Home and Mediterranean Fleets was resumed in March 1939. When the Fleet entered the harbour, many of the new ships of the accelerating rearmament programme were present. Among them were the large Tribal destroyers and the Town class cruisers. But the first of the new aircraft carriers, HMS *Ark Royal*, which had visited Gibraltar a few weeks before on its shake-down cruise, was still working-up and had not yet joined the Home Fleet.

Notes and References

(1) *Achernar, Algenib, Algol, Altair, Arcturus, Crucis, Corvi, Cygni* sold on 17 May 1919, but the *Antares* was retained until 1921. (Colledge 2)

(2) Colledge 1:544; Somner 19-20, 46, 49.

(3) *Brassey's 1920-21* 6.

(4) Patterson 218.

(5) Gonzalez 42; Somner 27.

(6) *Brassey's 1927* 26; *Brassey's 1923* 390.

(7) Winton *Glorious* 29-31.

(8) Harker 27.

(9) *Gibraltar Directory 1939* 351-352.

(10) Salas 1:161.

(11) *Gibraltar Chronicle* passim.

(12) Gretton 58-59.

(13) Gretton 204.

(14) Gretton 60-61; Cervera 60-61; Alcofar 265-270.

(15) Gretton 111.

(16) Salas 1:516.

(17) Cervera 67-68.

(18) McKay; *Gibraltar Directory 1939* 361; Gretton 255-257; Winton *Glorious* 68.

(19) Alcofar 255-256, 258-262; Winton 69; Giorgerini 352-354; Roskill 1:307.

(20) Alcofar 179-186; *Gibraltar Directory 1939* 360-362.

(21) Gretton 427-428; Cervera 89-90.

(22) Gretton 431-437; Cervera 91; Palao 77-80; Benady *Police* 28.

(23) Chalmers 379-380.

(24) FO.371/19173.

(25) Elliott Ms 10, 11, 15.

(26) Elliott Ms 16.

(27) Fairbairn 71.

(28) Edwards 252-253.

CHAPTER XI

WAR

The outbreak of war in 1939 gave Rear-Admiral H A Woodehouse at Gibraltar, responsibility, in his role as Flag Officer North Atlantic Command, for an area of ocean which stretched out over a thousand miles into the Atlantic, from the north of Portugal to Dakar in the south, and included the islands Of Azores, Madeira and Canaries. To patrol this area he had under his command the old light cruisers HMS *Capetown* and *Colombo*, the 13th Destroyer Flotilla commanded by Captain F de Winton in the leader HMS *Keppel*, with the 25th Division of HMS *Velox*, *Vidette*, *Vortigern* and *Watchman* and the 26th Division consisting of HMS *Active*, *Douglas*, *Wishart* and *Wrestler*. He also had two submarines, two minesweepers and some tugs and harbour craft. Some of the destroyers had been in reserve at Gibraltar before they were mobilised; *Douglas* was a leader serving as a private ship and *Wrestler* was in dock having asdic fitted. In addition the old destroyer *Wryneck* went into dock that month to be converted into an escort vessel, her torpedo tubes were to be removed and AA armament increased.[1]

The land defences had been little modified since the previous war, some of the 9.2-inch guns had been updated to Mark X on Mark V mountings, but their number had been reduced to eight, and the 6-inch guns to ten; and even these were not all fully manned. The miscellaneous QFs had been replaced by six twin 6-pounder mountings, two on each of the Admiralty moles. In later years naval 4-inch guns and mobile heavy howitzers, 25-pounders and anti-tank guns were added. In 1939 the AA armament consisted of eight mobile 3-inch. It was later increased to 16, and supplemented as the war progressed by 24 3.7-inch, and 36 40-mm Bofors, as well as 24 20-mm Oerlikons (borrowed from the Navy) and 60 rocket projectors. There were three infantry battalions in the garrison, later increased to six.[2]

At the beginning of the war, Gibraltar was not too well defended, as she had no fighter squadron, and her only aircraft were three Swordfish float planes of No 3 AA Cooperation Unit of the RAF which were housed on Gun Wharf and were used to tow targets for the AA gunners. Much depended on the attitude of Italy and Spain. Italy had signed a 'pact of steel' with Germany the previous May and formed an alliance normally referred to as the 'Axis'. Would she now join in the fighting? Within a few weeks it became clear that she would not, just yet. Franco, who had recently been victorious in the Civil War thanks to the generous help given to him by his German and Italian allies, had to be considered a potential supporter of the Axis, but he was isolated geographically for the time being. Therefore, although Gibraltar was secure for the present, long-term prospects might not be so bright. Gibraltar's defences were too weak to withstand a determined attack from the Spanish mainland.[3]

Like all other stations, the North Atlantic Command was responsible for control of the adjacent waters. It had to protect Allied shipping from submarines and surface raiders which had to be sought out and destroyed. In addition, the economic blockade had to be enforced by intercepting enemy merchant ships and preventing the carriage of contraband, to and from enemy destinations, in neutral bottoms. The Navy was only responsible for the interception of ships at sea and sending them to Gibraltar and further action regarding the ships and their cargoes depended on the Prize Court and the MEW. Arrangements were also made to censor the correspondence between Europe and the Americas carried on board the Italian mail steamers which were all forced to call at Gibraltar, and a special censorship section 200 strong operated at the King George V Hospital with living quarters in Loreto Convent. Even diplomatic mail was secretly opened by a special section, but mails to and from Germany had to be diverted to Britain for examination because of lack of facilities at Gibraltar.[4]

In 1938, the military historian, Captain Liddell Hart had advised the Secretary of State for War, that in wartime, 'a friendly Spain is desirable, a neutral Spain is vital.' Much care was therefore taken to bring this about. The Spanish economy was still suffering from the devastating effects of three years of civil war and the country was close to starvation.

The MEW used Britain's control of the sea routes to counter Franco's naturally pro-Axis proclivities. With the cooperation of the USA, a system of 'controlled assistance' was established, help was given for Spain to obtain the necessary food and oil from overseas, but only enough for current consumption was allowed through. No stocks were allowed to be built up. So at all times right through the war, Spain was just a step away from starvation and complete economic collapse which she could only avert by not throwing in her hand with the Axis, for otherwise the RN would have severed her vital supply line which brought in the essential food and fuel from the New World on an instalment basis. This policy worked remarkably well and was to ensure Gibraltar's continued survival and use as an important naval base right through the war.[5]

As the war did not spread immediately into the Mediterranean, RAF Squadron 202, which flew Saro London flying boats from Kalafrana in Malta, was ordered to Gibraltar on 9 September 1939. It arrived within 24 hours and was operational the next day. The ground staff arrived in HMS *Shropshire* on the 13th. Thus 200 Group RAF was formed, it depended on the AOC Middle East, but was under Navy control at Gibraltar, and the operation room was in the Admiralty Tower. The administrative offices were temporarily set up in the Bristol Hotel. The flying boats were moored in the harbour. There was no slipway but No 20 shed in the North Mole was converted into a maintenance workshop. The flying boats were assisted in their patrols by the floatplanes of No.3 AACU. At first, the Londons returned to Malta for their 60-hour inspection. But even after Gun Wharf was organised, and the aircraft were lifted out of the water for servicing, by a crane, they still had to be flown back to the UK for major inspections.[6]

Within a few weeks all enemy merchant shipping had disappeared from the area so *Capetown* and *Colombo* went to other stations, but when information was received that a German merchant ship was leaving Cadiz harbour, she was shadowed by a London aircraft until she was intercepted by HMS *Wishart*; the *Glucksburg* then ran herself aground.[7]

As in the previous war, Gibraltar became an important assembly port for convoys. The first convoy, an important one of eight ships, left Gibraltar for Capetown the day before war was declared, and HG1, the first of the cycle of regular convoys to Britain, left on 26 September. By that time, outwards convoys from the United Kingdom, had already been started. At this stage of the war they were organised into OA convoys starting at Southend, and OB convoys starting in Liverpool. Southbound ships would rendezvous off the Scillies and there be formed into OG convoys. They would then proceed under an ocean escort until they were met by the local escorts to the west of the Strait and the ships proceeding further south would continue on their own.

In the first few months of the war, the convoys generally reached their destination without loss, but ships with a speed of over 15 knots sailed independently, as did those merchant vessels that could not make 9 knots. A group of the latter, returning from Gibraltar, was attacked by submarines off Cape Finisterre on 17 October and three ships were sunk. Starting in July 1940 the OG convoys were formed in the Clyde or Mersey under local anti-submarine escorts, but for the bulk of their journey they were protected by only one or two sloops, until they were met by destroyers from Gibraltar.[8]

In November 1939, Woodehouse was replaced as Flag Officer North Atlantic Command by Vice Admiral Sir Dudley North, the most senior officer to fly his flag ashore at Gibraltar since St Vincent, 150 years before. This underlined the increased importance of Gibraltar as a naval base. North moved into The Mount and held open house for the officers of the RN, and occasional French warships that came under his command. Living in these opulent surroundings, North and his successors enjoyed an unusual luxury in wartime Gibraltar - fresh milk. There was none to be obtained except from the cow that was kept in The Mount's garden to supply the Admiral's table, the Governor and a few other exalted officials.[9]

The local patrol force was strengthened and by May 1940 it consisted of four trawlers fitted with asdic, four minesweeping trawlers, five ABS and five tugs. The anti-submarine trawler HMS *Kingston Cornelian* had been sunk in a collision to the east of Gibraltar the previous 5 January. A minesweeping force was maintained at Gibraltar but there are no records of mines being laid. The centre of the Bay was too deep for ground mines, and the busy western shore was too overlooked by the defences for such operations to be conducted successfully. Instead the Italians tried some of their secret weapons with a certain amount of success, but an account of this merits a chapter on its own (see chapter 12).[10]

On 10 May, Germany launched the attack on the Low Countries and France, and the following day the National Government was formed with Churchill as Prime Minister. On the 16th the War Cabinet decided to evacuate all non-combatants at Gibraltar who were not involved in essential services. The evacuation of the Gibraltarians to French Morocco started on the 21st, and on the same day the first party of English women and children were homeward-bound on SS *Dorsetshire*. Three days later, Operation Dynamo - the evacuation from Dunkerque - commenced. All those evacuated to Britain had left within four days, but the evacuation of 13,000 Gibraltarians took longer and the last ship did not leave until 24 June, which was the day that France sued for peace.[11] The captain of the Cormorant wrote,

Main Street which had always seemed rather lively was almost dead. All the Indian shopkeepers had gone and their colourful shops were closed down. So were the dance halls. The Naafi was the one bright spot. The Rock had become a ghostly gloomy place.

Italy entered the war on 10 June and that evening, the six Italian merchant ships in the Bay tried to scuttle themselves. The *Pagao* succeeded and the tanker *Olterra* beached herself in Spanish waters; we shall hear more of her later. The Royal Navy managed to salvage two of the ships. Two days later shots were fired at the Italian submarine *Capellini* discovered cruising on the surface in the dark, but before she could be seriously damaged she had taken temporary refuge in the port of Ceuta.[12] The Mediterranean Fleet had moved to its wartime base at Alexandria and the control of the western basin now seemed to be in the hands of the powerful Italian Navy. The Admiralty considered withdrawing the whole of the Fleet to the west, but as this would have entailed the loss of Malta and probably, Egypt also, a powerful detached squadron was ordered to Gibraltar on 23 June to plug the hole. In the first instance Force H consisted of the battle-cruiser HMS *Hood*, the battleships HMS *Valiant* and *Resolution*, the aircraft carrier HMS *Ark*

Royal, and the destroyers of the 8th Flotilla HMS *Faulknor, Fearless, Foresight, Forester, Foxhound, Escapade* and *Escort.* Force H was able to call on the services of the 13th Flotilla and other detached ships in the area when available, including the cruiser HMS *Enterprise.* Vice Admiral Sir James Somerville arrived in Gibraltar on the 30th in the cruiser HMS *Arethusa* to assume command.[13]

Under the terms of the Armistice published on 25 June, French warships were to assemble where they could be demilitarised and disarmed under German or Italian control, and Churchill was afraid that once they were disarmed the Nazis would take them over and use them against Britain. Churchill, who in naval matters often thought in simplistic terms, feared, that in a few months, the four new and three reconstructed French battleships would join the six new and four reconstructed battleships of the Axis, against which the Royal Navy would only be able to deploy five new and six reconstructed ships. The Royal Navy would be outclassed, the control of the sea routes might be lost and Britain's defeat at sea would follow.

North was sent in HMS *Douglas* on the 23rd to meet the French Vice Admiral Gensoul at Mers-el-Kebir and he found the atmosphere one of stupefied misery, but having entered into an Armistice the French felt they had to abide by its terms, though Gensoul was distressed at the possibility of any cleavage between France and Britain. Before North left, Gensoul gave his word of honour that though he could not turn them over to the RN, 'the Germans would not get his ships, that he had made arrangements to blow their bottoms out if the Germans tried to take them.' Vice-Admiral Wells, who had flown from HMS *Ark Royal* to Casablanca, returned with a similar message. The admirals, including Somerville, were convinced that the French Navy would honour its promises but Churchill insisted that action had to be taken to ensure Britain's survival. With the benefit of hindsight we can now say that the admirals were right, but Churchill was not the only one to get it wrong. In November 1940 Hitler was convinced that Vichy was on the point of entering the war on the side of the Germans.[14]

On 2 July, Force H left Gibraltar for Mers-el-Kebir. Somerville's instructions were to offer Gensoul a number of options:

1	To sail to British harbours to continue the fight;
2	To sail to British ports with reduced crews;
3	To sail to a French port in the West Indies or to the USA;
4	Or sink their ships.

If none of these alternatives was accepted he was to put Operation Anvil into effect and sink the French battleships at their moorings. As might have been expected when Captain Power of the *Ark Royal*, who spoke perfect French and acted as intermediary, presented this ultimatum, Gensoul's reaction was negative. At 5.30 on the evening of the 3rd, after the deadline, which had been extended several times, finally expired, Somerville, with a heavy heart, ordered his battleships to open fire. In a few minutes the *Bretagne* had blown up and the *Dunkerque* and *Provence* were seriously damaged. After 36 salvoes Sommerville halted his fire to enable the French sailors to leave the sinking ships, but the *Strasboug* managed to get out of harbour with five destroyers and make its way safely to Toulon, although she was attacked by torpedo bombers from the *Ark Royal*. The French dead numbered almost 1,500 and there were no British casualties.[15]

Force H returned to Gibraltar sad at this massacre of their former comrades and friends, but this unfortunate operation had two important results. The threat of British aggression against French territory meant that the French warships were not demilitarised but retained their crews, who, when the Germans tried to seize them at Toulon in 1942, very honourably destroyed them. It also undoubtedly helped to convince Franco that Britain was not yet finished.

The bombardment of Mers-el-Kebir was to start a period of confrontation between Britain and the Vichy French forces, and led to the first serious air raid on Gibraltar on the night of 18 July when French aeroplanes dropped bombs which killed three civilians, including a nun at Loreto Convent, and injured eleven. But this was not the only direct consequence. For some days before, a convoy of fifteen British merchant ships with their holds fitted with accommodation for troops, had arrived in Casablanca. On board were 15,000 French servicemen rescued from Dunkirk, who wished to return home. The convoy was received with hostility and the British were accused of *Assassinat criminel des matelots français à Oran*. When the soldiers were disembarked the

French authorities insisted that the ships take on board the Gibraltarian evacuees.

Conditions in the ships were terrible. The holds had been left in a nauseating state, the stores were exhausted, there were no sanitary facilities for so many people, and the field kitchens used on the way out had been taken ashore. Nevertheless each of the vessels embarked over 800 of the evacuees and carried them on deck to Gibraltar. There, the authorities did not wish them to land, as the Germans were at the Pyrenees and might appear at the frontier at any moment. But Creighton, who was responsible for the convoy, insisted that the ships had to be properly prepared before they could accommodate old people, children and invalids for the three weeks that the journey to England took in wartime, and the evacuees were landed while the dockyard carried out the necessary alterations. Ships started sailing with evacuees on the 26th of July and the main convoy left on the 30th.[16]

All these events were watched closely by German officers. When France had sued for an armistice, Franco became convinced that the war would soon be at an end and he was enthusiastic about joining his German friends in their victory. German officers were allowed to reconnoitre the Rock and, by 25 July, a number were conducting a careful survey from the vantage points of the Spanish commander's office in La Linea and the lighthouse in Punta Carnero. Preliminary plans were drawn up for an assault which included 167 guns, to give them a three-to-one superiority over the defenders. But the German forces were busy consolidating their position in France and the projected assault on mainland Britain had priority, so no action was taken immediately. Britain's stubborn resistance made Franco want to ensure that the war was really nearing its end before he intervened, as the parlous state of Spain's economy would not allow for more than a few weeks' hostilities.[17]

By the time Franco met Hitler at Hendaye on 23 October, the Battle of Britain had been won and the duration of the war had obviously been considerably prolonged. Franco tried every artifice to sidle out of any firm commitment. After two hours of evasive private discussion between the two men, Hitler is reported to have said that he would rather have a tooth extracted than have another meeting with Franco. The point was, as Franco's foreign minister, Serrano Suñer, told Ribbentrop, Spain could not afford to do anything to endanger the delivery of 250,000 tons of foodstuffs coming from Canada. So by the time that the plans for Operation Felix, the capture of Gibraltar, were drawn up a few weeks later, there was no chance of the cooperation by Spain which was essential to its success. Though undoubtedly Franco would have still come in on the side of the Germans at any time that he felt that the war was really coming to an end, in order to secure a share of the spoils.[18]

Force H engaged in a few incursions into the Mediterranean and while returning from the first one on 11 July, the destroyer HMS *Escort* was hit by a torpedo fired by the Italian submarine *Marconi* and holed abreast the forward boiler-room, when she was north of Ceuta. She sank under tow before she could be brought into harbour. On the 31st of the month Force H left on Operation Hurry, to escort the carrier *Argus* to a position off Tunisia where she flew off 12 RAF Hurricanes for Malta. They were the first of these fighters sent to that beleaguered island and they were guided on their way by two Skuas from *Ark Royal*. The aircraft carrier also flew off a force of Swordfish during the night to bomb the harbour and airfield at Cagliari in Sardinia. Spares and ground equipment for the Hurricanes were taken to Malta by the submarines HMS *Pandora* and *Perseus*.

Somerville afterwards returned to Scapa Flow with the *Hood* and *Valiant*, and hoisted his flag on HMS *Renown*, a smaller ship, but she had been recently modernised and had better protection against bombs and an excellent AA battery. When the *Renown* arrived at Gibraltar on 20 August her guns were in action that very night when there was a raid by Italian aircraft. One plane approached from the north to bomb the harbour and after dropping its bombs continued south. When off Europa Point it was caught by the searchlights and was hit by a salvo from the battle-cruiser's starboard 4.5-inch battery. The tail fell off and then the port wing and it spiralled down into the sea. On 27 August the cruiser HMS *Sheffield* arrived and she proved a great asset to Force H as she was one of the first of the Royal Navy's ships to be fitted with early warning radar.[19]

On the 30th Force H left harbour, escorting a force of warships which were to join Admiral Cunningham's Fleet in the eastern Mediterranean:

the new aircraft carrier HMS *Illustrious,* the battleship HMS *Valiant,* the AA cruisers HMS *Cardiff* and *Curlew,* and destroyers. Operation Hats was combined with the passing of a convoy into Malta by the Mediterranean Fleet. Once again the *Ark's* Stringbags (as the Swordfish was affectionately called by its crews) took part in another night attack on Sardinia. A few days after they had returned to Gibraltar they left on 7 September with the battleships *Resolution* and *Barham* to take part in Operation Menace against Dakar. As the *Sheffield* had been detached on convoy protection duties, Force H now consisted only of *Renown* and destroyers.[20]

A number of Italian submarines passed through the Strait to operate against shipping in the Atlantic and a base was established in Bordeaux. Anti-submarine patrols in the Strait were therefore strengthened and in the early hours of the morning of 11 September the destroyers *Hotspur,* *Griffin* and *Encounter* on a routine anti-submarine sweep 120 miles into the Mediterranean encountered French Force Y of three cruisers of the *Georges Leygues* class and three *Le Fantasque* class destroyers. They started shadowing the French ships and alerted Gibraltar by wireless, this signal was immediately relayed to the Admiralty. The information had already reached London from other sources and North ordered the destroyers to resume their normal patrol. At 7.30 that morning, Force Y sighted two other destroyers patrolling in the Strait and at 8 they exchanged signals with the Lloyd's Signal Station. That afternoon they berthed in Casablanca. North and Sommerville, confident that Force Y was not heading for a port occupied by the Germans, had seen no reason to interfere.[21]

The *Renown,* which had been at an hour's notice to steam out of harbour, was stood down, but at 13.07 orders were received from the Admiralty to proceed to sea and obtain contact with the French. At 16.30 the *Renown* left harbour with the destroyers HMS *Griffin, Vidette* and *Velox,* but it was too late as Force Y was already entering Casablanca harbour by that time. That afternoon, one of the Londons was shot down by French fighters whilst on reconnaissance. Sommerville was ordered to patrol off Casablanca to stop Force Y from proceeding to Dakar. The admiral established a patrol off the coast with the *Renown* and six destroyers, but Force Y, with the assistance of air reconnaissance, managed to evade him, and reached Dakar unhindered; though HMS *Vidette* did have a short encounter with the much larger *Le Malin.* On the 14th, *Renown* was back in Gibraltar.

Operation Menace which started on the 23rd, was a failure and Churchill and the Admiralty thought that this was due to the additional reinforcements brought by Force Y, so North and Sommerville were blamed and on 15 October North was relieved from his command. This was perhaps just the excuse needed by the First Sea Lord to get rid of North whom he thought lacking in aggression and enterprise. Somerville also almost lost his command the following February, but the instructions to strike his flag were countermanded after they had been sent out.[22]

On 1 January 1941 North was replaced by Vice-Admiral Sir Frederick Edward-Collins. Somerville who had to work closely with him, resented North's replacement and never got on with his successor. He did not find him congenial company as he thought he lacked a sense of humour and had become stout and lethargic. Somerville was known for his fondness for physical exercise and his long walks up the Rock and he used to refer to his chair-bound colleague as 'Fat Fred'. Captain Roskill, the naval historian, considered Collins one of Churchill's bad appointments.[23]

The French retaliated for the attack on Dakar on the 24th September. At 12.30 pm a number of Vichy Glenn Martin bombers appeared over the Rock, taking advantage of the cover afforded by a high Levanter cloud, and bombed for over two hours. *Renown* had steam up and was a tremendous sight making her way out of harbour with all her 44 AA guns plus machine-guns firing. More than 150 bombs were dropped, twelve fell in the dockyard and twenty in the harbour, 55 fell ashore and 75 appear to have been deliberately jettisoned in the Bay. That afternoon four destroyers emerged from Casablanca and attacked HMS *Wishart* and *Wrestler* which were on patrol, but were driven away.[24]

The following day there was another air raid in the afternoon which started at 2pm and went on for three hours. The only warship of any size in the harbour was the destroyer HMS *Firedrake,* moored by the Tower and she shot down one of the bombers. This was a heavier raid than the day before but fortunately two-thirds of the bombs were jettisoned over the water. This appears to have been done deliberately, as the large number of deserters who arrived in Gibraltar showed how widespread pro-Ally feelings were among French officers. Only two or three bombs fell in the upper part of town and a few more near the Rock Hotel. The anti-submarine trawler HMS *Stella Sirius* which was moored at the South Mole was sunk, but Vichy admitted to the loss of a dozen bombers.[25]

Off Dakar, HMS *Resolution* was torpedoed by a French submarine during Operation Menace and after being patched up in Sierra Leone she had to go to Gibraltar, where she entered No 1 Dock after it had been vacated by her sister ship HMS Royal *Sovereign*.[26]

There were still no fighter aircraft at the airfield which continued to be run by the Navy until the end of 1941. In 1939 the Spanish Government had been assured that only an emergency landing ground was planned for the occasional training of the disembarked aircraft of the FAA, and this was adhered to. RAF Martin Marylands of 431 Reconnaissance Flight, on their way to Malta, were forbidden to stage at Gibraltar in September 1940 and had to make their way over occupied France. Nevertheless *Ark Royal* landed some of her aircraft whenever she was in harbour. The old grandstand was in the way of flying operations and an officer of one of the *Ark's* squadrons arranged to blow it up with the help of an RE major, who took time off from tunnelling for the purpose. The airfield received a number of French planes in 1940, which were flown over from North Africa by officers who wished to join the Free French, but it was not until March 1941 that Churchill gave the go-ahead for the landing ground to be used for staging Wellington bombers and Bombay transport planes for North Africa and Malta, as well as other long-range aircraft.[27] The Governor, Lord Gort, wrote to King George VI on 11 June,

> Although we are not supposed to use the aerodrome for operational purposes, the friendliness of the Spanish authorities has, so far, prevented any representations being made about the increasing bomber and fighter aircraft landings which take place. For instance 26 aircraft are due to arrive here today.[28]

In later years, the pro-Axis Suñer was to state that Franco, by his acquiesence to the use of the Neutral Ground as an airfield, had, in effect, made a present of it to Britain.

Squadron 202 had been assisted by the Sunderlands of 204 for a time and in May 1941 their London flying boats began to be replaced by Catalinas. Arrangements were made for the RAF to take over land newly reclaimed in front of the Naval Depot Cinema (the World War I hangar) to build a new hangar and slipway. The hangar at New Camp, a conspicuous silver building on the edge of the slipway, was completed in September 1941. Work to extend the airfield's runway into the sea started in December 1941, and with the appointment of Air Commodore Simpson as the first AOC, Gibraltar, on the 21st, No.200 Group was disbanded and the Gibraltar air station became part of Coastal Command. During 1941 a detachment of 233 squadron, which flew Hudsons on anti-submarine patrols, operated from North Front, though the Squadron was not officially posted at Gibraltar until June 1942.[29]

The constant routine patrolling of the Strait produced dividends. On 18 October 1940, the destroyers HMS *Firedrake*, *Vidette*, and *Wrestler* were patrolling off Alboran when they saw planes from Gibraltar dropping bombs on what appeared to be a calm and empty sea. The destroyers raced up, established asdic contact and attacked with their depth-charges. After making a number of attacks the Italian submarine *Durbo* came to the surface, the destroyers started firing but she had only come up to surrender. The destroyers lowered their boats to pick up the crew of the submarine which sank a few minutes later, so they returned triumphant to the Rock with their prisoners. On the 20th, the patrolling destroyers HMS *Hotspur, Gallant* and *Griffin* aided by a flying boat of 202 Squadron, sank her sister ship *Lafole* in the same area.[30]

Notes and References

(1) Roskill 1: 48, 584; Smith *Action Imminent* 114-115; *Gibraltar Directory 1939* 46.
(2) Hire Ms 27-75, 90-95; Ramsey 24; *Gibraltar Directory 1939* 50-51.
(3) Elliott Ms 23.
(4) Montgomery Hyde 33-35.
(5) Smyth 3; Medlicott 1:56, 529-548; Eccles passim.
(6) Elliott Ms 30-31.
(7) Elliott Ms 32.

(8)   Roskill 1:92-93; 344.
(9)   Gordon 229.
(10)   Smith ibid 117; Colledge 2:198.
(11)   Finlayson 232.
(12)   Finlayson 19; Plimmer 25; Cocchia 11-12.
(13)   Macintyre 54, 59; Smith ibid 121.
(14)   Macintyre 57; Plimmer 33-34, 39; Burdick 39.
(15)   Macintyre 59.
(16)   Creighton 99-111; Finlayson 34; Benady *Police* 30.
(17)   Burdick 26-27.
(18)   Burdick 50-52, 70.
(19)   Jameson 177-178, 185-188; *British Vessels Lost* 4; Smith *Hit First* 130; Bassett *Sheffield*
        52.
(20)   Jameson 191-192; Bassett *Sheffield* 55-58.
(21)   Roskill 1:347; Smith *Action Imminent* 169-187; Macintyre 80.
(22)   Macintyre 106-107; Smith ibid 202-205.
(23)   Macintyre 152. Roskill gives his judgement in his book *Churchill and the Admirals*
        page 280.
(24)   Smith *Hit First* 142-143.
(25)   Divine 72-77; *British ships Lost* 7.
(26)   Smith *Royal Sovereign* 83, 91.
(27)   Elliott MB 24-25, 27; Whiteley 21; Woods 25.
(28)   Colville 243.
(29)   Elliott MB 32-33; Fairbairn 71.
(30)   Roskill 1:601; Divine 79-80.

CHAPTER XII

PIGS AND CRABB

Although the heavy raids by Vichy French aircraft from Morocco were followed by a series of lighter and less effective raids by Italian aircraft right through until 1943, the amount of damage they caused was not great. It was left to a new secret weapon developed by the Italian Navy to pose a real threat.

The Italians had been fascinated by the possibilities of small explosive boats ever since one of these machines had destroyed the Austrian Dreadnought *Viribus Unitis* in the closing days of World War I. In 1935 during the Abyssinian crisis, two young engineer officers of the submarine flotilla at La Spezia, Elios Toschi and Teseo Tesei, had designed a small piloted torpedo which proved practical and promising. Several were built.

It is recorded that Tesei had to abandon one which went out of control during a practice immersion and on returning to the surface complained that 'That maiale (pig) got away again!' and *Maiale* was to become the weapon's semi-official designation. Interest in the invention disappeared with the end of the Abyssinian War and the machines constructed were secretly locked away, until the approach of a European war in 1938 led to further experimenting and the building of improved piloted torpedoes.[1]

The *Maiale*, or SLC, to give its official designation, was the size of an ordinary torpedo, 22 feet long with a diameter of 21 inches. Two men would sit astride it with their feet in stirrups, the pilot sat at the controls behind a windscreen fitted with a wiper. The machine was driven by counter-rotating propellers powered by an electric motor working from batteries and it could achieve a maximum speed of 2.5 miles an hour and had a range of 10 miles. The detachable warhead was 71 inches long and carried 300 kilos of explosives, the body contained motor, batteries and trimming tanks. The controls were simple and course was changed by moving a lever left or right, and another lever guided ascent and descent. The idea was for the crew to take the torpedo below a target anchored in shallow water, and there fix the warhead by clamps to the bilge keel on either side, while the craft rested on the bottom underneath. The explosive warhead would then be detached and the attackers would make their getaway, detonation being effected by a time fuse.[2]

The crew wore a wet suit designed by Commander Belloni which was therefore known as the 'Belloni overall' and which encased the wearer completely apart from the head and hands. Breathing under water was through a mouthpiece connected by a corrugated rubber tube to a breathing bag, which reduced the pressure of oxygen supplied from bottles which stored it at high-pressure. Air exhaled went through the same tube into the breathing bag and then into a canister of sodium crystals which eliminated the carbon dioxide produced in respiration. Spare breathing gear was carried in an external locker behind the crew's seats.[3]

At the end of August 1940, the submarine *Iride*, whilst carrying some of the guided torpedoes to attack Alexandria, was caught by a torpedo carrying Swordfish on the surface, in the shallow waters of the Gulf of Bomba, where the submarine could not submerge, and destroyed. Two other submarines, *Gondar* and *Scire* were fitted with three large cylinders on deck (two forward and one aft), in place of their guns, to carry three SLCs which it was intended they should launch within range of their targets. The *Gondar* was sunk off Alexandria in September, after being hunted for some hours by HMAS *Stuart* and aircraft of 203 Squadron, but her sister ship was to be more successful.[4]

On 21 October 1940, *Scire* left La Spezia under the command of Prince Junio Valerio Borghese to attack Force H at Gibraltar. It was not intended that the submarine should wait for the SLCs after they had finished their attack, but their crews were to make their way to Spain and from there be repatriated to Italy. On the 29th she reached the Strait and submerged off the entrance to the Bay. She came to the surface in the evening and tried to enter but approaching boats caused her to submerge again, so she slowly made her way under water to the north of the Bay and came to rest on the bottom at a depth of 15 metres, within 400 yards of the mouth of the Guadarranque. The divers emerged at 2am to open the canisters and launch the torpedoes. There were mechanical defects and it took a long time to prepare the SLCs for launching, but eventually they were ready and 40 minutes later the submarine made her way out of the Bay still submerged, leaving the attackers to their own devices.[5]

The trawler HMS *Clyne Castle*, whilst engaged in an early morning sweep in the Bay, found a black object caught in her sweeping gear. At first it was thought to be a mine, but it was eventually discovered to be an Italian frogman and the captain of the trawler came to the conclusion that the sweeping gear had knocked him off his 'bicycle'. This was not correct, though the 92nd Trawler Group which never succeeded in sweeping any mines in Gibraltar had at least swept up one Italian attacker. The sequence of events that had led to this discovery was as follows.[6]

One of the attacking craft had an encounter with a patrol boat which picked it out in its searchlights and it had to dive suddenly. It went down so deep that its tanks were stoved in and it had to be abandoned. The crew made their way safely to Spain. Another had made its way safely through the shipping outside the harbour and had reached the north entrance when the breathing gear malfunctioned. The spare masks were found to be unserviceable, so the warhead was detached and sunk and the craft was beached on the Playa del Espigon after it had been sighted by *Clyne Castle*. The two men took off their suits in the water and when they landed, contacted an agent waiting for them who whisked thcm away to safety. Their torpedo was later found by the Spanish authorities and sent to the naval base at San Fernando for examination.

The third craft was more successful. It negotiated its way to the north entrance, proceeding very slowly, because water had damaged the batteries. It took 3 hours and 40 minutes to reach the defensive 'gate' at the entrance to the harbour. It consisted of large buoys, moored 15 feet apart and connected by heavy iron bars set with sharp spikes every few feet.

Lieutenant Birrindelli guided his craft on the surface through these obstructions, unseen by the sentries on the mole, whose voices he could hear clearly in the dark. At this stage his crewman, Paccagnini's, breathing gear failed and he had to leave the craft. He was the man caught up in the sweeping gear of the trawler whilst trying to swim to a Spanish beach. In the meantime Birrindelli proceeded alone to attack the *Barham*. But his craft hit bottom and refused to budge although the engine was still running. He was now 70 metres from his target, and despite desperate attempts to pull the SLC manually towards the battleship's keel, he was unsuccessful and he gave up half an hour later. He therefore set the time switch for the explosives and started swimming to Spain, leaving his wet suit hanging on the harbour 'gate'. However, when he was off the Commercial Mole he had an attack of cramp and had to go ashore. It was now daylight and he tried to merge with the seamen and labourers on the Mole. He was negotiating to buy himself a passage to Spain on a small boat when he was spotted and arrested by two policemen. The explosive charge detonated while he was being interrogated but caused no damage.[7]

The attack had been bedevilled by technical faults and had been unsuccessful, but the authorities at Gibraltar were now alerted to the dangers of attack by human torpedoes. As there were neither the men nor craft in the harbour to mount regular patrols all visiting warships had to make a contribution. HMS *Sheffield*, for example, fitted out her No 1 motor boat with three depth-charges and two Lewis guns to patrol when she was in harbour. But later, anti-personnel charges were fashioned from old round cigarette tins filled with one and a quarter pounds of TNT and the lid taped down with a fuse protruding.[8]

By June 1941 Fairmile MLs had arrived at Gibraltar to take over the patrol work. Later on they were supplemented by 72-foot HDMLs, which in war conditions could not make the journey from Britain under their own power but were brought out on the decks of merchant ships. However, in March 1943, *HDML 1229* did arrive under her own power in the teeth of a strong gale. She was one of three launches which formed the deck cargo of SS *City of Christchurch*, which was sunk by a Condor off the coast of Portugal. As the ship sank the HDMLs were cut loose. One sank, another broke her back, but *1229* stayed afloat. She was manned by sailors from the escorting Canadian corvette *Morden* and made a successful two-day passage at 9 knots.[9]

In spite of the initial setbacks, the Italian Navy decided to proceed with its plans to build and train special units to attack the Royal Navy in its harbours. On 15 March 1941, these were formed into the X MAS (10th Light Flotilla), which was divided into two divisions, one for operations on the surface and the other for operations underwater was placed under the command of Borghese.

In May *Scire* attempted another attack on Gibraltar. This time the crews of the SLCs were not transported on board the submarine. In order that they should be more rested and effective, they travelled to Cadiz as civilian tourists and were transferred to the submarine there. After passing through the Strait, the *Scire* entered Cadiz Bay on 23 May and spent the day lying on the bottom. That evening Borghese carefully made his way alongside the Italian tanker *Fulgor* which had been anchored in the harbour since the entry of Italy into the war and acted as a supply ship for Italian submarines operating in the Atlantic. After the crews for the human torpedoes and fresh supplies had been taken on board, she set off again before morning, without being seen. The submarine entered Gibraltar Bay on the 26th and came to rest that night outside the mouth of the Guadarranque in 10 metres of water.

Three SLCs were again launched, but shortly after leaving the submarine one of them broke down and the crew and warhead were transferred to the other two. As they had been informed that there were no warships in the harbour they tried to fix their charges on merchant ships in the open road. The ships were at anchor in water too deep for the attacking craft to rest on the seabed so the human torpedoes had to be kept level, just below the surface, during the crucial minutes that the charges were being transferred to the hulls of the targets. This proved tricky and both craft plunged to the bottom in deep water and were lost with their warheads. The attack was again a failure but all the six crewmen landed safely in Spain and were flown back to Italy by the civilian airline LATI, now known as Alitalia.[10]

This attack passed unnoticed as far as Gibraltar was concerned, but other attacks on Malta and Alexandria, at this time, led to the defences being reinforced. Anti-personnel charges were dropped periodically from boats to scare off undersea attackers and Holman projectors were improvised so that the charges could also be fired from the Moles.

Borghese, newly promoted to lieutenant-commander, decided to have another try at attacking Gibraltar in September 1941. He was more confident this time, as the many mechanical defects of the SLCs had been ironed out. Events were to prove him right. The crew of the *Scire* luxuriated in hot baths and enjoyed brandy and bananas on board the tanker *Fulgor* in Cadiz harbour. And the *Scire* set off once again for Gibraltar Bay with *Maiali* and operators on board. She passed a convoy heading west on the way but did not attack because she had to concentrate on her main task of launching her charges. Once again she ran into the Bay at night to the sound of charges being exploded in Gibraltar harbour every half hour. At 1am, on 20 September, she launched her three craft and returned to La Spezia.

The presence of patrol boats and the charges being exploded at the harbour entrance caused the commander of one of the SLCs to attack a laden storage hulk *Fiona Shell*, 2,444 tons, which was at anchor outside the harbour. The charge was duly placed below the funnel and after an interval it exploded and the vessel broke in two and sank. The second crew exploded their charge below M V *Durham* of 10,900 tons, which did not sink. The third commanded by Lieutenant Visintini ignored the anti-personnel charges, which he did not find very alarming and entered the harbour through the north entrance. There were a considerable number of warships assembled in the harbour for convoy Halberd for Malta, but Visintini felt that there was too much boat traffic to reach the south of the harbour unseen as the warships were guarded by constantly exploding charges, so he fixed his warhead to the RFA *Denbydale* at the Detached Mole. The tanker was seriously damaged and despite being patched up she never went to sea again, though she was not broken up until 1955. Visintini had left the harbour by the time his warhead detonated and he and the other five attackers landed safely in Spain and were whisked away. Borghese was promoted to Commander for this successful operation.[11]

The Italian Navy also developed small charges that could be suspended to the belts of swimmers and fixed to the bottom of enemy ships. The *Mignatta* or *Leech* carried an explosive charge of 2 kilograms surrounded by rubber rings that would form a vacuum and fasten it to the hull by air pressure. It was detonated by a time mechanism. An 'assault swimmer' could carry four or five of these artefacts. The *Baulilla* or *Explosive Cylinder* was an improved version and consisted of a canister containing 4.5 kilograms of high explosive which was fixed to the bilge keels by two clamps. It was detonated by either a time or a space fuse. The latter was a small propeller set in motion by the vessel's passage through the sea after it had attained a speed of over 5 knots, and after it had covered a given number of miles it released the lock of the firing clock. After the RN learnt about these weapons and started slipping a cable along the hull to dislodge them, they were redesigned with a cover around which the cable would slip without catching. The clamps were also booby trapped, in case divers tried to remove them manually.

Sabotage groups were set up at Malaga, Barcelona, Lisbon and Oporto. But the most effective of these operated from the Italian SS *Gaeta* in Huelva harbour. British intelligence soon found out about the activities of the Italian frogmen and it became necessary to investigate the bottoms of all ships that arrived at Gibraltar, loaded with metal ores from Huelva, to join convoys for Britain. Lieutenant William Bailey who was Electrical Officer Minesweepers, organised a group of volunteer divers to search the ships below the water line. They had no proper diving gear and had to improvise. Commander Belloni, the inventor of the wet-suit was subsequently very scathing about the RN sending out its volunteer divers without proper equipment. They wore weighted gym shoes to keep them upright, and a heavy woollen suit to keep out the cold which was not very effective. They did not even have proper breathing equipment and had to borrow sixteen Davis Submerged Escape Apparatus from the submarine depot ship *Maidstone*. Bailey or his assistant, Leading Seaman Bell, examined the bottom of every ship arriving from Spain and cleared them of explosive charges. For this unpleasant and dangerous task they were awarded a miserly half a crown a dive, each side of a ship searched being counted as a separate dive.[12]

As access to and from the Spanish shore was so easy, it seemed unnecessary for submarines to have to make the hazardous trip into the Bay, which became increasingly more dangerous as counter-measures were stepped up. The inventor Ramognino had joined the Italian Navy with a design for fast speedboats that could be used to take the divers to their targets. In the company of Lieutenant Visintini, he investigated the possibilities of setting up a base in Gibraltar Bay for these craft. Ramognino had recently married a Spanish girl called Conchita and the couple bought a house in Puente Mayorga called Villa Carmela, which overlooked, what was in those days before the refinery was built, a deserted beach. Ostensibly this was for the benefit of Conchita's weak health which would benefit from plenty of fresh sea air. The Villa was quickly prepared for the reception of Gamma frogmen of the 10th Light Flotilla, and a new window was put in from which shipping could be observed, disguised on the outside, by a cage for budgerigars.

In July 1942 a dozen swimmers, with full diving equipment and three *Leeches* per man, were sent to Spain. Six of them went to the Italian submarine depot Betasom at Bordeau and from there were smuggled into Spain either concealed in the bottom of lorries, or on foot across the Pyrenees. The others signed on as crew of a cargo steamer and jumped ship at Barcelona, to the consternation of the captain who had not been let into the secret.

On the night of the 13th they sortied from the Villa in their wet suits carrying their *Bugs* and went down to the beach. There they put on their flippers and breathing masks and swam the half mile or so to the vessels anchored in the roadstead. The time fuses were then set and the frogmen returned safely to the beach, although one had been wounded in the foot by the propeller of a patrolling craft, and another had severe back injuries caused by the explosion of one of the defences charges. They sank their suits and gear before landing. One of the frogmen reached the beach at La Linea on his own and losing his way walked all the way to the Italian consulate at Algeciras, from where he was taken back to Villa Carmela, where he found four of his colleagues. The other seven had been apprehended by the Guardia Civil when they returned to the beach, but were eventually released at the request of the Italian consul. From Villa Carmela they were transferred to the *Fulgor* in Cadiz from where they were eventually repatriated.

In the morning the charges started exploding: three ships, *Shuna* of 1,494 tons, *Empire Snipe* of 2,497, and *Baron Douglas* of 3,899, were badly damaged and had to be beached, and the *Meta* was also damaged. Bailey and Bell spent a busy day examining the numerous other merchant ships anchored in the Bay.[13]

On 15 September there was another attack by three frogmen. One was unable to attach his explosives because of the activities of the three defending launches and escorting small boats, which had their searchlights on and kept dropping charges. The other two fixed their charges on the same ship by mistake, and the SS *Ravens Point* 1,787 tons, was severely damaged.[14]

Whilst setting up the Villa Carmela headquarters, Ramognino and Visintini had come up with another plan. The tanker *Olterra* which had been scuttled on the day Italy entered the war was still fast aground on the Spanish shore with a small caretaker party on board. Arrangements were now made for a Spanish company to salvage her, pump her out, and move her to Algeciras harbour. The professed intention was to sell her to a Spanish shipping line. The Admiralty warned that if the ship left territorial waters she would be arrested regardless of the flag flown, but this of course did not matter as she was not meant to go to sea. She was moored to the inside of the sea mole at Algeciras. Her engines having been for a long time under water were of course useless, so she had a good excuse for remaining there. The skipper and chief engineer stayed on board but the other members of the crew were replaced by navy men sent out from Italy under the guise of a replacement crew and workmen to repair the ship. A lot of work went on virtually under the windows of the British Consulate. The ship was careened and the bows were raised out of the water 'to repair' them, when in fact, under protective canvas, a door was being cut under the waterline, which, with a chamber behind, would enable frogmen and SLCs to emerge without being seen once the ship was back on an even keel. Human torpedoes were dismantled and sent out under the guise of spare parts for the machinery, and operational crews joined the ship. All this of course took time, but by the end of 1942 the secret base on the *Olterra* was ready to commence operations. There was one more piece of equipment required, and that was a powerful pair of binoculars to watch British shipping in the Bay, so one was stolen from the window of the British Consulate and fitted up inside the bridge.[15]

At this stage the most famous of the RN divers at Gibraltar entered the scene. In November 1942 Lieutenant Lionel P K Crabb RNVR arrived at Gibraltar as Mine Disposal Officer. He was 32 years old and was known to his friends as Buster and to those who served under him as Tadpole. He had been commissioned the year before but was subsequently found unfit to serve at sea, for health reasons. On reporting at Admiralty Tower he found that the only mines discovered in Gibraltar were under the keels of ships and he therefore felt duty-bound to join Bailey's group. He was a poor swimmer and had no experience of diving but he took to it like the proverbial duck, and when Bailey, after being awarded the GM, was invalided home, he took charge of the Underwater Working Party which never numbered more than six divers. The ratings shared quarters at Jumper's Bastion with the Army Bomb Disposal Squad.

Within a few weeks of starting to dive Crabb removed one of the new *Explosive Cylinders* a green torpedo-shaped object about three foot long, from the keel of the SS *Willowdale* which had arrived from Huelva with a valuable cargo of wolfram. He then towed it to the airfield, still crowded with aircraft taking part in Torch, and successfully dismantled it. This was of course not known to the RAF, who otherwise would have objected to having their valuable aircraft endangered in this way. In July 1943 Crabb was involved in salvaging papers and other belongings from the Liberator carrying General Sikorski, which had crashed into the sea off Eastern Beach on take-off. But his main work was of course inspecting ships in the harbour and keeping a watch for Italian frogmen.[16]

After this, the Deputy Defence Security Officer at Gibraltar, Colonel Kirby Green, started a Counter Sabotage Service of divers, to accompany merchant ships that went into Spanish ports in order to protect the cargoes and hulls of these ships from sabotage. The unit consisted of 20 men under Harry Allen who had been a boatswain with the MacAndrew Line and it achieved one success when the men on duty were alerted to bombs being placed among the cargo of a ship loading oranges in Valencia, when one exploded prematurely on the quayside. But as Italy joined the allies shortly after, there was an end to sabotage of allied shipping in the Spanish ports. But not before Lord Rothschild was awarded the GM for defusing a bomb which reached a Polish military camp in Leicestershire in a consignment of Spanish onions.[17]

One of the volunteers for this work was a young former merchant navy seaman, Maurice Featherstone. Maurice had been on board the SS *Clan MacWhirter* when she was torpedoed and sunk by U-156, 250 miles north-west of the island of Madeira, at midnight on 26 August 1942. The survivors were taken to Madeira where they became friendly with the Gibraltarians who had been evacuated there. Maurice met Irene de Torres, he fell in love with her and was determined to marry her. The crew of the *Clan MacWhirter* were taken to Lisbon and then to Gibraltar, and when he arrived there, he decided to find employment locally and wait for Irene to return after the war. They were married in 1945. Maurice was subsequently elected to the City Council in 1956 and was a member of the House of Assembly from 1969 to 1989. He became Minister of Public Works, and subsequently Minister of Health in the AACR government under Sir Joshua Hassan.[18]

By December 1942 the *Olterra* was fully organised and on the 7th, after Force H had entered harbour, a party of three SLCs left to attack them. The targets were the battleship HMS *Nelson* and aircraft carriers HMS *Formidable* and *Furious*. Visintini, the leader of the party had studied the methods of the defence and the random scattering of explosive charges, and decided that they were not as dangerous as they appeared. Events were to prove him wrong. One of the attacking craft was spotted by a sentry when it surfaced outside the Detached Mole at 11.30pm, and the alarm was given. It was pursued by a patrol boat which showered its wake with charges. A rating lit the fuses by hand and then threw them into the water. The crew had to scuttle their SLC and after getting rid of their diving gear climbed on board a US merchant vessel. But they were evasive when interrogated and left their captors with the impression that they had been brought into the Bay by submarine. The defences were now well and truly roused and Visintini's craft seems to have received a direct hit from one of the charges as it was entering the harbour and sank. Both crew members were killed. The strong reaction of the defence left the third boat no alternative but to return to *Olterra*. But much to the pilot's shock he found when he had docked, that his crewman was missing. So the 10th Flotilla suffered five casualties that night without achieving any positive results.

The scuttling of one of the craft had been seen from the mole and attempts were made to retrieve it. There was a diving bell in the Dockyard, dating from the beginning of the century. It consisted of a specially built barge with a rectangular open-bottomed chamber which could be lowered until it was 40 feet below the surface and the divers could then enter it through a shaft leading from the barge. Crabb took his place in the bell with the local divers and they searched the outside of the harbour for more than a week without any success, before giving up. The bodies of Visintini and his companion were in the intervening time recovered and Crabb arranged for his brave antagonists to have formal burial at sea. There was a fellow feeling between the opposing divers which was little understood by other personnel on the Rock.[19]

It is recorded that Dr Elvio Moscatelli who commanded the operation of the SLCs from the *Olterra* and was also at the same time intelligence and medical officer, made numerous successful reconnaissances amongst the ships anchored outside the harbour, in one of the bumboats from Algeciras that came to sell fruit to the ships. Two of the Gibraltar RN divers also went into Algeciras in disguise, in the boat that brought water regularly into Gibraltar, as the supply from the water catchments was not able to cope with the demands of the greatly increased wartime garrison. They reported back to Crabb who started having suspicions about the *Olterra* but he was denied permission to slip in one night and examine its hull under water.

It took the *Olterra* some time to prepare a new operation after the disastrous December sortie, and it was not until 8 May 1943 that the 'Great Bear' flotilla, now commanded by Lieutenant-Commander Notari, was again operational and another attack was launched. At dawn there was an explosion on board the US Liberty ship *Pat Harrison* of 7,000 tons which was severely damaged as was the British SS *Mahsud* of 7,500. The *Pat Harrison* stayed afloat because the time clock of a *Baulillo* placed on the bilge keel for good measure, stopped when the torpedo warhead exploded. She was beached successfully as was the *Mahsud* but the *Camerata* of 4,875 tons was a total loss. There were no malfunctions on this operation and the three craft used in the attack returned to their depot ship safely.[20]

On 3 August the 'Great bear' flotilla launched their next operation, again with three attacking craft. Notari came across a new type of defence when he attacked the steamer *Stanridge* of 6,000 tons. This was a curtain of barbed wire that was lowered round the hull of ships at anchor. It was supposed to keep frogmen away by entangling their gear and tearing their wet suits; but Notari managed to negotiate it with difficulty, although in the heat of the moment his craft plunged to the bottom and he lost his crewman. He, however, completed his attack and the *Stanridge* was badly damaged although the crewman was captured. PO Bell, one of the divers, was lucky to escape unhurt because he was just going to check the hull of the ship when the warhead exploded. The Norwegian tanker *Thoshvodi* later broke in two and sank, and the US Liberty ship *Harrison Gray Otis* was seriously damaged by an explosion.[21]

This was the most successful operation so far, but it was to be the last. For the capture of Sicily in August had led to the successful invasion of the Italian mainland on 3 September and Italy surrendered on the 7th. The Italian forces now joined the Allies but some continued to support Mussolini, who set up a breakaway republic in the north. Arrangements were immediately made to tow the *Olterra* to Gibraltar and although attempts had been made to sabotage the installation, Crabb managed to reconstruct one of the SLCs which he named *Emily* and he put it through its paces before it finally took a deep dive one day and became a total loss.[22]

The surrender of Italy meant that a massive operation that was being planned against Gibraltar was abandoned. This was to be a combined attack by a dozen explosive E boats and new type human-torpedoes which were to be brought in by three submarines; so after a time Crabb's diving team moved on to Italy. Crabb was awarded the GM for his work at Gibraltar and at the end of the war he was entrusted with clearing the canals of Venice that had been extensively mined by the retreating Germans. He was assisted in this work by many of his erstwhile antagonists, including Belloni, and they were successful in saving the many artistic monuments in the city from destruction by the heavy charges laid by the Germans. Even after he returned to civilian life Crabb continued diving for the Royal Navy and he disappeared in

Portsmouth harbour in April 1956, while secretly examining the underwater hull of the Russian cruiser *Ordzhonikidze* which had brought Bulganin and Kruschev to Britain.

Borghese, an unregenerated fascist, joined Mussolini's republican army and became second in command of his naval forces. At the end of the war he was sentenced to twelve years' imprisonment by the Italian authorities but shortly after was set free as part of a general amnesty. He entered politics as a neo fascist and was implicated in an abortive uprising in 1970 when he had to flee to Spain. He settled in Conil de la Frontera until his death in 1974.[23]

The development of another Italian secret weapon, designed specifically to attack Gibraltar, was also abandoned when Italy changed sides. This was a special glider carrying a massive amount of explosives, and it was intended to release a number of them a few miles from the Rock. It was expected that they would have a devastating effect if sufficient of them could be launched.

All activities in the harbour and Bay of Gibraltar were closely watched by agents on the coast of Spain and Morocco and the island of Alboran and promptly reported to Rome and Berlin. In addition, a number of Spanish boats were employed as spies or collaborated voluntarily out of sympathy with the Axis. Attempts were made to disguise the movements of RN warships, by sailing them to the west during daylight and then trying to double back through the Strait at night. But this did not always work.

In June 1942, the sortie of the convoy engaged in Operation Harpoon was notified to the Italian Supermarina in Rome by the Spanish steamer *Cabo Prior*, which crossed its path.[24] The following month the destroyers *Antelope* and *Westcott* which were escorting convoy HG85, stopped and searched a number of Spanish trawlers. The *Maria Luisa* was found to have powerful wireless equipment on board, and together with two other trawlers which had long been under suspicion, the *Primer Enrique* and *Segundo Enrique*, was sent into Gibraltar. The last of these boats was found to be equipped with H/F wireless and to carry 'suspicious documents'. The naval historian P C Smith adds an interesting footnote to the story of these two trawlers,

By another remarkable coincidence *both* these ships foundered under tow of British warships on the way back from Gibraltar to the UK, the *Segundo Enrique* astern of the trawler *Stella Carina* and the *Primier Enrique* in company with the corvette *Geranium*, on 3rd September 1942 in position 36 23' N, 8 43' W.[25]

When the trawlers HMS *Honjo* and *Erin* blew up in Gibraltar harbour, on 18 January 1942, suspicions were aroused that this was the work of Italian frogmen but no confirmation of this has been found. It is more likely that they were destroyed by explosives placed in their bunkers by saboteurs in the pay of the enemy. The following June the security services received information that, Luis Lopez Cordon-Cuenca, a Spaniard who came to Gibraltar daily to work as an assistant in the Wembley Fruit Shop in Main Street and also at times worked on maintenance in the Dockyard, was a paid German agent and was smuggling bombs in. He was arrested, as was another Spaniard, José Martinez Muñoz, who was accused of placing a bomb which exploded in the fuel enclosure in Coaling Island on the 30th. Bombs were found hidden in the Fruit Shop and in the Imperial Cafe. Both men were executed in the Moorish Castle on 11 January 1944, by the Home Office executioner Albert Pierrepoint, who was flown out to Gibraltar.[26]

These were not the first spies caught in Gibraltar. On 5 February 1942, José Estella Key, who was born in Gibraltar but had Falangist connections, was arrested and found to have in his possession papers listing ship and aircraft movements which he confessed he was going to pass to the *Abwehr*. He was sent to England to be tried at the Old Bailey and was hanged at Wandsworth Prison the following 7 July.[27]

Another abortive attempt to employ a secret weapon in the area was the German Operation Bodden of 1941. This was a plan to supplement the information on maritime traffic in the Strait obtained from Italian and German coast watchers in Spanish uniforms, and the Spanish boats, by a system of infra-red bolometers which detected the heat emissions of ships. Information about this was received though Ultra intercepts and in order that the source should not be revealed it was attributed to a mythical agent referred to as 'el Hatto'. Buildings to house the equipment were to be erected at nine sites north of the Strait and at five on the coast of Morocco and the system was expected to come into force in April 1942. At least one of the stations was operational by February. The First Sea Lord proposed that the stations should be destroyed by parties of saboteurs landed from submarines, but direct action was turned down by the Chiefs of Staff who feared counter-action against Gibraltar. The Ambassador to Spain was asked to approach Franco personally about this and obtained a promise that they would be removed. However, implementation was slow and the SOE put forward a plan for putting the stations out of action but this was also turned down for political reasons and further approaches were made to the Spanish Government in October. The last of the bolometers was removed before the end of the year.[28]

There appears to have been at least one attack carried out on one of these infra-red search-lights mounted in a villa at 4 Rue Falaise in the International Zone of Tangier. SOE arranged for two of its agents, a Spanish communist and a Jewish barman, to push 38 pounds of explosives through the bars of the basement window of the villa, which was blown up and the and the equipment destroyed.[29]

In 1943, other German installations in Spain enjoyed greater longevity. These were the *Sonne* radio navigation beacons which were mounted at Lugo and Seville and enabled German submarines and aircraft, within a radius of 1,000 miles, to pinpoint their position. As the beacons had been nominally sold to Spain after they had been erected it was difficult to complain, but it was soon found that this did not matter as they were equally useful to the Allied aircraft hunting U-boats. The equipment was dubbed Consol which is Spanish for 'with sun' as *Sonne* is German for sun. After the war the stations were kept operational to assist navigation and in addition a captured transmitter was erected at Bushmills in Northern Ireland.[30]

Notes and References

(1)   Borghese 14-17, 20; Cocchia 180; Brou 9.
(2)   Borghese 24; Brou 9.
(3)   Borghese 25.
(4)   Borghese 35, 40-41; Roskill 1:601.
(5)   Borghese 59-63.
(6)   Lund *Out Sweeps!* 46-47.
(7)   Borghese 63-71.
(8)   Bassett *Sheffield* 58; Pugh 33-34.
(9)   Pope 40, 95.
(10)   Borghese 85-95.
(11)   Borghese 85-95.
(12)   Borghese 28-29, 248; Pugh 19, 21-22, 32, 54-56; Brou 33-34.
(13)   Borghese 207-212; Pugh 5; *British Vessels Lost* 80.
(14)   Borghese 220.
(15)   Borghese 213-217.
(16)   Pugh 12, 25-31.
(17)   Conversation with Maurice Featherstone; West *MI5* 378-379, 392.
(18)   Rohwer 118.
(19)   Borghese 223; Pugh 37-42.
(20)   Borghese 241-244; Pugh 56-58; *British Vessels Lost* 48, 62.
(21)   Borghese 256-258; Pugh 70-74.
(22)   Pugh 77.
(23)   Alcofar 205.
(24)   Sierra 356.
(25)   Smith *Wild Swan* 228.
(26)   Ramsey 36-38; *British Vessels Lost* 21.
(27)   West MI5 342, 379, 380-381; Ramsey 36.
(28)   Hinsley 2:719-722; R V Jones 254-259.
(29)   West *MI6* 264-267.
(30)   Price 190-192.

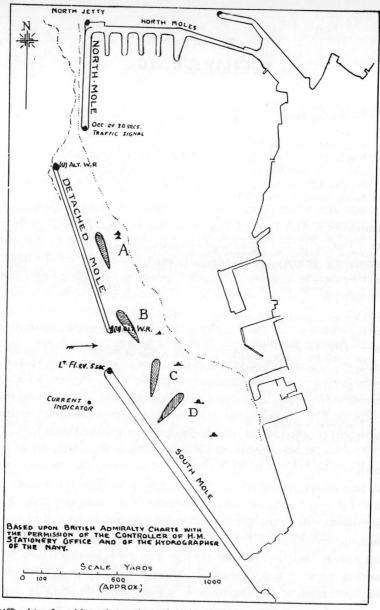

Difficulties faced by a large ship when berthing alongside the South Mole, from *On the Bridge* by Captain JAG Troup RN.

A   Ship proceeding as desired
B   Bow deflected by flood stream
C   Flood acting on stern combined with excess starboard wheel at B
D   A possible result

CHAPTER XIII

FORCE H

For two and a half years, from its formation in June 1940 until the invasion of French North Africa in November 1942, Force H guarded the entrance to the Mediterranean from its base at Gibraltar and exercised a decisive control over the adjacent waters. It kept the Italian fleet bottled in the Mediterranean, pursued German raiders that appeared in the nearby Atlantic, conducted a number of convoy operations which were vital in keeping Malta supplied, and finally, heavily reinforced, it escorted the fleet that invaded Algeria and ensured the success of the Torch landings. The Gibraltar Dockyard was kept busy refitting and repairing the ships of the Force as well as giving running repairs to the many warships damaged in the Malta convoys. In some cases the damage to the ships was so extensive that it was beyond the resources of the Dockyard but ships were patched up sufficiently so that they could proceed to long and extensive repairs in the UK or USA.

The commander of Force H during the first 18 months of its existence was Vice-Admiral Sir James Somerville, an effective and efficient officer. He was careful in husbanding his ships and would not enter into any operations without considering the risks very fully. His caution was at times anathema to Churchill but it certainly was a valuable asset during this period. For during the 18 months between March 1941 and August 1942, the RN lost no less than two aircraft carriers and another two were badly damaged, as well as two cruisers and twelve destroyers sunk, in the operations to supply Malta. In addition, four battleships, one carrier, twelve cruisers and 43 destroyers were lost during the same period, in other operations world-wide.

Although he was considered a strict disciplinarian, Somerville had a sense of humour. Lieutenant Ted Sworder RNVR who commanded the 92nd Trawler Group at Gibraltar, was once summoned to the quarterdeck of the flagship HMS Hood by the angry admiral. He later recounted their conversation,

'Are you in command of these trawlers?'
'Yes sir.'
'Do you have any naval discipline at all on board?'
'Well sir, they are all fishermen and very good at handling sweep-wires at sea, but they have never been in a Naval port before and know very little of naval etiquette.'
'Naval etiquette be damned! Do you know what happened to me this morning?'
Apparently he had stopped to look at my ships and the two stokers up the funnel stopped work to look at him, one saying, 'I wonder who he is?' The admiral overhearing the remark said, 'Why have you stopped painting - haven't you seen an admiral before?' There was a deathly silence and then one of the stokers replied, 'No, guv'nor - and if you are one we don't want to see any more!'
When the admiral finished speaking I thought 'This is the end of my Naval career', but the chief-of-staff roared with laughter, which broke the tension. The admiral turned to me 'I am not really giving you a bottle', he said, 'but I thought you ought to know.'[1]

In November 1940 arrangements were made to pass the battleship HMS *Barham* and cruisers HMS *Berwick* and *Glasgow* to the eastern Mediterranean; the ships also carried reinforcements for Malta. Somerville had to shift his flag to HMS *Ark Royal* for this operation as the pocket-battleship *Admiral Scheer* had broken out into the Atlantic and sunk the AMC *Jervis Bay* whilst it was escorting a convoy, and HMS *Renown* was sent to escort other convoys in the area. Operation Coat went off without a hitch and the *Ark's* Stringbags gave the airfield and seaplane base at Cagliari a pasting.

But a few days later there was a disaster. HMS *Argus* was to fly off more Hurricanes to reinforce Malta, but unfortunately when calculating the range of the aircraft not sufficient allowance was made for the strong head winds. The first group of six Hurricanes set off guided by a Skua and two of the fighters ran out of fuel and had to ditch 30 miles short of Malta although one of the pilots was rescued by a Sunderland. The second group consisting of the same number of planes was lost with all its pilots.[2]

A few days later, while the leader HMS *Faulknor* was on patrol in the Strait, she intercepted a French blockade runner *Charles Plumier* and took her into Gibraltar. The captured ship was renamed *Largs* and joined the Navy as an ocean boarding vessel. In 1942 she was converted into a headquarters landing ship and played an important part in the landings in Europe.[3]

After the *Renown* returned, Force H set out with another convoy of two fast merchant ships carrying 20,000 tons of supplies for Malta, the *New Zealand Star* with an urgently needed cargo of tanks for the 8th Army, and the cruisers *Manchester* and *Southampton* crowded with RAF personnel for Egypt. The convoy formed up west of Gibraltar on the morning of 25th November. When the ships had been escorted to the Sicilian Channel, Force H was due to meet the battleship HMS *Ramillies* and the cruiser HMS *Berwick* which were on their way back to the UK from Alexandria. No reaction was expected from the Italian fleet as three of its battleships had been badly damaged by aerial torpedoes at Taranto the week before. But on the morning of the 27th, when the two British squadrons met, air reconnaissance showed that the Italian fleet was out in force. It consisted of the new battleship *Vittorio Veneto*, an older battleship and seven 8-inch cruisers, and was considerably stronger than Force H. The 43,000 ton *Vittorio Veneto* on her own, should have been able to make mincemeat out of the old *Renown*, but lacking proper air reconnaissance, Admiral Iachino had no idea of the strength of the fleet facing him.

Somerville steamed towards the Italians, while the slow *Ramillies* tried to catch up by cutting corners but still trailed behind. At 12.20 action was joined between the opposing cruisers. The *Renown* added her salvos a few minutes later and the enemy started retiring back to his bases. The Italian admiral did not know that the *Ramillies* had not joined up with Force H, and he also feared that Somerville had a third battleship with him; the watchers at Gibraltar had apparently omitted to inform him that the *Royal Sovereign* was in dry dock at the time. As the enemy ships were considerably faster and were increasing their lead, Somerville gave up the pursuit after an hour. An attack by torpedo-Swordfish from the *Ark Royal* was unsuccessful as were later high-level bombing attacks on Force H by the Regia Aeronautics. The engagement was indecisive but the convoy got through which was the main purpose of the operation. However the Italians claimed the Battle of Cape Spartivento as a victory and Churchill expressed his dissatisfaction with Somerville's behaviour. When the admiral returned to Gibraltar he found himself faced with a Board of Enquiry before he had a chance to make his report, but the Board fully vindicated his conduct of the operation.[4]

In December, Force H was sent back into the Atlantic to patrol off the Azores as the German cruiser *Hipper* had attacked a troop convoy in the Atlantic. Force H rounded up the scattered convoy but the German raider was not located. The *Renown* was however, damaged by the heavy seas and 30 feet of plating over her starboard bulge was torn off, so she had to go into No 1 Dock as soon as she returned to Gibraltar to have this gash repaired. While she was under repair, the destroyers brought in a French convoy of three ships escorted by an armed trawler, which were suspected of running contraband goods for the Germans.

On 7 January 1941 Force H, reinforced by the battleship *Malaya*, left Gibraltar escorting Convoy Excess into the Mediterranean. This consisted of one ship for Malta and three for Alexandria and was run in conjunction with MW5 from the east escorted by the Mediterranean Fleet. Force H returned to Gibraltar, with the empty merchant vessels from the previous Malta convoy, without incident, though it was attacked by Italian high-level bombers. But the Mediterranean Fleet ran foul of the German Fliegerkorps X, which had been recently stationed in Sicily in order to neutralise Malta and rest control of the central Mediterranean from the RN. The dive bombers put the carrier HMS *Illustrious* out of action (though she managed to get to Alexandria after being patched up at Malta) and sank the cruiser HMS *Southampton*.

On 31 January Force H left Gibraltar on its most ambitious sortie so far. In order to preserve secrecy the ships were given sealed orders which were not opened until they were at sea and the operation was disguised as a sortie against Vichy shipping. After the fast section, composed of

Renown, Ark Royal and *Sheffield* screened by two destroyers, had carried out an unsuccessful air strike against the Tirso Dam in Sardinia, they met up with the *Malaya* and the other eight destroyers, to the north of the Balearic islands. But they then ran into a violent north-west gale and had to abandon the remainder of the operation and return to Gibraltar.

On 6 February, they sailed to the west escorting HG53, but during the night they doubled back, passed through the Strait and proceeded with the postponed plan for the bombardment of Genoa. Force H sailed through the channel between Mallorca and Ibiza. In spite of the attempted deception, Iachino knew of their destination and set out to intercept them with three battleships, three heavy cruisers and ten destroyers, but although the two fleets got within 40 miles of each other, Force H was not sighted and made landfall at Portofino at 6.45 am on the 9th. The *Renown, Malaya* and *Sheffield* turned north to bombard Genoa. Fire was opened at 7.15 and in half an hour 273 15-inch, 782 6-inch and 400 4.5-inch (some 400 tons of shells) were fired at the docks and the Ansaldo industrial complex to the east of the city. The battleship *Duilio*, in dry dock, repairing damage received at Taranto the previous November, was missed, but four merchant ships were sunk and another sixteen damaged and a number of warehouses were gutted. A few overs landed on the main shopping street of XX Settembre, and some houses were demolished. One shell landed in the ancient cathedral but fortunately did not explode. There were 72 civilian dead and 226 wounded. The *Ark Royal* had been detached earlier and twelve of her aircraft carried out attacks against the refinery at Leghorn, one pilot lost his bearings and attacked the railway station at Pisa instead. He later claimed to have straightened the leaning tower! Four Swordfish also laid magnetic mines at the entrance to the naval base of La Spezia.

Somerville now had to extricate Force H from its difficult position close to the enemy's air bases. So joining up with the *Ark Royal* the squadron sailed into the Gulf of Lyons. Iachino was still at sea looking for them but was badly served by his air reconnaissance and although he got within 35 miles of Force H and his superior speed should have enabled him to make contact, he ended up pursuing a French convoy by mistake. The misty weather conditions were undoubtedly a help and the air attacks were surprisingly light; Force H was safely back in Gibraltar on the 11th.[5]

They had only been back in Gibraltar for a couple of days when they were ordered to leave harbour as a radio message had been received from a merchant ship in the Atlantic that she was being attacked by a surface raider. This was the pocket battleship *Admiral Scheer* but it got away. The battlecruisers *Scharnhorst* and *Gneisenau* were also in the area, as was the cruiser *Hipper*, and Force H spent the next few weeks searching for them and protecting valuable Atlantic convoys. On 20 March, an aircraft from the *Ark* finally located the German battlecruisers. But unfortunately the aircraft's radio broke down and by the time it had returned to the carrier and reported its sighting, the coming of darkness and deteriorating weather conditions meant that the German ships were not located again and thus managed to get into Brest unharmed. After returning to Gibraltar to refuel Force H continued its long patrol, but the enemy did not come out again. The operation was not entirely fruitless as a number of supply ships and blockade runners were sunk.

The victorious advance of the 8th Army in Libya which secured air bases along that coast meant that Malta had been supplied for some weeks from Alexandria under the escort of the main fleet, but Rommel's successful break-out in March and recapture of much of the coast line meant that Malta had to be supplied again from the west. Between April and November 1941 *Ark Royal* flew off Hurricanes for Malta on eleven occasions, five times in company with the *Furious*, once with the *Argus* and once with HMS *Victorious*. On 14 June the two fleet carriers flew off 47 Hurricane fighters from a position south of the Balearics, which rendezvoused with four Hudsons of 200 Squadron, temporarily based at Gibraltar, that escorted them to Malta; 45 of the fighters landed safely.[6]

The aircraft were brought to Gibraltar by other carriers and then landed and loaded onto the *Ark* for the last stage of the journey. However, it was soon decided to save effort by mooring the incoming carrier astern of the *Ark* and then building a temporary bridge along which the fighters would be man-handled. A total of 325 Hurricanes were flown to Malta from the ships under the protection of Force H of which 305 arrived safely. Eighteen Swordfish and Albacore torpedo bombers were also delivered.[7]

Force H had just returned from one of these operations when news was received that the *Bismarck* had broken out into the Atlantic and sunk HMS *Hood* on 24 May. That very day Force H was ordered to proceed to a suspected refuelling point in the central Atlantic. The shadowing cruisers then lost contact with the *Bismark* and for over 30 hours the RN and RAF scoured the sea for her. She was obviously heading for Brest and the *Renown*, *Ark Royal* and *Sheffield*, punching their way north into the teeth of a gale were the only ships in a position to intercept her. Their escorting destroyers had returned to Gibraltar to refuel. The lightly armoured *Renown* was no match for the German mammoth but it was hoped that Swordfish from the *Ark* would be able to slow her down so that the heavy ships of the Home fleet could catch up with her. At daylight on the 26th the *Ark* started flying off her search aircraft. Weather conditions at this time were atrocious with the flight deck rising and falling 56 feet as the ship pitched in the heavy seas, and the wind touching 50 knots, nevertheless ten aircraft were launched safely, although several touched the wave-tops before they were airborne. At 10.30 *Bismark* was sighted by a Catalina which gave out an erroneous position and then lost her, but at 11.14 she was sighted by one of the Swordfish piloted by Flight-Lieutenant J V Hartley which was then joined by another aircraft and they remained in contact and reported her course to Force H which was 70 miles to the east.

A striking force of 15 Swordfish armed with torpedoes was immediately prepared and HMS *Sheffield* was ordered to press ahead and make radar contact. At 2.50pm the strike force took off and a ship showed on their radar. In the murky conditions, the attacking aircraft did not realise until too late, that it was the *Sheffield*. Fortunately, the cruiser was able to avoid the torpedoes and reported that no less than five had been exploded prematurely by their magnetic pistols. The flyers made their crestfallen way back to the *Ark* and three aircraft were badly damaged in landing. However, there was no time for delay, and another strike of 15 Swordfish was prepared, but this time the torpedoes were fitted with contact pistols.

At 7.15 pm the Swordfish took off, four were from 810 Squadron, four from 818 and three from 820. Half an hour later they sighted the *Sheffield* which directed them to their quarry, which was only 12 miles ahead. At 8.47 the attacks started and at 9.05 the *Bismarck* was hit aft in the steering compartment by a torpedo which destroyed her steering gear and jammed her rudder hard a-starboard. She was no longer able to manoeuvre. Another torpedo hit her armoured belt but did no damage, but the battleship was no longer able to continue her course towards the French coast. During the night, the 4th Destroyer Flotilla under Captain Vian attacked with torpedoes, scoring two hits, and kept the German battleship under surveillance. Although the weather conditions continued to deteriorate the *Ark* prepared a striking force of 12 aircraft for the following day, but it was not required, because during the night the Home Fleet battleships HMS *King George V* and *Rodney* caught up with the *Bismarck*. They used their heavy guns to reduce her to a flaming mass and the *Rodney* even fired her ten 24.5 inch torpedoes and scored at least one hit; the only known instance of a Dreadnought torpedoing another. The coup de grace was given by the cruiser HMS *Dorsetshire* with her torpedoes.[8]

One of the FAA officers who took part in the attack on *Bismarck* has described the triumphal return of Force H to Gibraltar:

> Our entry into Gibraltar will always live in my memory. Black Watch pipes played us into harbour, and every resident and serviceman had the day off. Every mole, every wharf, every window was full of flags and people, and as we moved gracefully to our usual berth, boats laden with sightseers, buzzed, sailed or rowed around us. A small ray of sunshine in a rather depressing part of the war. That evening came what we'd hoped for, a signal from *Sheffield* - 'Request the pleasure of your company for drinks tomorrow noon. All is forgiven and forgotten'. What a charming gesture![9]

After the formation of Force H, the number of submarines at Gibraltar was gradually increased and the 8th Submarine Flotilla came into being. This had the dual role of patrolling the Western Mediterranean and protecting the Atlantic convoys, and HMS *Maidstone*, was stationed at Gibraltar to serve as depot ship for the flotilla. In 1941, the RN and Dutch submarines of the 8th Flotilla scored a number of successes. At the end of May, HMS *Clyde* sank the 3,000 ton freighter *San Marco* in Sardinian waters, another 2,000 ton vessel further south and on her way back to Gibraltar destroyed a 1,000 ton Italian schooner by gunfire and took the crew prisoner. Her sister ship HMS *Severn* sank a 1,300 ton merchant ship in the Tyrrhenian Sea and rescued survivors, and in early July sank the 3,000 ton *Ugo Bassi* off Sardinia; on 7 August she also sank the Italian submarine *Michele Bianchi*. The Dutch *0.24* fired a salvo of torpedoes at the 7,000 ton tanker *Fianona* which broke surface and the Italian ship was able to avoid them, so she therefore surfaced and sank her by gunfire; and *0.23* sank a 5,000 ton tanker off Leghorn. In November *0.21* sank *U-95* 20 miles NE of Alboran.

For a time the Gibraltar submarines were relieved of their Atlantic patrol duties in protection of convoys, in order that they should have more time to run 'Magic Carpet' operations carrying supplies to Malta and *Severn* was specially converted for the purpose. Submarines from Alexandria also took part in replenishment operations. Boats coming out from the UK to join the 10th Flotilla at Malta or the 1st at Alexandria normally conducted a shake-down patrol from Gibraltar, along the Spanish coast, so as to get used to conditions in the Mediterranean; and damaged submarines from Malta were sent to Gibraltar to effect repairs, including HMS *Unbeaten* and the Polish *Sokol*.[10]

It became necessary to run another convoy to Malta in July, and Force H received substantial reinforcements for operation Substance. In addition to the cruiser HMS *Hermione* which had replaced the *Sheffield*, the French liner *Pasteur* was in the harbour full of troops which were transshipped to the cruisers HMS *Manchester* and *Arethusa*, and the fast personnel carrier *Leinster*, the 8th Destroyer flotilla, now consisting of HMS *Faulknor, Duncan, Fearless, Firedrake, Foresight, Forester, Foxhound* and *Fury*, and the *Cossack, Maori* and *Sikh* of the 6th. On the night of the 20th the convoy from the UK of six transports escorted by HMS *Edinburgh*, flagship of Rear-Admiral Syfret of the 18th Cruiser Squadron, HMS *Nelson*, the minelayer HMS *Manxman* and the destroyers HMS *Lightning, Nestor, Farndale, Avon Vale* and *Eridge* passed through the Strait. Force H sailed out to join them, in a thick fog, but the *Leinster* went aground alongside and had to be left behind.

Fortunately, most of the German aircraft had been withdrawn from Sicily to the Russian front, but the Italian torpedo aircraft were persistent and on the 23rd, in spite of the valiant efforts of the *Ark's* Fulmars, hit the *Fearless* amidships and she was brought to a standstill and had to be abandoned and sunk. The *Manchester* was also hit but in spite of heavy damage and with 38 dead, she was still able to limp back to Gibraltar under escort. Although Beaufighters from Malta took over the air cover that evening, the *Firedrake* was hit by a bomb and disabled, but she was successfully towed back to Gibraltar by the *Eridge*.

That evening the heavy ships had to turn back to keep company with the *Ark Royal* which was unable to operate its aircraft in the confined and mined waters of the Skerki Channel. But the convoy continued under Syfret with the *Hermione* in company and although ambushed by E-boats off Cape Bonn, which torpedoed and sank the transport *Sydney Star*, the rest of the ships reached Valetta harbour the following afternoon. The following day Syfret returned escorting the six empty transports and the supply ship *Breconshire* and successfully joined up with Force H. The Italian fleet did not intervene and the *Ark's* fighters dealt successfully with the air attacks and all the ships returned safely to Gibraltar. But there was to be no rest for the tired crews, the troops from the *Leinster* and *Manchester* still had to be taken to Malta, and they were embarked on the *Hermione, Arethusa, Manxman* and two destroyers to be transported, while aircraft from the *Ark* created a diversion to the north of Sardinia by bombing the aerodrome of Alghero. The operation went off successfully and there was an added bonus when the *Hermione* rammed and sank the Italian submarine *Tembien*.[11]

The *Renown* had to return home for extensive repairs to the covering of her bulges and the *Nelson* remained behind as flagship. The crews were at last able to have a rest and Somerville who was a great exponent of physical exercise got his skiff into the water to row round the harbour. On one occasion he rowed up to the *Firedrake* which had not yet entered dry dock and found that he was able to row right into her boiler room through the huge gap on her side. She was patched up in the Dockyard and then went to Boston Navy Yard for full repairs.[12]

Halberd, the next convoy operation to Malta, did not take place until September, but that did not mean that Force H was idle in the meantime, and two runs were made to fly aircraft to Malta. As action by the main Italian fleet was expected, Force H which was now made up of HMS *Nelson, Ark Royal, Hermione* and *Euryalus,* was strongly reinforced for Halberd by the new battleship HMS *Prince of Wales,* HMS *Rodney, Edinburgh, Sheffield* and *Kenya.* The convoy of nine merchant ships passed the Strait during the night of 24/25 September, and a number of warships entered harbour in the dark to refuel. Others refuelled under way from the RFA *Brown Ranger.* There were a total of eighteen destroyers in the escort, six of them were new ships of the L class and two were Tribals replacing the previous losses of the 13th Flotilla. On the afternoon of the 27th, as they were approaching the Skerki Bank, the Italian torpedo bombers commenced their attacks and in spite of the efforts of the defending Fulmars the *Nelson* was hit forward but maintained station. However, when news was received that the Italian fleet was out in force, the *Nelson* had to stay with the convoy as her speed had dropped to 14 knots, whilst the other battleships with the *Edinburgh* and *Sheffield* sought them out. But although at one stage the opposing forces were within 50 miles of each other they did not make contact and a strike force from the *Ark Royal* did not succeed in finding the enemy ships. A late evening torpedo attack by Italian Savoia aircraft badly damaged the freighter *Imperial Star* which had to be abandoned and sunk, but the rest of the convoy reached Malta safely. *Nelson* was escorted back to Gibraltar, while the rest of Force H waited for the convoy escorts to return from Malta after they had refuelled; in spite of air and submarine attacks they all reached Gibraltar safely. On the way back HMS *Gurkha* and *Legion* sank the Italian submarine *Adua.*[13]

Somerville now had to shift his flag to the *Rodney* and the *Nelson* returned home to be repaired. Whilst engaged in another operation to fly aircraft to Malta from *Ark Royal* Somerville received notification that he had been appointed a Knight Commander of the Order of the British Empire. He was already a Knight Commander of the Order of the Bath, and this led Andrew Cunningham to signal him from Alexandria, 'What twice a knight at your age?' The *Rodney* did not stay long with Force H and in October Somerville had to shift his flag again, this time back to the old unmodernised battleship *Malaya.*

When Italy entered the war in 1940 she possessed 110 submarines which constituted the largest force of its kind in the world. It was considered the elite and best trained part of her navy and it was therefore ironic that the design of the boats that constituted her submarine fleet was extremely antiquated. The Italian navy had built a substantial number of large comfortable boats which were slow and carried few torpedo reloads. They were not equipped with asdic, their large and imposing conning towers and bridges made them very noisy under water and they took up to two minutes to crash-dive, which was four times as long as the best submarines of the other navies. It is hardly surprising therefore, that although it scored a few successes the Italian submarine fleet was on the whole ineffective, and during the first 18 months of war had only succeeded in sinking three major RN warships the cruiser HMS *Bonaventure*, the AA cruiser HMS *Calypso*, and the destroyer HMS *Escort* near Gibraltar. Germany decided to remedy this situation by introducing her U-boats into the Mediterranean.[14]

At the end of September three U-boats attempted the passage, another three in October, more in November and December until, by the end of the year, over thirty had been sent to the Mediterranean. The Strait was difficult to guard because of its great depth, and strong currents which produced layers of water of different temperatures and density that deflected asdic echoes, and the complication of Spanish territorial waters on either side. In addition the large number of fishing boats that showed up on radar screens made discovery by night very difficult. But the defences did their best. Already, the 8th Destroyer Flotilla had destroyed *U-138* when it tried to enter the Strait the previous July, and now a further five were sunk. On 19 October the corvette *Mallow* and sloop *Rochester* sank *U-204* off Cape Spartel; on 16 November the corvette *Marigold* sank *U-433* 30 miles SE of Marbella; and on 28 November, *0-21* sank *U-95* as has been related. Two more U-boats were sunk the following month. *U-208* was sunk west of Gibraltar by the corvette *Bluebell*, on the 11th; and *U-451* by a Swordfish of 812 Squadron operating from the airfield on the 21st. Another five were badly damaged and had to return to Bordeaux without attempting the passage but nevertheless there were now some 20 U-boats operating inside the Mediterranean and they soon made their presence felt.[15]

On 10 November, Force H sailed with the *Malaya, Ark Royal* and *Argus* to fly off another reinforcement of 37 Hurricanes for Malta. The operation on the 12th went off fairly smoothly, 34 of the fighters landed safely and Force H returned to Gibraltar. The three major warships proceeded in line ahead, with the *Ark Royal* following the flagship and the *Argus* bringing up the rear. The following day at 3.30pm Force H had passed Alboran and the *Ark Royal*, having just flown off a patrol and landed some aircraft, had altered her course slightly to allow another to land, when she was suddenly shaken by a tremendous explosion, aircraft parked on the deck were seen to bounce with the force of the impact. She had been hit by a torpedo on the starboard side abreast the bridge. The *Ark Royal* took a list to starboard but continued steaming at 22 knots. Action stations were ordered by bugle, her engines were stopped and she was brought to a standstill. The destroyer *Legion* nosed up to the stricken carrier and in half an hour took off 1,487 of her crew, who were not needed on board. The destroyer rejoined the screen with eight times her normal complement on board.

Oil fuel was pumped from the starboard to the port tanks and at 5 o'clock the list had been stabilised at 17°. The destroyer *Laforey* now came alongside, and she pumped water so that the *Ark's* port boilers, which had not been flooded, could be relit. That evening, the Dutch rescue tug *Thames* arrived from Gibraltar and took her in tow. For four hours she continued to be towed slowly and at 2am the following morning Gibraltar was only 30 miles away when the port boiler room flooded, the furnace was extinguished, the electricity supply failed and the pumps stopped. The Dockyard tug *St Day* now arrived and joined the tow and the *Laforey* came alongside again and supplied power for the pumps to be restarted, but it was too late, it was impossible to keep the list under control and it continued to increase. At 4.30 it was 35° and the ship was abandoned. At 6.13am the most famous ship in the modern Royal Navy sank 25 miles east of Gibraltar in 1,000 fathoms. *U-81* had succeeded where many had tried and failed. The sinking of a modern warship by a single torpedo showed deficiencies in design and poor damage control, and the captain of the *Ark* was found negligent at the subsequent court martial.[16]

The *Ark Royal's* surviving aircraft operated for a time from Gibraltar airfield. The radar-equipped Swordfish were particularly welcomed as the six Hudsons of 233 Squadron, then at Gibraltar, were not equipped for night operations and as we have seen an aircraft of 812 Squadron sank a U boat the following month. In addition to her other squadrons (807 Fulmar and 813 Swordfish) the FAA formed Swordfish squadron 824 specially to operate from the North Front.[17]

The sinking of the *Ark Royal* reduced the strength of Force H to such an extent that for a time it did not get involved in any operations into the Mediterranean. Fortunately, the launching of Operation Crusader by the 8th Army in November 1941, led to the recapture of a large part of the Lybian coast and Malta was kept supplied from the east. After Japan's entry into the war in December Somerville was appointed to the command of the Eastern Fleet. Early in the new year he took passage in HMS *Hermione* for England and handed over command of Force H to Rear-Admiral Neville Syfret.

The first important operation of Force H under Syfret's command was in distant waters, when he was sent with HMS *Hermione* to take charge of the invasion of Madagascar in May 1942. For this operation Force H was reinforced by carriers from the Eastern Fleet. By May, the troops were well entrenched ashore and Syfret returned to Gibraltar.

Malta's Hurricane fighters were constantly being decimated by attacks from the German and Italian air forces and it was decided to reinforce them with Spitfires. In March 1942, the carriers HMS *Eagle* and *Argus* were escorted to within range of the island and they flew off 15 Spitfires. The *Eagle* returned twice that month, but she was slow and old and she did not have a large capacity, so the US carrier *Wasp* which was with the Home Fleet at Scapa Flow was sent out. On 20 April the *Wasp* flew off 47 Spitfires from a position north of Algiers and all landed safely apart from one that deliberately crash-landed in Algeria. Unfortunately, the enemy air forces were waiting for the reinforcements and they were attacked as soon as they had landed at Malta. After three days only half a dozen Spitfires remained serviceable. So on 9 May, the *Wasp* and *Eagle* flew off another 64. Sixty of these landed safely, and with previous experience in mind they were immediately refuelled and sent back into the air with fresh pilots to meet the expected onslaught. This plan worked but the rate of attrition of the fighters was high and reinforcements had to be continually flown in. The *Eagle* and *Furious* made a total of 13 trips between March and October 1942, and together with those carried by the *Wasp*, a total of 375 Spitfires were flown off, of which 367 landed safely at Malta.[18]

Rommel's last campaign in the Libyan desert started at the end of May and his lightning advance once again deprived the RAF of the bases from which air cover could be given to the convoys sent from Alexandria to Malta. The fast minelayer HMS *Welshman* was disguised as one of the large French three-funnelled destroyers and made a number of trips from Gibraltar carrying urgent supplies. In June Force H was substantially reinforced for Operation Harpoon, and as Syfret had not yet returned from Madagascar, the operation was commanded by Vice-Admiral A T B Curteis. The main force was composed of HMS *Malaya*, *Eagle*, *Liverpool* and *Charybdis* and eight destroyers, and protected a convoy of five cargo ships and one tanker. The close escort consisted of the AA cruiser HMS *Cairo*, the five fleet destroyers, HMS *Bedouin*, *Ithuriel*, *Marne*, *Matchless* and *Partridge*, the four 'Hunts' HMS *Blankney*, *Middleton*, *Badsworth* and the Polish *Kujawiak*, four fleet minesweepers and six MLs. Events were to show that the close escort was not strong enough to confront successfully the hazards that would face the convoy.

On the 14th, they were within range of the enemy and the air attacks started. The *Liverpool* was hit in the engine room by a bomb and virtually disabled but the destroyer *Antelope* managed to tow her all the way back to Gibraltar, though this took three days. One of the merchantmen was sunk. That evening, Force H reached the narrows between Sicily and Sardinia and the covering force turned back to await the return of the close escort which continued with the convoy. The following day the convoy was off Pantellaria and although cover was given by fighters based on Malta it was severely harassed by air attacks. A strong Italian squadron consisting of two light cruisers and five destroyers also appeared, but the RN ships put up a spirited defence with their 4-inch and 4.7-inch guns. The convoy was covered with a smoke screen and the five fleet destroyers steamed at full speed towards the enemy causing them sufficient damage to make them turn away. The Italians did not press their advantage and made off, although the *Bedouin* was sunk in the fighting and the *Partridge* and *Cairo* badly damaged. In the meantime the convoy suffered from the air attacks and one of the ships was sunk and another two (including the tanker) were so severely damaged, that with the prospect of the Italian surface squadron returning it was deemed necessary to sink them, and only two cargo ships reached Malta. On the way into harbour, the *Kujawiak* hit a mine and sank and others were damaged, but all the surviving destroyers and the *Cairo* managed to rejoin Force H apart from *Matchless* and *Badsworth* which had to be dry docked.

At this stage there were doubts whether Malta could continue to hold out because of lack of food and fuel. Harpoon had only landed 25,000 tons of supplies and no fuel, and the Vigorous convoy, which had been run in conjunction from Alexandria, had been turned back. Although ammunition and aviation fuel was constantly being transported by submarines and the *Welshman*, the food stocks were depleted and unless replenished the island might have to surrender. Another determined effort was required.[19]

In August, Force H received substantial reinforcements from the Home Fleet. This became possible because the Russian convoys which had hitherto had precedence over Malta had been suspended during the summer months as the long hours of daylight in northern latitudes made them too hazardous. Syfret had under his direct command a covering force consisting of HMS *Nelson* and *Rodney*, the cruisers HMS *Phoebe*, *Charybdis*, *Sirius*, nineteen destroyers and the aircraft carriers HMS *Victorious*, *Indomitable*, and *Eagle* were to provide air cover. In addition HMS *Furious* would fly Spitfire reinforcements for the garrison. In view of the experience gained in Harpoon, Force X under Rear-Admiral H M Burrough, which would act as close escort, was made strong enough to counter any interference by Italian surface warships, and consisted of the cruisers HMS *Nigeria*, *Kenya*, *Manchester*, and *Cairo* and ten destroyers.

On 3 August, the main body of the escort joined the fourteen merchant ships off the Clyde and together they passed through the Strait in dense fog on the night of the 10th. That afternoon the convoy was sighted and was henceforth kept under observation by enemy aircraft in spite of the efforts of the carriers' fighters. The following day *Furious* flew off 38 Spitfires 550 miles from Malta and steamed back to Gibraltar at speed with an escort of three destroyers, one of which, HMS *Wolverine* rammed and destroyed the Italian submarine *Dagabur* on the way. She embarked a further 32 Spitfires at Gibraltar which she flew off on the 17th.

That day the *Eagle* was struck by four torpedoes fired by *U-73* and sank in a few minutes. Then heavy air attacks commenced and the following day one of the merchant ships was damaged and had to leave the convoy. She later sank close to the Tunisian coast. In the afternoon of the 12th, the convoy was attacked by submarines and although many torpedoes were fired none of the ships were damaged but HMS *Ithuriel* rammed and sank the Italian submarine *Cobalto*. That evening HMS *Foresight* was hit by an aerial torpedo and had to be abandoned. The convoy reached the entrance to the Skerki Channel and during the night the main force hauled off to await the return of the close escort from Malta. The Italian submarine *Axum* then sank HMS *Cairo* and damaged HMS *Nigeria*, which had to return to Gibraltar. Burrough had to shift his flag to the destroyer HMS *Ashanti*. The convoy was then attacked by the submarine *Alagi* which sank a merchant ship and damaged HMS *Kenya*, but the cruiser was able to continue with the convoy. A second cargo ship was also sunk. In the early hours an attack by E boats developed, and HMS *Manchester* was hit by a torpedo which destroyed her propeller shafts. After she had lain immobile for some hours her captain scuttled her. (A court martial held after the war ruled that he had acted prematurely.) Four more merchant ships were also sunk.

At daylight on the 13th German bombers appeared and damaged and stopped three of the surviving ships including the vital tanker *Ohio*. Only three undamaged merchant ships entered Valetta harbour that day. One of the ships crippled by the Germans sank but the *Ohio* managed to struggle slowly into harbour in the early hours of the 15th, thanks to the heroic efforts of the destroyer *Penn* and the minesweepers *Rye* and *Ledbury* and her own crew. Her master Captain D W Mason was later awarded the GC; 55,000 tons of supplies had been delivered, including the *Ohio's* precious cargo of fuel. This enabled Malta to survive until the sea routes to the east were opened again. Although the population and garrison continued to suffer severe privations for a further six months until supplies started arriving regularly.[20]

A heavy price had been paid. The *Eagle, Manchester, Cairo, Foresight* and nine merchant ships had been sunk and in addition the *Ohio* was a write-off. The *Indomitable, Nigeria* and *Kenya* were heavily damaged and were out of the war for months, (the *Nigeria* was sent to be repaired in Charleston, South Carolina, and was not operational again until the following July) but Malta had been saved through the valiant efforts of Force H.

Notes and References

(1) Lund *Out Sweeps!* 45-46.
(2) Jameson 231.
(3) Smith *Destroyer Leader* 87.
(4) Roskill 1:301-304.
(5) Macintyre 107-115; Smith *Hit First* 179-186; Bassett *Sheffield* 76-81; Sierra 168.
(6) Vella 239; Apps 50-51; Fairbairn 71.
(7) Woods 84, 98.
(8) Macintyre 130-133; Jameson 294-307; Thompson 48-49.
(9) Woods 98.
(10) Mars 90, 124-125, 145-146; Cremer 217.
(11) Macintyre 135-142; Smith *Fighting Flotilla* 109; Roskill 1:601.
(12) Macintyre 144; Divine 166.
(13) Smith *Fighting Flotilla*, 110; Macintyre 152-159.
(14) Georgerini 536-537; Sierra 291.
(15) Cremer 216-217.
(16) Jameson 328-348; Macintyre 166-168.
(17) Roskill 1:474.
(18) Vella 135-136, 239.
(19) Roskill 2:63-66; Smith *Pedestal* 22-27.
(20) Roskill 2:301-305; Smith *Pedestal* passim.

CHAPTER XIV

CONVOYS AND TORCH

After the surrender of France, the German Navy established bases along her Atlantic coast which were better placed to attack shipping in the south west approaches of the British Isles; convoys to and from Sierra Leone and Gibraltar suffered heavily. A base for Condor long distance bombers was also established at Mérignac near Bordeaux. The threat posed by these aircraft was revealed when on 12 October 1940 one attacked the small coaster *Starling* five miles from Cadiz and she had to retreat into harbour with twelve casualties. That stragglers and ships sailing independently would be vulnerable to attack by aircraft was only to be expected, but that the aircraft were even successful against ships sailing in convoy showed the sad lack of adequate AA armament of the corvettes and most other RN escorts vessels. The Free French sloop *Savorgnan de Brazza* demonstrated the effectiveness of an adequate armament when she formed part of the escort of convoy KMS11 in March 1943 and with her substantial AA armament of 3 5.5-inch, 8 37-mm, 3 25-mm, 2 20-mm and 12 machine-guns, shot down two Condors.[1]

Most Flower class corvettes carried nothing more lethal to aircraft than a few machine-guns although a number also had a single 2-pounder pompom. But by 1943, the new wartime construction coming into service and the assistance of the US Navy, which had brought a reduction in the burden shouldered by the Royal Navy, permitted an AA cruiser to be stationed at Gibraltar to accompany the convoys. In 1943, HMS *Scylla* commanded by the historian Captain Donald Macintyre, was stationed at Gibraltar for the purpose. She accompanied convoys up to 44°N, where she would take over the southbound convoy which was also escorted by a cruiser and the two would exchange their charges. In the words of an American merchant skipper, a Limey cruiser brought us down here [to Gibraltar] from Cape Finisterre. Boy! Could that ship chuck shells into the air! We were attacked by aircraft, and when that baby went out, way in front of the convoy and opened fire, she was just one great sheet of flame. The Heinies never got anyway near the convoy when she was around, I'm telling you.[2]

Nevertheless, the really important role of the Focke-Wulf Condor was reconnaissance, and summoning up U-boats whenever they sighted a convoy. Many of the OG and HG convoys suffered grievously. The most tragic was undoubtedly OG71 which sailed on 13 August 1941 with 21 merchant ships, one salvage tug, and an apparently strong escort of the sloop HMS *Leith*, the Norwegian destroyer *Bath* (ex US four-stacker) and five corvettes HMS *Bluebell, Campanula, Campion, Hydrangea* and *Wallflower*. The escort was later joined by a sixth corvette, HMS *Zinnia* and, in addition, the destroyer HMS *Wanderer* was ordered on the 18th to sweep behind the convoy to attack any U-boats that were following it. On the 17th, while still to the west of Ireland the convoy had been sighted by a Condor, and the next day was attacked by two Junkers 88; their bombs fell wide but henceforth the convoy was kept under continual observation from the air.

The U-boats began to close in. At 1am on the morning of the 19th, *U-204* sighted RNN *Bath* astern of the convoy and hit her amidships with two torpedoes. She sank quickly and less than 50 out of her crew of 130 were saved. *U-559* then sank the cargo ship *Alva* and *U-210* sank, first the Vice-Commodore's ship *Ciscar*, and then the Commodore's *Aguila*, in quick succession. On board the *Aguila* were 22 Wrens who had been posted to Gibraltar, and though a few were picked up by the tug they too were drowned when the *Empire Oak* was sunk three nights later. None of the Wrens survived to reach Gibraltar. The convoy was still four days from Gibraltar and seriously threatened, so the next day the escort was strengthened by three additional destroyers, HMS *Gurkha, Lance* and *Boreas*, and the *Hydrangea* which had a large number of seriously wounded on board, was sent on ahead at full speed. Although still kept under observation by Condors, the convoy was not disturbed that night or the following, but radio transmissions showed that it was being tracked by at least eight U-boats. HMS *Wyvern* joined the escort on the 22nd but that night the tug *Empire Oak* was sunk by *U-564*.

It was the night after that, the wolf pack caught up again. The *Clonlara* was sunk by *U-564*, then *U-201* attacked and sank the *Stork* and *Aldergrove* in quick succession, and *U-564* attacked again and sank the corvette *Zinnia*, and then shelled and set on fire one of the merchant ships that had trailed behind. The escort did their best but none of the attacking submarines was damaged and the depth-charges killed many of the survivors from the sunken ships struggling in the oily waters. HMS *Vidette* joined the escort during the day but the *Gurkha* and *Lance* were short of fuel and had to leave for Gibraltar. The convoy was now at the latitude of Lisbon and it was still surrounded by U-boats so the Admiralty sent a signal: 'All ships of OG71 are to be escorted to Tagus and instructed to proceed to Lisbon'. The merchant ships took refuge in the neutral harbour while the defeated escorts continued to Gibraltar with the wounded survivors they had picked up from the sea. The author Nicholas Monsarrat was a lieutenant aboard the *Campanula* and his experience of this convoy features in his book *The Cruel Sea*.[3]

Convoy HG73, which left Gibraltar on 17 September, did not fare much better although it was escorted by ten destroyers and corvettes. Out of the 25 ships that formed the convoy, nine were sunk, including four survivors from OG71, the catapult ship *Springbank*, and Commodore Creighton's ship *Avoceta* which was carrying 128 refugees, of which 60 were babies and young children; from a total of 168 people on board, only 28 were saved. That autumn all U-boats operating in the North Atlantic were concentrated against the Gibraltar convoys.[4]

The Admiralty was aware of the need for small aircraft carriers to protect convoys, but shipbuilding resources did not stretch to the provision of these essential vessels during the first two years of war. Every ship that could float was urgently required and none could be spared for conversion. In 1941 an order was placed for eighteen escort carriers with US shipyards and as an interim measure a number of ships were fitted with a catapult on which a fighter would be carried. This meant that in many cases the fighter, out of range of land airfields, would have to be ditched after its flight, an expensive procedure but the need for protection was urgent. The old seaplane carrier HMS *Pegasus* was fitted to carry three Fulmars and on 3 December 1940 she sailed with OG47, and subsequently three other ships were also converted as Fighter Catapult Ships under the white ensign. A large number of merchant ships were also taken in hand to have a catapult fixed on their forecastle. They were designated CAM and carried a fighter whilst engaged on their normal commercial journeys. One accompanied each OG and HG convoy until in 1942 the number was increased to two. A small reserve of three Hurricanes for these CAM ships was established at North Front in September 1941.

The capture of the 5,337 ton German blockade runner *Hanover* was a windfall, and it was decided, in 1941, to give her a flying deck. She had no hangar and no aircraft lifts, but accommodated six Wildcat fighters parked on deck. Renamed HMS *Audacity* she was the first of the escort carriers to enter service when she was commissioned in June of that year. In September she sailed with OG74. Her Wildcats performed sterling service in buzzing U-boats which came to the surface near the convoy and making them stay down, so that they could not continue the pursuit of their prey. One of her aircraft destroyed a Condor which attacked the tug *Thames* and rescue ship *Walmer Castle* while they were picking up survivors away from the convoy, though the latter ship had been set on fire and sank. Before docking at Gibraltar, *Audacity* flew off her aircraft to North Front. Her maiden trip had proved successful. Her return trip was uneventful, but one of her aircraft skidded over the side although the pilot was saved.[5]

The *Audacity's* next convoy was OG76. At midday on 8 November a Condor was destroyed, although it shot down one of the attacking Wildcats, and a few hours later the *Audacity's* pilots scored another kill. Like other convoys, the air defence was bedevilled by the failure of RAF pilots to display their IFF, and there were numerous abortive launchings. Fortunately the navy pilots were better at aircraft recognition than the gunners on the merchant ships who, during the war, shot down more than one RAF plane under these circumstances.[6]

After she had arrived in Gibraltar, *Audacity* stayed in harbour for a month, waiting for the next convoy and she sailed with HG76 on 14 December. This was a large convoy of 32 ships and the escort commander was that great U-boat hunter, Commander F J Walker. The second day out, the destroyer HMAS *Nestor* sank *U-127* 35 miles from Cape St Vincent. That afternoon one of the fighters attacked *U-131* which shot it down but Walker rushed to the scene with HMS *Stork, Blankney, Exmoor,* and *Stanley* and sank the submarine by gunfire as it had been damaged and was unable to submerge. The next morning *Stanley* sank *U-431* but that night she was in her turn sunk by a U-boat she was attacking. Walker's *Stork* steamed up and began dropping depth-charges and the submarine surfaced 200 yards away. As the *Stork* was unable to depress her guns sufficiently to hit her, Walker sank *U-574* by ramming. Later, several Condors were sighted and *Audacity's* aircraft shot one down and drove the others away.

The following day, the 21st, the *Audacity's* aircraft discovered a number of U-boats surrounding the convoy and Walker decided to press for home as quickly as possible. That night *Audacity* took station outside the convoy and was hit by two torpedoes from *U-751* and sank; but HMS *Deptford* managed to dispose of another attacking submarine *U-567*. Though HG76 had lost air support from *Audacity* it was now within range of the RAF bases in Britain, and the convoy arrived without any further losses. Only two of the 32 merchants ships convoyed had been sunk, and *Audacity* had proved the value of escort carriers. It was another 18 months before the back of the U-boat campaign was finally broken, but it was now clear that the defeat of the submarine depended on adequate air cover and as this gradually became a reality the situation improved.[7]

When Nicholas Monsarrat arrived in Gibraltar after the nightmare of OG71, he found it a haven of peace, and in his autobiography he recalls,

I swam in what truly seemed a rich man's playground, Rosia Bay, not quite shadowed by the Rock, in the warm Mediterranean water which really could caress an exhausted body. We travelled round the town by gharry, a light, springy, slightly crazy four-wheeled cab topped by a linen awning. There was no black-out. We took our *apéritif* - Tio Pepe sherry - on a balcony overlooking Main Street, crammed with the eddying to- and-fro of the evening parade. We dined *a l'espagnole* off onion soup and *paella* and dripping melon and roughish Algerian wine, while at our back the bristling honeycombed fortress of the Rock stood guard, and seemed by its very name to restore our honour.[8]

Although the civilian population had been evacuated in 1940 Gibraltar had much the appearance of normality and sailors on their way home could stock up with luxuries not available in wartime Britain - nylons, bananas and other goodies. There was no blackout, though in order to preserve discipline there was curfew at 10 o'clock and nobody was allowed in the street after that without special permission.

Leisure activities were organised strictly on class lines, which no doubt were originally set by social habits, but this did not hold in the war-time citizens' forces when many middle class conscripts were serving in the ranks. It caused much discontent and was to lead to the overwhelming Labour victory in the 1945 election and the ousting of Churchill's government.

Officers did particularly well, they (and petty officers) could put on mufti and visit nearby La Linea or Algeciras; they found Gibraltar a very pleasant station. They could patronise the Yacht Club; and the bars of the Grand, Bristol and Rock Hotels were reserved for officers as well as the Capitol Bar in Main Street. Though Monsarrat seems to have sipped his sherry on the balcony of one of the leading gentlemen's clubs, either the Casino Calpe or the new Gibraltar Club, both of which had premises on a first floor in Main Street.

Other ranks were not allowed to visit Spain but they had the run of the Garrison Recreation Rooms. Sometimes there were dances in the Assembly Rooms (since demolished to make room for the Queen's Hotel) in spite of the scarcity of female dancing partners, and they had the run of the bars in town although the members of the girlie bands were now older and less attractive. Perhaps this was because most of the pre-war girls were enemy nationals and they were either not allowed into Gibraltar or else had gone home to engage in war work! The only thing really scarce (apart from women) was beer, which had to be imported from UK, and with 40,000 men on the Rock in addition to several thousands in the ships in the harbour, supplies tended to run out very quickly after a 'beer ship' arrived and the men had to console themselves with 'Red Biddy' - red wine from Spain or North Africa - which was always in plentiful supply.

For other entertainment there was sport in the Naval Grounds, the Army also had sports fields at Europa Point, and there was a civilian football ground at North Front. There were three cinemas - Theatre Royal, Rialto and Naval, and occasional visits by well known actors and singers arranged by ENSA. There were also amateur theatricals, and a production of James Elroy Flecker's *Hassan* by Major Anthony Quayle RA, who was on the staff at the Convent, was long remembered.

There were also facilities for the more serious minded. The Garrison Library was of course reserved for officers except that there was a record concert of classical music every Sunday evening which was attended by all ranks and professionally compéred by a corporal on the Convent staff. The civilian Exchange and Commercial Library (its building has now become the House of Assembly) was reserved for other ranks, and Lieutenant-General Sir Noel Mason-MacFarlane, who was the governor at the time, founded the Gibraltar Literary and Debating Society in 1943 which became the Mecca for those interested in politics and the platform for a fiery communist CPO from *Cormorant*. Although a haven from the war for the visiting matelot, Gibraltar was nevertheless an exceedingly boring place for the ordinary pongo who had to spend years on end within the confined area of the Rock.[9]

In April 1942, although the war with Italy was still in progress, four large Italian liners anchored half a mile from the Detached Mole. They were painted white all over, had two large red cross flags painted on either side, and a large Italian flag on the sides of the hulls and funnels. Arrangements had been made to repatriate the Italian civilians from East Africa (Eritrea, Ethiopia and Somaliland) and the ships were fitted out as hospital ships for the purpose. They were not allowed through the Suez Canal but had to sail right round Africa and they called at Gibraltar to take on a British SNO, who commanded the operation, and in addition each vessel had a naval party of an officer and four signal ratings and a military armed guard of an officer and seven men. Two Italian tankers were allowed to leave their neutral port of refuge, in the Canaries, and fitted with similar markings and guard, in order to bring oil fuel from the West Indies for the use of the hospital ships. In all, the four ships did three round trips, and had just returned from the last one when Italy surrendered to the allies. The *Giulio Cesare* and *Duilio* were scuttled in Trieste harbour to stop them falling into the hands of the Germans, the *Vulcania* was sunk at sea, but the *Saturnia* got away and became an American troopship.[10]

MI6 and SOE were very active in Gibraltar, both in counter-espionage, and dealing with escapees and intelligence agents in the Peninsula and occupied Europe. These services, as we shall see had virtually their own private navy operating from Gibraltar. The head of NI at Gibraltar was Commander Grenville Pyke-Nott but his exploits were limited in comparison with the exploits of Charles the Bold in the previous war. The senior NI officer in the Iberian Peninsula was Captain Alan H Hillgarth, who had retired from the Navy before the war and was British Vice-Consul at Palma de Mallorca during the Civil War. During that time he was involved in much humanitarian work, including the bloodless surrender of the Republicans in Minorca, and built up good personal relations with the Nationalists. He was recruited by NI at the outbreak of war and was Naval Attaché in Madrid from 1939 to 1943. He ran a very effective information network but, like Thorobold, has left no record of his activities. It is known however that through the good offices of his friend Juan March he organised a large fund to help ten of Franco's generals take steps to make sure that Spain did not enter the war on the side of Germany. The leading light in this group was Lieutenant-General Antonio Aranda, who had been one of Franco's most successful generals but was strongly anti-Falangist.[11]

Perhaps the most unique units to operate from the Naval base during the war were two 20 ton Spanish built fishing boats *Seawolf* and *Seadog* commanded by a couple of young Polish lieutenants and crewed by sailors whom General Sikorski described as 'too rough even for the Polish navy'. They were used by SOE to take their agents to the south of France and bring off escaped prisoners of war and RAF pilots shot down over occupied Europe. Their speed was 6 or 7 knots and the round trip would take up to a fortnight. These 38 foot, narrow beamed craft, with a single lateen sail and a diesel engine, had very meagre accommodation, a small compartment containing four cots forward, a wheelhouse just big enough for two men to stand in and a tiny cabin aft with room for just one cot, but there were occasions when they had more than 20 passengers. They would embark them at Gibraltar (their passengers were always referred to as Joeys) and when about two miles out everybody on board would turn out to paint the sides and structure in the colours of a normal Spanish fishing boat. On the way back, the returning passengers would have to turn out to paint everything in grey Navy paint, and they would raise the white ensign before reaching harbour, so that their clandestine activities should not be guessed at. For a time HMS *Fidelity*, a former French cargo ship was tried for agent running but she was too large and too obvious for undercover operations. Other vessels that operated with the Gibraltar Auxiliary Patrol were the ex-French trawler HMS *Tarana* and ex-Scottish Fishery Protection vessel HMS *Minna*, both commanded by RNR lieutenants. In the spring of 1942 all the boats engaged in clandestine operations along the coast of southern France and north-west Africa were amalgamated into a single Coast Watching Flotilla.[12]

Not all SOE operations proved a success. In March 1942 a bomb was being transported to Tangier, in the diplomatic mail carried by the ferry *Rescue*, in order to be placed on a Vichy dredger. The bag carrying the bomb had just been placed on the quayside at Tangier when it exploded prematurely. One civilian died and there were a number injured.[13]

A mystery surrounds Operation Banana which was conducted by the Secret Intelligence Services in conjunction with the American OSS. During and after the Spanish Civil War, a number of left-wing activists took refuge in Gibraltar. In 1940 the bulk of the civilian population of Gibraltar was evacuated but 400 of these men were allowed to stay on. It is fairly obvious that these activists were kept on hand in case Spain entered the war on the side of the Axis, and they could then be infiltrated back to organise guerrilla and sabotage activities. What is remarkable is that the file among the Gibraltar papers at the Public Records Office, instead of being opened after thirty years is sealed for the unusually long time of 75 years, and in 1954 the copies held by the Gibraltar Government were burnt on instructions from the Foreign Office.

In July 1943 a team of these anti-Franco Spaniards was successfully landed near Malaga by HMS *Tarana*. They established themselves ashore successfully and a further team was due to be landed in

September. In the interim Sir Samuel Hoare, the Ambassador in Madrid, heard of it and insisted that this operation to destabilise the Franco regime be cancelled. The second landing did not take place, the reception committee waited on the beach until they were captured by a police patrol. Under torture they admitted the existence of the Banana network, the police arrested 261 and 22 of them were executed for plotting against Franco. Was the 'passing police patrol' there by chance? Does the Public Records Office file explain what really happened?[14]

In July 1942, agreement was reached between American and British planners on operation Torch, the invasion of French North Africa. By then the Gibraltar airfield had been considerably lengthened and in March 1942 the Coastal Command detachment had been strengthened by the addition of two further squadrons of Hudsons - nos 500 and 608. The airport was to be crucial as General Eisenhower who commanded the operation explained,

> Land-based aircraft had to take almost the entire load of providing air protection, and the only available spot from which this could be done was Gibraltar. This made Gibraltar the focal point of our air umbrella and this in turn fixed the distance to which we could safely proceed into the Mediterranean with surface ships.[15]

The date of the multiple invasion of the coasts of Algeria and Morocco was fixed for the end of October but was later set back. On 25 September the Catalina in which a courier was travelling, bearing full details of the operation for General MacFarlane, was attacked by German aircraft and forced into the sea before it could reach Gibraltar. Some hours later the body of the courier was washed ashore at Cadiz, still clutching a sealed container with the plans. The body was returned with the package unopened but there was concern that it might have been tampered with and a copy handed to the Germans; the date for the invasion in the document was 4 November. However it was decided to continue with the operation as planned although for other reasons the date was altered to 8 November. Surprisingly, the Germans were not informed of the details of the plans.[16]

Above: The Naval Picket House at the entrance to Main Street. The shore patrols operated from here and drunks invariably ended up here. On this occasion in 1953 the drunks seem to be in charge as the White Ensign is flying upside down - see inset. *(Photo Stuart Brown)*

Below: The Bland ferry SS *Gibel Tarik* remembered by many as the Tangier ferry between 1949 and 1954. She figured in the Alec Guiness film 'Captain's Paradise'. Originally HM Minesweeper *Ford* of the Hunt class, she was converted to a car ferry and renamed *Forde* in 1928. During World War II she served as a salvage vessel. *(Photo courtesy John Gaggero)*

Above: The Old Naval Hospital. *(Photo John Farmar)*

Below: The entrance to the Victualling Yard with Parson's Lodge behind.
(Photo John Farmar)

Above: The explosion in the barge alongside the *Bedenham*.
(Photo Elio Bado, courtesy Gibraltar Museum)

Below: The explosion seen from New Camp.
(Photo Norman Cumming, courtesy Gibraltar Museum)

Above: The *Bedenham* after the explosion.
(Photo courtesy Gibraltar Museum)
Below: The wreckage on Gun Wharf after the explosion.
(Photo courtesy Gibraltar Museum)

Above: HMS *Childers*.
Below: HMS *Gambia*.

Above: HMS *Vanguard* at the New Mole.
Below: HMS *Hermes* in the Bay.

Above: The boom defence vessel RMAS *Moorland*.

Below: The harbour tug RMAS *Dexterous*

Above: The French destroyers *Guepratte* and *Kersaint* astern of HMS *Jutland*
with two Dutch destroyers of the Friesland class alongside.
Below: The RFA *Eddybeach* leaves harbour in 1962 for the last time.

Above: The Mediterranean Fleet in harbour.
Below: HMS *Bulwark* comes alongside.

A fine aerial view of one of the last concentrations of big ships in the harbour

Above: The ships of Exercise Spring Train in the harbour, April 1982, before news of the Argentinean invasion of the Falklands was received.
Below: HMS *Plymouth* returns from Falklands

Above: HMS *Boxer*, a type 22 frigate of the Broadsword class.
Below: HMS *Beaver*, a sister ship.

Above: HMS *Active*, a type 21 frigate.
Below: Sister ship HMS *Avenger*.

HMS *Invincible*

Above: HMS *Ark Royal*.
Below: HMS *Hart* with the Admiralty Tower behind; the quay alongside is reserved for use by the Royal Navy. *(Photo John Farmar)*

Above: HMS Rooke and the new extension to Coaling Island.
(Photo Johan Farmar)
Below: The new reclamation in the harbour. *(Photo John Farmar)*

Before the invasion it was thought necessary for the Deputy Allied Commander and chief planner, Major-General Mark Clark, to confer with some French officers who were favourably disposed to the operation, at an isolated spot near Algiers. The submarine HMS *Seraph* of the 8th Flotilla which had already operated on this coast with a party that charted the prospective landing beaches, was detailed to take him there. Clark flew to Gibraltar in a Flying Fortress on 19 October, and removing his hat and coat, so that he should not be identified by German spies from across the frontier, he was whisked by car to HMS *Maidstone*, and then boarded the *Seraph*. The submarine surfaced at the rendezvous near Algiers before dawn on the 21st, but the meeting had been postponed at the last moment until that evening, so they lay on the seabed all day. That night, Clark and his party were taken ashore in folboats and the *Seraph* waited submerged offshore. In the early hours of the 23rd they picked up the party, who had a stirring time hiding from the French police, and headed for home. But Clark was in a hurry so the submarine made a rendezvous with a Catalina which flew him back to Gibraltar.[17]

As the date of the invasion drew nearer it was necessary to send a submarine to the south coast of France to pick up General Giraud, who was a supporter of the allies, as it was hoped that his influence would secure the support of the French forces when the invasion started. Giraud had insisted that he should be picked up by an American submarine, but as there were none in the Mediterranean it was decided to send *Seraph* again, but under the American flag. Captain Wright USN was appointed to command her but as he had no experience of submarines, the real captain, Lieutenant Jewel RN, remained in full control. Giraud was duly picked up from a boat on 4 November, while his staff was embarked by HMS *Sybil* another member of the 8th. Both submarines returned safely to Gibraltar.[18]

On 24 November, *Seraph* left Gibraltar on her first regular war patrol and during the two weeks she was out she sank two Axis supply ships and two transports, but when her patrol was over she did not return to Gibraltar as by then *Maidstone* and the 8th had moved to Algiers to be nearer the seat of operations. *Seraph* was later involved in another famous undercover operation. After being refitted at Blyth in April

1943, she embarked a canister, in which was a corpse in the full uniform of an officer of the Royal Marines, carrying false plans. This was operation Mincemeat or 'the man who never was', dreamt up by Lieutenant-Commander Montagu of NI in order to mislead the Germans about the approaching invasion of Sicily. On the 19th the *Seraph* surfaced a mile from a beach near the mouth of the Huelva river and the body was duly consigned to the waves so that it should wash up ashore. When he reached Gibraltar, Jewell sent Montagu a postcard: 'Parcel delivered safely'. The *Seraph* then continued to her base at Algiers. For his part in Torch, Jewell was awarded the MBE and missed receiving a higher US award, as there was an arrangement between the British and US governments during the war, that only one award should be made for a single operation.[19]

Torch was a large and complex operation involving over 1,400 ships, of which 160 were RN warships, and Admiral Sir Andrew Cunningham was the overall naval commander. The plan involved landing in three areas, at Algiers, Oran and Casablanca, and 70,000 assault troops were used to capture the three ports. The attack on Algiers was by a combined British and American force and was followed up by the British 1st Army; Oran was to be an entirely American operation; so was the Casablanca landing which was conducted by troops sailing directly from the States. The landing at Algiers was covered by the Eastern Task Force under Vice-Admiral Sir Harold Burrough, and at Oran by the Central Task Force under Commodore T H Troubridge. The Western Task Force that covered the Casablanca landings was entirely USN and was commanded by Rear-Admiral H K Hewitt. The whole operation was covered by Force H under Vice-Admiral Sir Neville Syfret.[20]

The requirements of Torch put a heavy strain on the Allies' shipping resources and the whole system of convoys had to be changed, OG89 which sailed on 31 August 1942 and HG89 which sailed on 17 September were the last of the series and though the numbering continued to be used until October 1943 they henceforth sailed as part of the KMS convoys. For a time the commercial convoys from UK to the Strait were numbered KX (the return convoys were of course XK). But subsequently the special series meant to differentiate Torch military convoys from commercial ones, came to be applied to all convoys to and from the Strait; the designation for the convoys to Gibraltar became KMS (UK to Med Slow) and the fast convoys, mostly trooping, were designated KMF. The return convoys were of course MKS and MKF. The direct convoys from the USA to the Strait were designated UG/GU with the suffix F and S for fast and slow respectively. Eventually other convoys were established, CG/GC between Casablanca and Gibraltar, and when the navigation of the Mediterranean opened up in 1943 the through convoys from Gibraltar were designated GTX (Gibraltar-Tripoli-Alexandria) and the return convoys were XTG. The first one sailed on 24 May 1943. Other local Mediterranean convoys starting from Gibraltar were numbered TE. The special tanker convoys from Trinidad to Gibraltar that were run in 1943 became TM, and the ones to and from Sierra Leone RS/SR.[21]

The first convoys for Torch sailed from the Clyde on 22 October and Task Force 34 (UGF1) had already left the USA. Force H, which had to protect the invasion force from interference by the Italian (or Vichy French navies), was considerably strengthened with ships from the Home Fleet, and consisted of the battleships HMS *Duke of York, Rodney* and *Renown,* carriers HMS *Victorious, Formidable* and *Furious,* the cruisers HMS *Bermuda, Argonaut* and *Sirius,* and seventeen destroyers. The Algiers and Oran support groups each had in addition, two escort carriers, two or three cruisers, 13 destroyers, AA ships and many minor vessels. At Gibraltar there were also 2 destroyers, 4 corvettes, 13 A/S and 5 M/S trawlers, HMS *Maidstone* with 7 submarines, 1 minelayer, 25 MLs, 32 motor minesweepers, 3 salvage vessels, 4 tugs, and a supply reserve of 23 cargo ships, 18 tankers and 6 landing craft.[22]

In the meantime the airfield at North Front became crammed with aircraft and this provoked air raids. Italian aircraft, which normally flew over at lunchtime on reconnaissance, and were dubbed 'Prying Percy', dropped bombs on North Front. They did no damage but a stick of anti-personnel bombs fell on La Linea on 20 October, which caused casualties and a great deal of panic. At the end of the month, some 200 Spitfire and Hurricane fighters were delivered which had to be assembled to support the ground forces in North Africa; 121 of the fighters were ready by 7 November. Over 400 fighters were assembled at Gibraltar during November and dispatched to the front.[23]

Admiral Cunningham arrived at Gibraltar in the *Scylla* on 1 November, his headquarters were inside the Rock, but he stayed at the Mount as a guest of Edward-Collins;[24] four days later five Flying Fortresses landed, bringing Eisenhower and his staff, who set up their headquarters for the operation on the Rock. Eisenhower was accommodated in the Convent but he did not much like his invasion headquarters deep in the Rock,

> At Gibraltar our headquarters was established in the most dismal setting we occupied during the war. The subterranean passages under the Rock provided the sole available office space, and in them was located the signal equipment by which we expected to keep in touch with the commanders of the three assault forces. The eternal darkness of the tunnels was here and there partially pierced by feeble electric bulbs. Damp, cold air in block-long passages was heavy with stagnation that did not noticeably respond to the clattering efforts of electric fans. Through the arched ceilings came a constant drip, drip, drip of surface water that faithfully but drearily ticked off the seconds of the interminable, almost unendurable, wait which always occurs between completion of a military plan and the moment action begins.[25]

The convoys and their covering warships, some 340 ships in all, started passing through the Strait on the night of 5 November, and the following night Cunningham went to Europa Point to see the major part of the darkened ships sliding silently past. The convoys had eluded the U-boats sent out to intercept them but they were undoubtedly detected by the Axis coast watchers; however they were presumed to be heading for Malta or the Libyan coast.

The landings at Algiers took place at 1 in the morning of the 8th and met no resistance; but HMS *Broke* and *Malcolm* which were carrying American troops to prevent the sabotage of the harbour installations met with strong resistance from the French Navy. *Malcolm* was heavily hit in her boiler room and had to withdraw but the *Broke* managed to part the boom on her fourth attempt. Resistance continued and although HMS *Zetland* towed the damaged *Broke* out of the harbour they met rough seas and she sank the following day. There was strong resistance that day but that evening a cease fire was declared and the following morning Admiral Burrough entered the harbour in his flagship HMS *Bulolo*.

The attack on Oran started at the same time, but here resistance was stronger, the sloops HMS *Walney* and *Hartland* (both ex-US Coast Guard cutters) were sunk when they tried to rush the harbour. Captain Peters who commanded them was awarded a posthumous VC. The fighting was fierce and went on for two days, and HMS *Rodney* had to give gunfire support and the cruisers HMS *Aurora* and *Jamaica* engaged French destroyers that sortied from the harbour. *Tramontaine* and *Tornade* were sunk, *Epervier* was driven ashore in flames and *Typhon* retired back into the harbour where she was scuttled.[26] Oran did not capitulate until noon on the 10th.[27]

Within four days the Allied army was well established on shore. On the 12th there was an unopposed landing at Bone and within a few days the army was on the Tunisian frontier. Eisenhower moved from Gibraltar to Algiers on 24 November and Cunningham followed him the next day. By the middle of December Force H, consisting of the *Nelson*, *Rodney*, several aircraft carriers and destroyers, was dividing its time between Gibraltar and Mers-el-Kebir. On 23 January, Syfret was found to be suffering from acute appendicitis and sent to a hospital ship and Vice-Admiral sir Harold Burrough took over temporarily. On 4 March Vice-Admiral A U Willis took over command and raised his flag in the *Nelson* at Gibraltar, as he was expecting a break-out of German capital ships into the Atlantic which did not materialise. Henceforth the main field of operation of Force H was in the Mediterranean, and strongly reinforced it covered the invasion of Sicily. In October 1943, after the surrender of the Italian fleet, this famous force, which for more than two years had strong connections with Gibraltar, was disbanded.[28]

Malta with its large dockyard once again became the main RN base in the Mediterranean, but Gibraltar still played an important role as the focal point of convoys in and out of that sea. During 1942 an additional 23 U-boats were ordered into the Mediterranean, of which 16 got through, but 14 were sunk during the year. On 2 May, HMS *Wishart* and

Wrestler in conjunction with a Catalina of 202 Squadron sank *U-74* north of Oran and another flying boat of 202 sank the Italian *Veniero* off the Balearics. But it was the far ranging Hudsons operating out to a radius of 700 miles from North Front which could quickly follow up any information from Ultra or direction-finding stations, that achieved a great measure of success. On 1 May, 233 Squadron accounted for *U-573*; and during the first fortnight of Torch the Hudsons of 500 Squadron sank *U-595* on 14 November, *U-259* on the 15, and *U-331* on the 17 in conjunction with *Formidable's* 820 Squadron. The total German U-boat fleet in the Mediterranean at the end of 1942 was 23, which was only two more than at the beginning of the year.[29]

During 1943, another 22 U-boats were ordered to the Mediterranean of which 15 succeeded in getting through to the area of the Strait or beyond and two were damaged and had to turn back to their French base. The number sunk during the year was 25 and there were only 13 operational in the Mediterranean at the end of the year. Group 202 of Coastal Command at Gibraltar accounted for no less than seven of these as well as another six out in the Atlantic. When Hudson Squadron 608 moved to Blida in February 1943 it was replaced at North Front by No 48. The 'resident' Squadron 233 accounted for *U-167* on 6 April and *U-447* on 7 May, and shared *U-77* with Squadron 48 on 28 March. While 48 on its own, accounted for *U-442* on 12 February and *U-594* on 4 June; Squadron 500 sank *U-83* on 4 March; and a flying boat of 202 sank *U-620* on 14 February. Squadron 179 of Leigh Light Wellingtons was posted to Gibraltar during the year to keep the pressure up at night and sank another four German submarines on its own, *U-435* on 9 July, *U-134* on 24 August, *U-566* on 24 October, and *U-211* on 19 November; in addition *U-617* was sunk in cooperation with HMS *Hyacinth, Haarlem* and HMAS *Wollongong* on 11 September, and *U-340* on 1 November, in collaboration with HMS *Fleetwood, Active* and *Witherington*. The destroyer HMS *Douglas* and trawler HMS *Imperialist* also sank *U-732* south of Tarifa on 31 October, making a total of 14 U-boats sunk by the Gibraltar sea and air patrols during 1943.[30]

As has already been mentioned, the Strait produces very difficult conditions for detection by asdic, as the complex currents and the differences in water density act as barriers to discovery. The currents on the surface flow into the Mediterranean, but below 100 to 150 feet there is a strong counter-current flowing in the opposite direction which reaches a speed of 4.5 knots and this made the passage of the submarines of the time, with an underwater speed of 7 or 8 knots, virtually impossible. This meant that submarines trying to enter the Mediterranean had to travel above the 100 to 150 foot line, and were ideally placed for detection by a new invention. This was MAD (Magnetic Anomaly Detector) which could detect magnetic anomalies up to a range of 400 feet and the limitations imposed on the navigation of submarines by conditions in the Strait made it ideal for the area. It was anticipated that low-flying aircraft using this device would find it easy to detect any U-boats trying to make the passage.

US Navy Squadron VP-63 was equipped with Catalinas carrying the MAD equipment (Madcats) in a cone in the tail. The Madcats were armed with 65.5lb bombs filled with 25lbs of Torpex explosive. The bombs fitted with retro-rockets which propelled them at a speed which was the same as the forward speed of the aircraft in order to ensure that they hit the target just beneath. The Madcats also carried small floats with lights which were also rocket-propelled and could be fired at the same time and which marked the course of the target for any anti-submarine ships around. The squadron operated for over a year on the East Coast of the USA without achieving any kills but on 18 January 1944 it was stationed at Port Lyautey in order to operate in the Strait, which was considered an ideal area for the use of this weapon.

The tactic adopted was to have two Madcats flying a 'barrier patrol' at an altitude of less than 100 feet, round a course four miles long and one mile wide, south of Tarifa. The aircraft would follow each other round the course at a speed of 100 knots and it was anticipated that they would pass every point in the course once every three minutes.

Their first kill, on 24 February, was *U-761*, sunk south of Tarifa through the combined effects of the retro-bombs of two Madcats and depthcharges from the destroyers HMS *Anthony* and *Wishart*. The next U-boat to try the passage found the defences too strong and returned to base, but on 16 March, *U-392* was damaged by retro-bombs, within four miles of the previous kill, and finished off by the hedgehog of the destroyer HMS *Vanoc.* The frigate HMS *Affleck* collected debris from the U-boat.

After three more boats managed to evade the defences, *U-731* was finished-off on 15 May by the gunboat HMS *Kilmarnock* and trawler HMS *Blackfly*, after it had been damaged by the aircraft. Although 13 U-boats penetrated the Strait during 1944, they were quickly destroyed, either on passage or shortly after. In September the last two surviving U-boats in the Mediterranean were sunk in harbour at Salamis by American bombers and the U-boat campaign was over and convoys were no longer required within that sea.[31]

In 1944 the repatriation of the civilian population was begun and the town began to assume an air of normality, though there were still Nissen huts, for the large garrison, in every conceivable clear space in town, on the Walls and on the Rock. After D-Day when the Atlantic coast of France had been isolated and was abandoned by the deep-sea German naval and air forces, the war seemed very far from Gibraltar, and VE Day came almost as an anticlimax. But it was celebrated in fine style, with music and dancing at the Grand Parade in the Alameda, free food and tea and Saccone & Speed supplied 10,000 pints of free beer.

Notes and References

(1)   Poolman 24, 167-170; Jubelin 258-267.
(2)   Hughes 181-182.
(3)   Lund *Nightmare Convoy* passim.
(4)   Lund *Nightmare Convoy* 105-106; Creighton 137-149.
(5)   Poolman 41, 53, 118, 124, 162.
(6)   Poolman 137-141.
(7)   Poolman 141-149.
(8)   Monsarrat 115.
(9)   Glasfurd 8.
(10)   Glasfurd, Foreword, 9, 17, 19-20, 131.
(11)   Hinsley 2:15; West *MI6* 230.
(12)   Foot 91; Hampshire 147, 149-150.
(13)   Somner 35; West *MI6* 260-261.
(14)   Finlayson 10-11, 145-146; West *MI6* 354-355.
(15)   Eisenhower 87.
(16)   Breuer 55; Roskill 2:314; G Jones 168.
(17)   Robertson 31-51; Breuer 72-80.

(18) Robertson 55-92.
(19) Montagu passim; Robertson 121-125.
(20) Roskill 2:313-314.
(21) Roskill 2:214-215, 453-456; 3:110.
(22) Roskill 2:316-317.
(23) Elliott Ms 41-42.
(24) Cunningham 482.
(25) Eisenhower 106.
(26) Brown *Losses* 72.
(27) Cunningham 483, 487-490; Hinsley 2:477-478.
(28) Roskill 3:184; Cunningham 491, 503, 512, 517, 522.
(29) Roskill 3:246-247.
(30) Cremer 220-225; Elliott Ms 45.
(31) Roskill 3:246; 4:107; Cremer 226-228; Hendrie 65-67; Price 192-197.

CHAPTER XV

AFTER THE WAR WAS OVER

The end of the war in Europe meant that many of the escort vessels in the RN and the older worn-out major warships were laid up, and the bulk of the active fleet was transferred to the Indian Ocean and the Pacific. A procession of these warships came through Gibraltar on their way east and after VJ Day, in August 1945, the process was reversed. A number of the ships called at Gibraltar for minor repairs and the Dockyard was kept busy, but after 1946 it began to be run down and the work force was reduced. Once again Malta became the main base in the Mediterranean and the fleet was based there. Although the Mediterranean Fleet now had a smaller establishment than before the war, it was still the RN's main detachment abroad. At the end of 1946 it was made up of one of the new light fleet carriers, 5 cruisers, 24 destroyers, 10 frigates, 10 submarines and 16 minesweepers. The number of minor vessels was inflated by the need to clear mines left over from the war and the attempt to stem Zionist immigration into Palestine.[1]

Nevertheless, financial problems were to bring further reductions in the strength of the Fleet, and eighteen months later, the Mediterranean station was down to the carrier, four cruisers, eleven destroyers, nine frigates and two submarines. This was considerably more than the active Home Fleet which at the time was reduced to one cruiser, two destroyers, half a dozen frigates and twenty submarines.

From now on, the maritime defence of the Mediterranean area was to be shared with the US Sixth Fleet, which, with its amphibious force and large carriers (later given a nuclear capability) was considerably stronger, although it had no permanent base. This arrangement was formalised by the signing of the North Atlantic Treaty in April 1949 and the setting up of NATO. Eventually the RN's CinC in the Mediterranean was given command of the area but it did not include the Sixth Fleet, a strike force under the American admiral appointed to the Southern European Command (COMNAVSOUTH), with headquarters at Naples. The Flag Officer Gibraltar (FOGIB) in his NATO role as COMGIBMED, was allocated an area under CINCAFMED, the RN's CinC Mediterranean, but was not part of IBERLANT covering the Atlantic coast of the Iberian Peninsula, although there was a certain amount of overlap in area and responsibilities.[2]

The role of Gibraltar's naval base since the late 40s has been to provide control and support facilities, and to protect the route that NATO supplies and reinforcements take from the USA to Southern Europe and the Mediterranean. The US Navy also has a base at Rota in Cadiz Bay under the US-Spanish Agreement of 1953. If a confrontation was to arise in the future with Fundamentalist Moslem states in North Africa, the Rock would still carry out the same role, but would also be in the front line. The role of the base has changed essentially in the last forty years in that it is no longer an independent responsibility assumed by the UK but a part of the cooperative effort of the member states of NATO, which now includes Spain. Although Spain is not part of the integrated military structure. In time of war, collaboration with the Spanish forces would be orchestrated by CINCIBERLANT and CINCSOUTH.

To enable Gibraltar to fulfil its role there is sophisticated electronic and electro-magnetic equipment which monitors all movements through the Strait, on the surface as well as beneath. Control of shipping in the Strait and the forces in the immediate vicinity (COMGIBMED's NATO area) is exercised by the maritime headquarters (MHQ) deep in the Rock.

When the MHQ was reorganised in 1964, the problem of adequate manning had to be faced, and, as it would be expensive and might even prove impractical in an emergency, to send out reservists from Britain, it was decided to form a local Headquarters Unit for the RNR. Recruitment went ahead and HMS Calpe was commissioned on 18 November 1965 with premises in the Dockyard. The establishment was named after the ancient Greek name for the Rock of Gibraltar and it was the third time the name has been used by the Royal Navy. The first *Calpe* was the polacre that took part in the Battle of Algeciras in 1801, and the second ship of that name was a Hunt class destroyer which was lent to Denmark in 1953 and renamed *Rolf Krake*. The premises of HMS *Calpe* were moved to the old USOC club house in Queensway in 1983. The unit has a nominal complement of 130 and consists of some 100 volunteers, including seventeen officers, who are trained to man the communications and plotting side of the MHQ, as well as undertaking diving and defence of ports and anchorages operations (DEFPA).[3]

There were other important changes. The Royal Navy base establishment was moved ashore onto land reclaimed during the war, and renamed HMS Rooke in June 1946. HMS *Hart* was sold in 1948 and the *Cormorant* was broken up in Malaga the following year. The reduction of the Army in Gibraltar led to a realignment of service responsibilities and the Navy became responsible for many of the services' facilities in Gibraltar. As a result of this, the Military Hospital was taken over in 1963 and became the Naval Hospital, and the previous hospital, which had been closed down and turned into quarters 40 years previously, was renamed the Old Naval Hospital. The Detached and North Moles were leased to the civilian authorities for commercial use and so were Jetties 1 and 2 and the extension to No 3, in what was formerly known as the Destroyer Pens.

The Home Fleet's spring cruises and joint exercises with the Mediterranean Fleet were resumed. The exercise for 1949 required the Mediterranean Fleet under the tactical command of Rear-Admiral Lord Mountbatten to pass the Strait of Gibraltar which was held by the much larger Home Fleet under Vice-Admiral G Russell. The ships approaching from the Mediterranean were spotted from the air, but by dividing up and hugging the Spanish shore, some managed to get through. As they were approaching Gibraltar, Mountbatten called for his flagship's Warrant Telegraphist. 'I've sent for you,' he told him, 'because I want to break your arm.' Suitably bandaged, the Telegraphist was put ashore with a concealed transmitter. He reported the movements of the opposing Home Fleet and even penetrated their headquarters and took notes of their plans. When this was revealed, it caused a furore. At the manoeuvres the following year, the Home Fleet was so anxious about Mountbatten's activities that a totally innocent passenger was refused permission to disembark at Gibraltar.[4]

There were other cruises coordinated with ships belonging to NATO allies. In 1950, for example, in addition to the spring cruise there was an autumn cruise of the combined Home Fleet and Training Squadron which left for Gibraltar on 14 September under Admiral Sir Philip Vian flying his flag in HMS *Vanguard.* There was an impressive array of more than twenty ships which included the carriers HMS *Indefatigable* and *Vengeance,* the cruisers HMS *Swiftsure* and *Cleopatra,* and destroyers. The ships did not return home until 7 December and during the time they were abroad they exercised with Canadian units (carrier HMCS *Magnificent* and destroyers HMCS *Huron,* and *Micmac*) and the Portuguese frigate *Diogo Gomez* and destroyers *Vouga* and *Dao.* French depot ship *Gustave Zede* and frigates *Tonkinois* and *La Surprise,* and the Dutch carrier *Karel Doorman,* destroyer *De Ruyter* and submarines *Tijgerhaai* and *Zwaardvis,* were also in Gibraltar at the same time. On 15 January 1951, Vian was back in Gibraltar, for two months, flying his flag in HMS *Indomitable,* to engage in joint exercises with the Mediterranean and Sixth Fleets.

On 24 April, a few weeks after the fleets had dispersed, the Naval Armament Carrier RFA *Bedenham* arrived with a cargo of 500 tons of mixed ammunition. She tied up at Gun Wharf. In the morning of the 27 she was unloading depth-charges into a lighter alongside when one of them ignited. Sub Officer George Henderson arrived with a fire appliance, and on his own, boarded the *Bedenham* and directed a jet of water into the burning ammunition in the lighter, while Captain St J Cronyn DSO RN and Chief Fire Officer Andrew Indoe organised the fire fighting arrangements on the quayside. But their efforts were of no avail. There was an explosion in the lighter and the fire spread to the ship. There then followed a violent explosion in *Bedenham* and a thick column of smoke rose, which, when seen from Algeciras, was higher than the Rock. The *Bedenham* broke in two. The bow was blown onto the Gun Wharf and the remainder of the ship then listed to port and sank. The crew of the *Bedenham* had abandoned the ship in time, but the captain and the Naval Armament Supply Officer who had remained on the bridge, were blown into the water and were subsequently rescued, severely shaken, but otherwise unharmed. However, thirteen people were killed, including Henderson and Indoe. In addition to Indoe and

Henderson another nine were killed in the Dockyard. Five were Gibraltarians: John Lane, Joseph Moss, Mr Perez, Florencio Ruiz, and Joseph Zammit. Four were Spaniards: Francisco Martín Amador, Carlos Muñoz Postigo, Laureano Escriba Rodriguez, and Bartolomé Delgado Marín. Another two were killed by flying debris at the top of Ragged Staff Hill: A Abudarham, a taxi driver and José Moreno Serrano, a vegetable vendor. Fifteen of the seriously injured were taken to the Military Hospital and sixteen to St Bernard's.

As may be imagined the explosion of several hundred tons of explosives shook the town very severely. Fortunately the high Line Wall protected the Alameda Housing Estate, though the roofs were damaged. Worse hit were the Grand Stores, which subsequently had to be demolished and the site was used for the John Mackintosh Hall. Other buildings badly affected included the Admiralty Tower, the Convent, King's Chapel, the Government Secretariat, Bristol Hotel, Cathedral of St Mary, (where the clock in the church tower was stopped at two minutes past ten by the force of the explosion) and St Andrew's Church. All the stained glass windows of the churches were destroyed by the explosion. In addition, most other buildings in town were damaged to a lesser extent, there was a great deal of broken glass and many cracks. The Admiralty assumed full responsibility for the damage and some £250,000 was paid out in indemnity.

Henderson was posthumously awarded the George Cross and Indoe the King's Police and Fire Service Medal. Captain Cronyn was made a CBE. There were five awards of the George Medal: to Surgeon-Lieutenant J G H Sheppard RN and Leading Sick Berth Attendant M Hughes, for hastening to succour the wounded while it was feared that another explosion would take place; to Chargeman Juan Manuel Cruz for continuing to help the injured though he himself was wounded, and to James Keen and PC Michael Orfila for helping with the fire-fighting after the first explosion. Two other PCs from the police launch *William Seed*, Joseph Baglietto and Michael Felices, were awarded the Colonial Police Medal for Gallantry. The British Empire Medal was awarded to Anthony Ballantine for assisting the injured though he himself had been wounded and Vicente Pisarello, a foreman, for conducting fire precautions. Those who received the King's

Commendation for their behaviour that day were: Alfredo Banda, David S Hutcheon, Cecil N Knowles, Alfred McGrail (who had his left hand amputated) and Francis J Parody. In addition other were commended by the Admiralty: C L Doughty, R J Coulter, M R Beattie, J Borg, C Veale, E Butler, B Ryan and L Consigliero.[5]

The RN at Gibraltar was subsequently peripherally involved in two other disasters. In March 1954, the troopship *Empire Windrush*, returning from the Far East with 1,481 troops and dependents, including many children, was gutted by a disastrous fire, north of Algiers. Although four of the crew were killed the passengers all successfully abandoned ship and were rescued and taken into Algiers. The burning ship was taken in tow by the Battle class destroyer HMS *Saintes* until the dockyard tug *Brigand* arrived from Gibraltar to tow the smoking hulk. The survivors were brought to Gibraltar by the carrier HMS *Triumph* and destroyer HMS *St Kitts* and each man received a present of cigarettes from Saccone & Speed when he landed. The passengers lost all their belongings but the Government compensated them for the loss of their kit and luggage.[6]

On 19 December 1963, the Greek liner SS *Lakonia* left Southampton with 651 cruise passengers, first port of call, Madeira. At midnight on Sunday 22nd, when the ship was 130 miles from Madeira, fire broke out. The alarm was given and an SOS was sent out within minutes, which was picked up by the US Coast Guards who activated a procedure known as Atlantic Merchant Vessel Report which had been organised in 1958 to deal with disasters at sea in the North Atlantic, and instructions were given to the US Air Force in the Azores to send Air Sea Rescue Neptunes. The planes arrived within a few hours and dropped twenty life rafts. Later other aircraft appeared on the scene including two Shackletons from Gibraltar. In the meantime, ships close by, had started to reach the burning *Lakonia.* The aircraft carrier HMS *Centaur* and the Norwegian salvage tug *Hercules* sailed from Gibraltar at 1.30am, to give assistance.

Fire fighting arrangements were bad and flames soon engulfed the vessel. An hour after the fire had been discovered the captain gave orders for the boats to be launched so that the passengers could be taken off. By 4.30am the survivors began to be rescued by the ships that had arrived on the scene. But, unfortunately, at least one of the lifeboats had overturned on launching, and there had already been a number of deaths. Between the fire and the chaos in the water, 98 passengers and 30 members of the crew died that night. All the next day the rescue work continued and most of the 918 survivors were landed in Madeira by the Argentinean liner *Salta* and the US cargo boat *Rio Grande*, but the British steamer *Montcalm* landed hers at Casablanca and the Belgian *Charlesville* at Tenerife.

The *Centaur*, which had steamed to the scene at 27 knots, arrived at 8.45 am on the 24th and she started searching the water for survivors, but only dead bodies were found. The *Lakonia* was still burning and Lieutenant-Commander Parry was winched on her quarterdeck by helicopter. He found that the deck was almost burnt through and only a six-foot strip remained intact between the stern and the swimming pool, but the edges were brittle and crumbling. The lower decks had been burned away and Parry could look down through three decks. It was obvious that there was nobody alive in this inferno so he was winched up again. The *Centaur* returned to Gibraltar with 58 bodies which were all finger-printed and photographed by the Gibraltar Police and their description was circulated among Police Forces abroad. All the dead were eventually identified, and though they were all interred in Gibraltar, some were later exhumed and returned to their native lands for burial.[7]

The closing of the border

The announcement that Queen Elizabeth II would visit Gibraltar during her six months Commonwealth Tour of 1953 and 1954 prompted the resurrection of Spanish claims to Gibraltar. Spain's post-war ostracism by the international community was coming to an end, and with Churchill back as Prime Minister, Franco felt that it was time to have the talks on the status of the Rock that he had been promised in 1940.[8] Rebuffed, the Spanish authorities started causing difficulties at the frontier. The British Government adopted a low key approach to the problem, and over a period of years this led to an improvement of relations between Britain and Spain and the measures making transit difficult were relaxed. In the words of one Prime Minister, Harold

Macmillan, Gibraltar was 'preserved in good heart and strength by wise and courteous diplomacy. We did not then think it necessary to prove our devotion to our own democratic ideals by heaping vain insults on the proudest people in Europe.'[9]

When Harold Wilson became Prime Minister in 1964 he was less tactful and voiced his strong disapproval of Spain's Fascist regime. Joint naval exercises which had been planned between the Royal Navy and the Spanish Navy were cancelled, as was the promised technical aid to enable Spain to build five Leander class frigates. The cancellation of the technical aid did not cause any serious setback as the US immediately took it over, and the design of the new frigates of the *Baleares* class was changed to that of the US Knox class. They were the first major warships built in Spain, in over 60 years, which were not of British design. But the insulting way in which Spain had been rebuffed caused the dispute over Gibraltar to flare up. Fuel was added to the flames by the UNO's insistence that talks should take place between Britain and Spain on the future 'decolonisation' of the Rock. These talks did not lead to any understanding and relations between Britain and Spain deteriorated as more severe restrictions were placed on transit at the frontier.

The impending break between Britain and Spain did not make sense in view of the strong economic bonds between the two countries and many behind the British and Spanish governments worked to defuse the situation. The formula that was eventually found was to hold a referendum in Gibraltar to establish the views of the Gibraltarians, in spite of the fact that it was perfectly clear that all political parties in Gibraltar were against a deal with Spain. When the referendum took place, more than 99% of the Gibraltarian electorate voted for maintaining the relationship with Britain as it existed at the time. But the referendum heightened emotions and feelings on both sides became inflamed. The net effect was to turn a confrontation between Britain and Spain into one between Spain and the people of Gibraltar. Whilst relations between Britain and Spain improved, the full wrath of the Spaniards was turned on the Gibraltarians and encouraged by a resolution passed in 1968 by the General Assembly of the United Nations, that Gibraltar should revert to Spain, the Spanish Government closed the frontier completely in 1969.[10]

Having brought about the confrontation with Franco, the Wilson Government was persuaded to stand back and let the Gibraltarians bear the full weight of Spain's hostility without involving the important British commercial interests. But the British Government did accept moral responsibility for Gibraltar's economic plight resulting from the closing of the frontier. Economic collapse was prevented by a policy of aid termed 'sustain and support' which enabled the people of Gibraltar to weather the storm. It is significant that Parliament was not given the chance to discuss fully the reasons for this aid, as funds were not voted specifically but were deflected from the Overseas Development Aid already authorised for Third World countries.

The closing of the frontier made life difficult in two ways. First of all there was a shortage of skilled workmen who had previously come in daily from Spain and the Dockyard was forced to recruit labour from Morocco which was less skilled. Also, life in Gibraltar became considerably less pleasant. Personnel stationed on the Rock could no longer visit Spain except by sea, either by going on the ferry to Tangier and from there to Algeciras, or else by yacht to ports outside the area of the Strait. British boats from Gibraltar were not allowed to call at Algeciras, Tarifa or Ceuta, without first obtaining permission from the Spanish authorities. There was also a shortage of fresh food until arrangements were made to import it from Morocco and Britain.

There were a number of confrontations between the Royal Navy and Spanish warships. The Spanish Navy instituted a patrol of the Rock to make sure that Spanish boats did not enter Gibraltar harbour and boats from Gibraltar did not make unauthorised visits to Spain. This patrol was normally maintained by one of the minesweepers built in Spain during World War II to German plans (they were similar to the German Navy's M-Bootes). They were coal burning and their worn-out machinery, together with the bad quality coal in their bunkers, made them progress under a dense pall of smoke. Inevitably, the boat on patrol was dubbed 'Smokey Joe'.

In November 1967 the minesweeper *Tambre* dropped anchor in British waters, the frigate HMS *Grenville* was sent to chase the intruder away, but the captain of the *Tambre* refused to weigh anchor, claiming that his ship was anchored in Spanish territorial waters. However the captain of HMS *Danae* had more success with the Spanish helicopter carrier *Dedalo* when she did the same thing the following March. The closure of the frontier in June 1969 led to more demonstrations by the Spanish forces and the number of RN warships present in Gibraltar harbour was increased. In October a squadron of six Spanish warships anchored at the head of the Bay. It consisted of the cruiser *Canarias*, the carrier *Dedalo* and four destroyers. The destroyer HMS *Diana* kept a watchful eye on them, while the carrier *Eagle* was carrying out a self-refit inside the harbour. Eventually the Spanish squadron sailed away to engage in joint manoeuvres with the French Navy, leaving the minesweeper *Lerez* on patrol.

The Army had supplied all governors of Gibraltar since 1707 (although Edward-Collins had acted in a temporary capacity in 1942) but it was now decided that the three services should take it in turn to appoint a senior officer to the post. In 1969 General Sir Gerald Lathbury was succeeded by Admiral of the Fleet Sir Varyl Begg, a former First Sea Lord, who held the position until he was succeeded by Marshal of the Royal Air Force Sir John Grandy in 1973. Sir Varyl Begg was the first admiral to become governor of Gibraltar since the Marques de Santa Cruz in the 16th century. In 1982 it was the RN's turn again and Admiral Sir David Williams succeeded General Sir William Jackson and held the post until 1985. The strict rotation between the services has been broken in recent years and when Admiral Sir Derek Reffell took over from Air Chief Marshal Sir Peter Terry in 1989 he was only once removed from his RN predecessor.

The closing of the Dockyard

By 1967, the Royal Navy's commitments in the Mediterranean had been considerably reduced and the flag of the CinC Mediterranean based in Malta was hauled down for the last time, after almost two centuries. In 1972, agreement was reached with the Government of Malta, to close the base there in 1979. It was obvious that the reduction in British defence commitments in the area would have repercussions on Gibraltar. In 1981 the British Government produced a White Paper on defence which stated that the Gibraltar Dockyard would close down in 1983 (though the date was later to be extended to the end of 1984) and that no further half-life refits of Leander frigates would be undertaken at Gibraltar after the end of the year. The announcement could not have come at a worse time. The frontier with Spain was still closed and the economy of Gibraltar was in crisis.[11] The Dockyard was one of the mainstays of the economy, as, 2,500, out of a working population of 12,000, worked for the Ministry of Defence, of which some 750 were employed by the Dockyard. This was therefore, a bombshell, as far as the Gibraltar Government was concerned, particularly as the economic implications threatened to undermine the stand taken against the Spanish claims to the Rock.

A long period of consultation followed. The British Government offered to give 'grant-aid' but as this would have entailed complete loss of local autonomy in financial matters, it was turned down by Gibraltar. A feasibility study was commissioned to consider the possibility of turning the Dockyard into a commercial institution owned by the Gibraltar Government. Eventually the British Government agreed to subsidise the change-over to commercial work provided that A & P Appledore were appointed managers of Gibraltar Ship Repair Ltd. Appledore had conducted the viability study of the Gibraltar commercialisation and was successfully managing ship repair yards in Dubai and Greece at the time.

The British Government agreed to hand over to the Government of Gibraltar the whole of the Dockyard, except for a section to be retained for the greatly reduced Naval base. In addition, they offered £28,000,000 of overseas Development Aid for the conversion and guaranteed £14,000,000 of naval work in the first few years, to help the new company get started. Two further sites for development, at Queensway and Rosia, were included in the package, and the cost to the British taxpayer of relocating the installations there, was a further £12,000,000.

To go commercial was a brave step to take considering that the ship building and repair industry in many parts of the world was going through financial problems. However, the Gibraltar Government felt that there was no chance of altering the decision to close the Dockyard and that they had secured good terms from Britain. The situation was serious, but *faute de mieux*, Gibraltar had secured the best deal possible.

The Unions did not see things in this light, they believed that the British Government had a moral commitment and could be forced to change its mind. They engaged in an energetic campaign against the deal which extended to industrial action against anything connected with the change-over. Appledore was blacked and its employees were not allowed into the Dockyard, so they were unable to quantify correctly the cost of converting and updating the installations. Unfortunately the Unions misjudged the determination of the British Government to close a dockyard which was no longer needed by a Royal Navy much reduced in size. The complete 'blacking' of Appledore until they eventually took over, was to have serious consequences, as it meant that the run-down state of the infrastructure was not discovered until the commercial company started operating and the financial provisions made for modernising the yard then proved totally inadequate.[12]

The privatisation scheme was still being studied, when the Argentinians occupied the Falkland Islands in April 1982. The RFA *Fort Austin* and the nuclear submarine HMS *Spartan* had been dispatched from Gibraltar as reinforcements a few days before; but when the Argentinian invasion took place the bulk of the active fleet was in Gibraltar, taking part in Exercise Spring Train. Ten destroyers and frigates were immediately sent to Ascension Island under the command of Rear-Admiral Sandy Woodward, as the vanguard of the fleet. The Sea Wolf equipped frigate, HMS *Battleaxe*, had to return to Britain for repairs that could not be carried out at Gibraltar, but the Dockyard worked very hard to prepare and arm the other vessels before they sailed south.

Feelings of patriotism caused the Gibraltar Trades Council to suspend their industrial action against commercialisation on 7 April, to enable the demands of the emergency to be met. The biggest job tackled was the conversion of the cruise ship *Uganda* into a 1,000 bed hospital ship. The ship was ordered to Gibraltar after she had landed her passengers, and the full conversion was carried out in the record time of 65 hours over the weekend, between Friday 16 April and Monday 19. A helicopter landing pad was added and full hospital facilities were installed, as well as a satellite communication system and provision for refuelling at sea. The surveying vessel HMS *Hecla* was also converted into a hospital support ship. Work connected with the Falklands War kept the Dockyard working a few months longer and the final date of closure was altered to 31 December 1984.[13]

In preparation for the change over, redundancy notices were issued to 776 Dockyard workers in November 1983, and recruitment for the new civilian company was started. From the beginning, the new Gibraltar Shiprepair Company Ltd (wholly owned by the Gibraltar Government and managed by Appleyard) was beset by labour disputes, and this had a demoralising effect on both the work force and management. And no doubt on prospective customers too, who had to be enticed to the Dockyard by attractive terms. The net result was that the losses were considerably higher than anticipated. The £28,000,000 grant had included £17,000,000 for alterations and equipment and £11,000,000 for trading capital and to cover the projected losses of the first two years, but as has been explained the expenses of conversion were higher than had been budgeted. By the beginning of 1986 there was only £300,000 of ODA money left which was frozen for a time because of the industrial unrest. The 1985 loss was £3,720,000 and another £3,311,000 was lost the following year, and £2,908,000 in 1987. More ODA money was pumped in and when this ran out the Gibraltar Government had to start subsidising the losses until by 1988 they had pumped in £4,000,000 which was largely spent on redundancy payments during the restructuring that took place in late 1987 and early 1988.

Morale in the Yard was not improved by the financial situation, and was further impaired by the large salaries the managers were receiving. The breaking point came when the ODA granted an Appledore subsidiary the contract for a computer programme. Although Appledore eventually spent more on the programme than they were paid they never got it to work properly and the Gibraltar Government gave them statutory notice of termination.

There were elections in Gibraltar and the GSLP Government that came into power in April 1988 was led by Joe Bossano, who as Union Leader had led the struggle against commercialisation. But in spite of the unpromising outlook, he tried to continue running the Dockyard on the established lines, although losses were running at £250,000 a month. The contract with Appledore was terminated and the cost-cutting exercise was continued. But it was too late, in 1989 the

Dockyard lost £7,900,000 and although this included certain capital items, losses were still larger than in previous years. In July 1991 the Dockyard was closed down, having lost some £26,000,000 since it was privatised. It became a casualty of the penchant for confrontation in Gibraltar's political life.

The following November, the Gibraltar Government negotiated with the Norwegian company Kvaerner to lease them the docks and repair facilities for three years, at nil rent, in the hope that with a small and dedicated labour force they might be able to make it a going concern, as there has been an upturn in the ship repair industry in recent years.

The Naval base today

The naval base is considerably smaller than previously and comprises the Admiralty Tower and wharf and workshops alongside (including the power station), Coaling Island, and the northern end of the South Mole for the docking of large ships and submarines. In addition there is living accommodation for personnel and barracks (including HMS Rooke), the Naval Hospital (now reduced to 35 beds), and ammunition stores and other installations inside the Rock. There is also a satellite communications receiver at Windmill Hill. The number of personnel in the base was reduced from 557 to 410 by 1986.

Although Britain is no longer a Mediterranean power she has retained a commitment to detail a frigate, when required, to the on-call NATO forces in the area. This NAVOCFORMED frigate is allocated to COMNAVSOUTH and is part of a force of some four or five warships from the RN and US Navy and Mediterranean NATO nations, which meet together regularly for exercises. In addition a frigate stationed in home waters is normally designated Gibraltar guard ship.

The Flag Officer Gibraltar comes directly under CINCFLEET at Northwood and the Royal Navy makes him responsible for an area extending from Corsica and Sardinia in the east to 20° West in the Atlantic. The seas round Gibraltar are still an important training area for the Royal Navy, particularly, the area of Alboran where the waters are deep and close to the base. Missile firing exercises are normally held to the west of the Strait where there is greater sea room and less maritime traffic.

FOGIB also has NATO responsibilities as COMGIBMED and comes under COMNAVSOUTH at Naples, though the area covered in this capacity is much more limited. Situated on the western edge of SACEUR (Europe) command, COMGIBMED borders on SACLANT (Atlantic) command, and most of the NATO exercises in which Gibraltar is involved are in conjunction with CINCIBERLANT at Lisbon.[14]

Today, Spain is a part of the southern area of NATO, but the unresolved political problems mean that she does not take part in any activities directed from Gibraltar, and Royal Navy ships participating in joint exercises with the Spanish Navy come directly under CINCFLEET at Northwood. There is never any Gibraltar involvement on these occasions.[15]

As the defence establishment in Gibraltar has shrunk over the years the Royal Navy has assumed greater responsibilities locally. In 1985 the Marine Craft Unit of the RAF was closed down and its air sea rescue duties were taken over by the RN. The high speed launches, HMAFV *Sunderland* and *Stirling*, were renamed HMS *Cormorant* and *Hart* as these names have been connected with Gibraltar since the days of the old depot ships at Coaling Island. The launches were run by the Navy for some time but were scrapped in 1991 and have been replaced by the search and rescue craft *Ranger* and *Trumpeter*. In addition the Navy is responsible for the Exocet missiles which would be deployed at Europa Point in an emergency. These missiles, in effect, replace the old 9.2-inch guns that used to command the passage of the Strait.[16]

In addition to becoming responsible for the hospital care of all service personnel at Gibraltar, the Royal Navy also took over the main role in running the officers' clubs. These have been run down over the years as the total number of officers of all services in Gibraltar has reduced. USOC was closed down in 1979 and the club house is now the headquarters of HMS Calpe.

The Garrison Library with its fine building and valuable collection of books on the history of Gibraltar has closed down its club facilities and lending library, because of lack of support. It is still used by the Services and the people of Gibraltar for special social functions, and the historic library collection is available to bona fide researchers, but the future of the institution remains uncertain. At one stage it was on the point of being handed over to the Gibraltar Heritage Trust but changes in the Ordinance that governed it made this impossible, and the negotiations were suspended. The Trustees of the Library are in a delicate situation as they have to safeguard the assets built up from contributions by members, in the two centuries since it was founded in 1793. Until a formula can be found that will protect the future of the Library the matter remains in limbo, for to allow the Library to be dismantled would be a breach of the terms under which the Garrison Library Trust was set up.

The military presence in Gibraltar has been greatly reduced as Britain's armed forces are cut-back after the end of the cold war. The Army has now withdrawn its resident battalion and it only maintains a nominal presence apart from the Gibraltar Regiment. The RAF's programme is similar and the airfield is due to be 'privatised' by 1998. The Royal Navy has therefore become the lynch-pin of the three services in Gibraltar. Although the Royal Navy's presence in the Mediterranean has almost disappeared Gibraltar still has a role to play in the NATO command structure on the southern flank of Europe. The base, though greatly reduced in size is still important and will continue to be so in the foreseeable future. Today it is the main Royal Navy base abroad and is considered a plum posting by many personnel. Service life in Gibraltar provides many of the amenities of life found in the United Kingdom. British newspapers are on sale the same day, there are BBC programmes on local television and first class radio provided by the British Forces Broadcasting Services and Gibraltar Broadcasting Company. At the same time there is Mediterranean sun and sea all the year round, and opportunities for weekends and holidays in Spain and Morocco. Above all nobody can visit Gibraltar without being conscious of its historical connection with the Royal Navy and the important part it has played in Naval history for three centuries.

An English speaking civilian community allows many opportunities for integration and engaging in joint undertakings in sport and other leisure activities, such as amateur dramatics. HMS Rooke received the Wilkinson Sword of Peace in 1988 for outstanding efforts in fostering good relations with the local civilian population. This sword has been presented annually since 1966 by Wilkinson Sword Ltd, to a unit of the three armed services which has established outstanding relations with its civilian host community. Rooke had carried out many projects of redecorating and refurbishing communal buildings, and had held many charitable functions and distributed the proceeds to local charities. Facilities had also been made available for sporting and social functions.

A great deal of money has been spent on improving facilities and amenities and the MHQ has recently been fully refurbished at the cost of £6,000,000. The Admiralty Tower, which had been shored-up since the *Bedenham* explosion, has been repaired and restored. The admiral is now CBF Gibraltar commanding all the three services on the Rock and the Admiralty Tower has become the control centre for all three services, replacing Fortress Headquarters.

Notes and References

(1)   Grove 22.
(2)   Grove 37, 54-55, 106; *Brassey's* 1958 10-12.
(3)   Beaver 54; *Gibraltar Government Report 1966* 82-83.
(4)   Ziegler 494-495.
(5)   *Gibraltar Chronicle* passim.
(6)   *Gibraltar Chronicle* 30 March 1954.
(7)   Marchbanks 13, 16, 29, 109, 114-115; Bond 176, 190-194; Benady *Police* 43-44.
(8)   Smyth, the bearer of the message was the Under-Secretary of State at the Foreign Office, R A Butler (266 n12O).
(9)   Macmillan 262.
(10)   Magauran 33.
(11)   A Canepa, election address, *Panorama* 16 January 1984.
(12)   J Bossano, election address, *Panorama* 23 January 1984.
(13)   Villar 33, 183; Brown 53, 67, 75, 82, 145; Grove 360.
(14)   *Gibraltar Chronicle* 16 October 1985, Rear-Admiral Dingemans, 18 November 1987.
(15)   *Gibraltar Chronicle* 8 April 1989.
(16)   *Gibraltar Chronicle* 2 September 1985, 12 October 1985.

APPENDIX I

The Sea Fight in the Road of Gibraltar

The news of the naval battle in Gibraltar Bay caused a great deal of excitement when it reached England and a pamphlet was published that same year which was a translation of a letter written by Ioris van Spilberg, the Commissary of the Dutch Fleet describing the events. The title page of the publication carried the following information (the spelling and punctuation have been modernised):

THE SEA FIGHT IN

the Road of Gibraltar the 25th April last, betwixt the King of Spain's carracks and galleons, and the Hollandish men of war, reported by a letter written aboard the Hollands Fleet, by a commander of the same, and faithfully translated into English.

The pamphlet was printed in London for John Hardie, and was sold by Robert Jackson at his shop under the Royal Exchange. The text read:

A COPIE OF A LETTER

written out of the Hollands Fleet at sea, the fourth of May 1607 NS.

Being under the height of 36 degrees, or afore the river of Lisbon, upon the tenth of April, our Admiral Jacob van Heemskerk and his Council determined and fully resolved, to enter into the said river with all our ships to assail and spoil the carracks and galleons lying there, but being certainly advertised[1] that the carracks were gone and the galleons, being 8 or 9, were wholly unrigged and their ordinance on shore, so as it would be two months before it could be ready, the aforesaid resolution was for the time stayed; and the rather for that diverse English and French ships coming out of Sanlucar and Cadiz, brought us certain[2] news that not long before their coming forth, fifteen Spanish ships of war of Sanlucar and Cadiz, had put to sea and were gone to the Straits of Gibraltar, being eleven galleons and the rest smaller ships as then made men of war.

1. advised
2. definite

235

A contemporary Dutch engraving of the battle. The tower in the foreground is a representation of the pentagonal Torre del Tuerto.

Whereupon we resolved to follow and find them out, but the wind being at east, we met a Flushinger called *Loy Sailmaker* that came out of the Straits the 22 of April and showed[1] us that the night before he had been in company with the Spanish Fleet, and that in the morning finding himself alone without company, he supposed they had taken their course for Cadiz, for with an easterly wind they might come out of the Straits.

Upon the 24 of April the wind coming westerly, we passed close by the bar of Sanlucar and Bay of Cadiz, but could not hear that the galleons had put in there, for we were resolved to set upon these galleons that lay within the Bay. But the same day, having otherwise determined, we sailed forward to the Straits of Gibraltar intending to find out those galleons of [the] Spanish Navy and assail them.

Upon the 25 of April, coming before the town of Tangier upon the coast of Barbary, lying in the mouth of the Straits, and finding the galleons not there, the Admiral sent for his Council on board his ship, where it was resolutely determined, that if the Spanish Navy were in the Bay of Gibraltar they would set upon them, although it were in their own haven and under shot both of the town and castle. And to [this] end we took order in what sort to assail them, which was, first, our Admiral with Captain Lambert Hendrickson of Rotterdam, being Rear Admiral, should set upon, assail and board the Spanish Admiral, and our Vice Admiral and Captain Bras of Horn, should fight with the Spanish Vice Admiral and so every one in order.

At last, coming to the Bay of Gibraltar and finding the Spanish Army[2] there, presently we began, with God's help, to proceed in our resolution in such order as time and place required, where we found 21 ships among which were some Frenchmen, Emdeners and other merchant ships; upon our approach weighed anchor and went nearer the town and lay by four other galleons, but the Vice Admiral lay still, having aboard 450 men (as the prisoners after certified us); the Admiral had 100 cavaliers out of the town that voluntarily came aboard to help him although he was well provided with men before.

1. told
2. Fleet

All this notwithstanding and although he had the advantage of the ordnance of the town and castles, yet our Admiral and Captain Lambert of Rotterdam valiantly boarded him, and the rest of our ships, as well as they could, set upon the rest of the galleons and also upon the Spanish Vice Admiral. And after we had fought in that most furious assault, both with ordnance and forceable boarding their ships 4 hours or thereabouts, by God's help we got the victory, all the galleons being spoiled, battered and burnt were driven aground. And among the rest, the Admiral of 800 tons, called *S Agustin*, wherein the general called Don Juan Alvares d'Avila, born in Astorga, was slain, being an old experienced soldier that had served at sea in Don John of Austria, his time, also the Vice Admiral was slain and the Colonel of the soldiers and all the captains of their Navy.

The galleons and the rest of the Spanish ships were presently burnt down to the water, whereof two did drive on shore but so spoiled that they were altogether unserviceable; the ensigns, streamers and pennants of the Admiral, Vice Admiral and other galleons we took with us and some other pillage but by reason of the terrible fire in the Spanish Vice Admiral and other galleons that were on fire and ran aground we could not bring any ship or ordnance away, for we were in great danger of fire ourselves, and diverse of us had work enough to do to quench the fire that had gotten into them, but God of His mercy preserved us.

Of all the men in the Spanish Army but few escaped, for the Road of Gibraltar showed as if it had been sowed with Spaniards that had lept overboard, and those that we took confessed that they were 4,000 men in the Navy. We took 50 prisoner, one whereof was the General's son called Juan Alvares d'Avila, captain of the galleon called *S Agustin*

In this fight we lost our valiant General Jacob van Heemskerk, who with an honourable and brave resolution undertook this fight with the aid of the Vice Admiral, Captain Lambert of Rotterdam, and Captain Peter Willemsen bravely overcame and by God's help vanquished their enemy.

The 26 of April we brought our ships [from] before the town and castle, for with their continual shooting they did us much hurt, and being without their reach we manned out some of our boats and sent them to the burnt ships which lay upon the shore, which the Spaniards on land perceiving went themselves to set the Admiral's ship on fire, which lay all shot and torn upon the strand, and so they did that which we meant to have done.

In this fight there was at least 8,000 great shot discharged and was hardily and furiously fought, being fearful and terrible to behold when the Spanish galleons began to burn, especially when fire came to their powder, it showed as if new clouds and lightning had risen out of the sea and mounted into the sky.

By a sailor called Goyer, an English man that gave himself out for one of Emden, that was taken prisoner by the Spanish general and set at liberty upon our approach to be advised and counselled by him what were best to be done. We were advertised[1] that the Admiral would not believe we dare be so bold to board him in the King's Bay or haven, and especially under the shot of the town and castle of Gibraltar, which contrary to their expectation we made them feel. The Spanish General had certain advice before of our coming how many ships of war we had and with provant[2] ships and soldiers.

Among other things that we took, we found the King's secret instructions signed with the King of Spain's own hand *Io el rey* whereby we perceived what unaccustomed tyranny the said King had commanded him to execute and torment the natural born inhabitants of the Netherlands, especially the Hollanders and Zealanders and all their adherents, tho' that other nations by this commission were not altogether exempted.

The 27 of April we set sail and put out of the Bay of Gibraltar, and made toward the coast of Barbary, first going to Ceuta and entered so far into the bay that they shot at us both from the town and other places on the shore. There the Portugalles[3] in great numbers got upon their horses, fearing to be dealt withal as they were at Gibraltar; but because of the unfitness and bad security of the place, we sailed further to the Bay of Tetuan, five miles from Ceuta, to rig our ships for that many of them were unfurnished of bowsprits, masts, sails, cordage and other things, that had been shot through and fired in boarding the Spanish

---

1. advised
2. definite details of

galleons. And coming before Tetuan (a place under the Turks' and Moors' command) we were very welcome unto them; and upon the 28 of April, the Governor with many Turkish gentlemen came aboard our ship, bidding us welcome, offering us all favour and friendship he could afford us, and to aid us with all we stood in need off, for our wounded men otherwise.[1] He and all his company and country seeming to be glad of the victory which (by God's help) we had obtained against the Spaniards.

The fourth of May, at Tetuan, five miles from Ceuta, upon the coast of Barbary, we newly rigged and prepared our ships (which were sore battered) of all necessaries, staying God's pleasure for an easterly wind, to pass the Straits, and once again to seek after our enemies, dividing our Fleet into four squadrons. The Admiral being accompanied with seven other ships of war and the like in every squadron.

The Admiral, Monsieur [sic] Heemskerk that was slain was a very wise and well experienced man, who with great pain, labour and industry had been twice in the cold Strait of Wegattes, and at the East Indies, where in his last voyage he overcame and took the great rich carracks coming from Malacho in China, with whom of good will and affection towards him, many men ventured their lives in this voyage as among others Ioris van Spilberg that hath been both in the East and West Indies and employed in this Fleet as Commissary, and one of the Council of War, general captain of the Zealand soldiers, and diverse other captains.

THE Names of the Spanish galleons that were spoiled and burnt with many other whereof the names are not known:

The Admiral - S Agustin
The Vice-Admiral - Nuestra Señora de la Vera [Cruz]
The Rear-Admiral - Nuestra Señora Madre de Dios
Nuestra Señora Madre de [la] Concepción

The S Anna	Nuestra Señora de la Regla
The S Cristóbal	Nuestra Señora de los Dolores
The S Miguel	Nuestra Señora del Rosario
Nuestra Señora de la O [?]	The S Pedro

Yours to command,
I. V. S.

1. likewise

APPENDIX II

Senior Naval officers at Gibraltar

Commissioners of the Dockyard at Gibraltar :-
1756 Captain Charles Colby (until the end of the Seven Years War
                                         in 1763
1793 " Harry Harmwood
1794 " Andrew Sutherland
1796 " John N Inglefield
1801 " Sir Alexander J Ball Bart
1803 " William A Otway
1805 " Robert G Middleton
1808 " William G Lobb
1811 " Percy Fraser
1813 " Isaac Wolley (until 9 Jan 1818 when he transferred
                                      to Malta)

Naval Officer in Charge :-
1821 M B Mends RN
1829 John Slight RN
1833 John Davidson (Clerk in Charge)
1842 Captain Sir John G Sinclair Bart
1846 " Hon George Grey
1856 " Frederick Warden CB
1862 " Erasmus Ommanney
1864 " James C Prevost
1869 " Augustus Phillimore
1874 " John D M'Crea
1878 " William H Edye
1881 " Hon Edward R Fremantle CB CMG
1883 " John C Purvis
1886 " Henry C St John
1888 " Claude E Buckle
1892 " Atwell P M Lake

1895	Captain	John A T Bruce
1898	"	Charles C Drury
1899	"	William H Pigott
1902	Rear-Admiral	Sir William A D Acland Bart CVO
1904	"	" Sir Edward Chichester Bart CB CMG
1906	"	" James E C Goodrich MVO
1909	"	" Frederick S Pelham
1912	"	" Frederick E E Brock CB
1915	"	" Bernard Currey
1917	"	" Heathcote S Grant CB
1919	"	" Sir Reginald Y Tyrwhitt Bart KCB DSO DCL
1921	"	" Henry B Pelly CB MVO
1923	"	" W Maurice Ellerton CB
1925	"	" R G A W Stapleton-Cotton CB CBE MVO
1927	"	" C S Townsend CB
1929	"	" Berwick Curtis CB CMG DSO
1931	"	" T M James CB MVO
1933	"	" F M Austin CB
1935	"	" Sir James M Pipon KBE CB CMG MVO
1937	"	" A E Evans CB OBE
1939	"	" N A Woodehouse CB
1939	Vice-Admiral	Sir Dudley North KCVO CB CSI CMG
1941	"	" Sir Frederick Edward-Collins KCB KCVO
1943	"	" Sir Harold M Burrough KCB KBE DSO
1945	Rear-Admiral	V A C Crutchley VC KCB DSC
1947	"	" E R Archer CB CBE
1949	"	" P W B Brooking CB DSO
1950	"	" The Rt Hon Lord Ashbourne CB DSO
1952	"	" St J A Micklethwait CB DSO**
1953	"	" H P Currey CB OBE
1956	"	" R S Foster-Brown CB
1959	"	" P F Powlett CB DSO* DSC
1962	"	" Errol Sinclair CB DSC
1964	"	" T W Best CB
1966	"	" M F Fell DSO DSC*
1968	"	" I W Jamieson DSC

1969	Rear-Admiral		A R B Sturdee CB DSC
1972	"	"	H W E Hollins
1974	"	"	Sefton Sandford CB
1976	"	"	Michael Stacey CB
1979	"	"	Gwynedd Pritchard CB
1981	"	"	D J Mackenzie CB
1983	"	"	George M F Vallings
1985	"	"	Peter G V Dingemans DSO
1987	"	"	Hon Nicholas J Hill-Norton
1990	"	"	Geoffrey W R Biggs
1992	"	"	Jeremy Sanders

BIBLIOGRAPHY

MANUSCRIPT SOURCES

PUBLIC RECORDS OFFICE, London.
Gibraltar papers - Co.91 Series.
Foreign Office papers - FO.371 series.

NATIONAL MARITIME MUSEUM, Greenwich.
Adm/A and Adm/B Series.

BRITISH LIBRARY, Bloomsbury.
Additional manuscripts (Ad Ms).

BIBLIOTECA NACIONAL, Madrid
Portillo, Alonso Fernandez del, *Historia de la muy noble y mas leal ciudad
de Gibraltar.* (c.1626)

GIBRALTAR MUSEUM
SH, *Journal of the Siege of Gibraltar from Febr. 11: 1726/27, to June
12.*(1727)
Hire, Major, *Brief History of the Rock Armament.* (typescript 1960)

GIBRALTAR GOVERNMENT ARCHIVES
Elliott, H M, *Flying from the Rock, The Story of Aviation at Gibraltar
1901-1945.* Intelligence Section, RAF Gibraltar, 1945.

PRINTED SOURCES

Ackermann, Paul, *Encyclopaedia of British Submarines 1901-1955.*
Maritime Books, Liskeard Cornwall 1989.
Alcofar Nassaes, J L, *La marina italiana en la guerra de España.* Editorial
Euros, Madrid 1975.
Anderson, R C, *The Journals of Sir Thomas Allin.* 2 vols. London NRS
LXXXIX, LXXX 1939-40.

Anon, *An Exact Journal of the Taking of Gibraltar.* London 1710 (?)
—— *An Authentic and Accurate Journal of the Late Siege of Gibraltar.* London 1785.

Apps, Michael, *Send her Victorious.* Purnell Book Services, London 1971.

Ayala, Ignacio Lopez de, *Historia da Gibraltar.* Madrid 1782.

Barbudo Duarte, Enrique, *Apresamiento de la esquadra francesa del almirante Rosily en la Bahia de Cadiz, el 14 de junio de 1808.* Colección Fragata, Cadiz 1987.

Basset, Ronald, *Battle-Cruisers.* Macmillan, London 1981.
—— *HMS Sheffield: The Life and Times of 'Old Shiny'.* Arms & Armour, London 1988.

Baugh, Daniel A, *British Naval Administration in the Age of Walpole.* Princeton University Press, New Jersey 1965.
—— *Naval Administration 1715-1750.* London NRS CXX 1977.

Baumber, Michael, *General-at-Sea: Robert Blake and the Seventeenth-Century Revolution in Naval Warfare.* John Murray, London 1989.

Beach, Edward L, *The United States Navy - a 200 year history.* Houghton Mifflin, Boston Mass, 1986.

Beesley, Patrick, *Room 40.* Hamish Hamilton, London 1982.

Benady, Tito M, 'The Settlement of Jews in Gibraltar.' *Transactions of the Jewish Historical Society of England XXVI* London 1979.
—— *History of the Gibraltar Police.* Medsun, Gibraltar 1980.

Benavides, Manuel D *El ultimo pirata del Mediterraneo.* Ediciones Roca, Mexico D F 1976.

Bertaut, Francois, 'Journal du voyage d'Espagne, 1659.' *Revue Hispanique XLVII,* New York-Paris 1922.

Bond, Geoffrey, *Lakonia.* Oldbourne, London 1966.

Borghese, Junio Valerio, *Sea Devils.* Andrew Melrose, London 1953.

Bowles, Thomas G, *Gibraltar a National Danger.* Sampson Low, London 1901.

Brassey's Naval Annual. 1886 to 1971 (82 volumes).

Brenton, Edward P, *Life and Correspondence of John Earl St Vincent.* London 1838.

Breuer, William B, *Operation Torch.* St Martin's Press, New York 1985.

British Vessels Lost At Sea. Patrick Stephens, Cambridge 1984.

Brou, Willy Ch, *The War Beneath the Sea*. Frederick Muller, London 1958.

Brown, David, *The Royal Navy and the Falklands War*. Arrow Books 1989.

—— *Warship Losses of World War Two*. Arms and Armour, London 1990.

Bryant, Arthur, *Samuel Pepys: The Years of Peril*. Collins, London 1948.

—— *Samuel Pepys: The Saviour of the Navy*. Collins, London 1949.

Burdick, Charles B, *Germany's Military Strategy and Spain in World War II*. Syracuse University Press, Syracuse NY 1968.

Cabrillana Ciézar, Nicolás, *Documentos notariales de Marbella (1536-1573)*. Archivo Historico Provincial de Málaga 1990.

Cardozo, Aaron, *Letters, testimonials &c &c*. London 1830.

Carlyle, Thomas, *The Letters and Speeches of Oliver Cromwell*. 3 vols. Methuen, London 1904.

Cavilla, Manuel, *Diccionario Yanito*. Medsun, Gibraltar 1978.

Cervera Perry, José, *La guerra naval Española (1936-39)*. Editorial San Martín, Madrid 1988.

Chalmers, W S, *The Life and Letters of David Beatty*. Hodder & Stoughton, London 1951.

Chappell, Edwin, *The Tangier Papers of Samuel Pepys*. NRS LXXIII. London 1935.

Charnock, John, *Biographia Navalis*. 6 vols. London 1794-98.

Chatterton, E Keble, *Sea Raiders*. Hurst & Blackett, London 1933.

—— *Seas of Adventure*. Hurst & Blackett, London 1936.

Clarke J. & M'Arthur, J, *The Life and Services of Horatio, Viscount Nelson*. 3 vols. London 1840.

Clowes, William L, *The Royal Navy: A History*. 7 vols. Sampson Low, London 1897-1903.

Coad, J G, *Historic Architecture of the Royal Navy*. Gollancz, London 1983.

—— *The Royal Dockyards 1690-1850*. Scolar Press, Aldershot Hants 1989.

Cocchia, Aldo, *Submarines Attacking*. William Kimber, London 1956.

Colledge, J J, *Ships of the Royal Navy*. 2 vols. David and Charles, Newton Abbot 1969.

Colville, John R, *Man of Valour; Field Marshal Lord Gort VC.* Collins, London 1972

Corbett, Julian S, *England in the Mediterranean.* 2 vols. Longmans, London 1904.

—— *England in the Seven Years War.* 2 vols. Longmans, London 1907.

Creighton, Kenelm, *Convoy Commodore.* William Kimber, London 1956.

Cremer, Peter, *U-Boat Commander.* Naval Institute Press, Annapolis Md, 1984.

Critchley, Mike, *British Warships and Auxiliaries.* Maritime Books, Liskeard Cornwall 1979-1992

Cunningham, Andrew B, *A Sailor's Odyssey.* Hutchinson, London 1951.

Dalton, Charles, *George the First's Army 1714-1727.* Eyre and Spottiswood, London 1910-1912.

Divine, A D, *Destroyer's War.* John Murray, London 1943.

Drinkwater, John, *A History of the Siege of Gibraltar 1779-1783.* John Murray, London 1905.

Duro, C Fernandez, *Armada Española desde la Union de los Reinos de Castilla y Leon.* 9 Vols. Madrid 1895-1903.

Eccles, David, *By Safe Hand.* Bodley Head, London 1983.

Edwards, Kenneth, *Uneasy Oceans.* George Routledge, London 1939.

Eisenhower, Dwight D, *Crusade in Europe.* Heinemann, London 1948.

Ellicott, J T & D M, *Gibraltar's City Hall.* Gibraltar 1949.

Elliott, Peter, *The Cross and the Ensign.* Patrick Stephens. Cambridge, 1980.

Fairbairn, Tony, *Action Stations Overseas.* Patrick Stephens, Sparkford Somerset 1991.

Finlayson, Tommy J, *The Fortress Came First.* Gibraltar Books, Grendon Northants 1991.

Foot, M R D, *SOE: the Special Operations Executive 1940-46.* BBC, London 1985.

Francis, David, *The First Peninsular War 1702-1713.* Ernest Benn, London 1975.

Fremantle, Edmund R, *The Navy as I have known it.* Cassell, London 1902.

Froude, J A, *Spanish Story of the Armada.* Alan Sutton, Gloucester 1988.
Gibraltar Chronicle. 1801 to date.

Giorgerini, Giorgio, *Da Matapan al Golfo Persico.* Arnoldo Mondadori Editore, Milan 1989.

Glasfurd, Alec, *Voyage to Berbera.* Sheppard Press, London 1947.

Gonzalez, A, 'History of the Gibraltar Dockyard.' *Gibraltar Society Journal,* Gibraltar 1930.

Gordon, Oliver L, *Fight it Out.* William Kimber, London 1957.

Granville, George, *The Expedition to Cadiz.* London 1724.

Gretton, Peter, *El factor olvidado.* Editorial San Martín, Madrid 1984.

Grosart, Alexander B, *The Voyage to Cadiz.* Camden Society New Series 32, 1883, Johnson Reprint, New York.

Grove, Eric J, *Vanguard to Trident.* Bodley Head, London 1987.

Hakluyt, Richard, *The Principall Navigations of the English Nation.* Everyman's Library 8 vols.

Halpern, Paul G, *The Naval War in the Mediterranean 1914-1918.* Allen & Unwin, London 1987.

——*The Royal Navy in the Mediterranean 1915-1918.* NRS CXXVI London 1987.

——*The Mediterranean Naval Situation, 1908-1914.* Harvard University Press, Cambridge Mass, 1971.

Hampshire, A Cecil, *Undercover Sailors.* William Kimber, London 1981.

Hannan, Bill, *Fifty Years of Naval Tugs,* Maritime Books, Liskeard, Cornwall 1984

Harker, Jack S, *HMNZS Achilles.* Collins, Auckland 1982.

Hendrie, Andrew, *Flying Cats.* Airlife, Shrewsbury 1988.

Hills, George, *Rock of Contention.* Robert Hale, London 1974.

Hinsley, F H, *British Intelligence in the Second World War.* 3 vols HMSO, London 1979 - 88.

Hornstein, Sari R, *The Restoration Navy and English Foreign Trade 1674-1688.* Scolar Press, Aldershot Hants 1991.

Hughes, Robert, *Through the Waters.* William Kimber 1956.

Hyde, H Montgomery, *Secret Intelligence Agent.* Constable, London 1982.

Jackson, William G F, *The Rock of the Gibraltarians.* Gibraltar Books, Grendon Northants 1990.

Jameson, William, *Ark Royal 1939-1941.* Hart-Davis, London 1957.

Jane's Fighting Ships 1914.

Jato, David, *Gibraltar decidió la guerra.* Ediciones Acervo, Barcelona 1978.

Jenkins, E H, *A History of the French Navy.* Macdonald and Jane's, London 1973.

Jones, Geoffrey, *Attacker.* William Kimber, London 1980.

Jones, R V, *Most Secret War.* Hamish Hamilton, London 1978.

Jubelin, André, *The Flying Sailor.* Hurst & Blackett, London 1953.

Kuenzel, Heinrich, *Leben und Briefwechsel des Landgrafen Georg von Hessen-Darmstadt.* London and Friedberg 1859.

Lantery, Raimundo de, *Un comerciante saboyano en el Cádiz de Carlos II.* Caja de Ahorros de Cádiz 1983.

Laughton, John K, *Memoirs relating to the Lord Torrington.* Camden Soc New Series 46, 1889. Johnson Reprint, New York.

Layman. R D, 'Naval Warfare in a New Dimension 1914-1918.' *Warship 1989.* Conway, London 1989.

Leadam, I S, volume 9 (1702-1760) in *The Political History of England.* ed W Hunt and R L Poole, 1909, Kraus Reprint, New York.

Le Fleming, H M, *Warships of World War I.* Ian Allan, London 1967.

Lumby, E W R, *Policy and Operations in the Mediterranean 1912-1914.* NRS CXV London 1970

Luna, José Carlos de, *Historia de Gibraltar.* Madrid 1944.

Lund, Paul & Ludlam, Harry, *Out Sweeps! Foulsham, London 1987.*

—— *Nightmare Convoy.* Foulsham, London 1987.

McConville, Sean, *A History of English Prison Administration.* vol 1, Routledge & Kegan Paul 1981.

McGuffie, T H, *The Siege of Gibraltar.* Batsford, London 1965.

Macintyre, Donald, *Fighting Admiral.* Evans Brothers, London 1961.

McKay, George, 'Mystery Torpedo.' *Warship World* vol 1 no 7, Liskeard Cornwall 1986.

Mackay, Ruddock, *Admiral Hawke.* Oxford University Press 1965.

Macmillan, Harold, *At the End of the Day.* Macmillan, London 1973.

Magauran, H C, *Rock Siege.* Medsun, Gibraltar 1986.

Mahan, Alfred T, *The Life of Nelson: The Embodiment of the Sea Power of Great Britain.* Haskell House, New York 1969.

Maríategui, E de, *El capitán Rojas.* CEDEX Centro de Estudios y Experimentación de Obras Publicas, Madrid 1985.

Mark, William, *At Sea with Nelson.* Sampson Low, London 1929.

Martin-Leake, Stephen, *The Life of Sir John Leake.* 2 vols. NRS LII, LIII London 1920-21

Marchbanks, David, *The Painted Ship.* Secker & Warburg, London 1964.

Marder, Arthur, *The Anatomy of British Seapower.* Putnam, London 1940.

—— *From the Dreadnought to Scapa Flow.* 5 vols. Oxford University Press, 1966-70.

Mars, Alastair, *British Submarines at War 1939-1945.* William Kimber, London 1971.

Medlicott, W N, *The Economic Blockade.* 2 vols. HMSO, London 1952-59.

Merriman, R D, *Queen Anne's Navy.* NRS CII London 1961.

Miles, Benedict, *Gibraltar Directory and Guidebook.* (1916 & 1939)

Monks, Noel, *That Day At Gibraltar.* Frederick Muller, London 1957.

Monsarrat, Nicholas, *Breaking Out.* (Life is a Four Letter Word part 2) Cassell, London 1970.

Montagu, Ewen, *The Man Who Never Was.* Evans Brothers, London 1956.

Morris, Roger, *The Royal Dockyards During the Revolutionary and Napoleonic Wars.* Leicester University Press 1983.

Navy List August 1914.

Nicolas, Nicholas H, *Despatches and Letters of Vice-Admiral Lord Viscount Nelson.* 7 vols. London 1844.

Padfield, Peter, *Rule Britania.* Routledge & Kegan Paul, London 1981.

Palao, George, *Our Forgotten Past.* Gibraltar 1977.

Panorama, weekly newspaper, Gibraltar

Pares, Richard, *Colonial Blockade and Neutral Rights.* Oxford University Press 1938.

Patterson, A Temple, *Tyrwhitt of the Harwich Force.* Macdonald, London 1973.

Plimmer, C & D, *A Matter of Expediency.* Quartet Books, London 1978.

Poolman, Kenneth, *Scourge of the Atlantic.* Book Club Associates, London 1979.

Pope, Dudley, *Flag 4.* William Kimber, London 1954.

Powell, J R, *The Letters of Robert Blake.* NRS LXXVI London 1937.

Preston, Anthony & Major, John, *Send a Gun Boat.* Longman's, London 1967.

Price, Alfred, *Aircraft Versus Submarine.* William Kimber, London 1973.

Pugh, Marshall, *Commander Crabb.* Macmillan, London 1956.

Ramsey, Winston, 'Gibraltar.' *After the Battle 21.* London 1978.

Ranft, B McL, *The Beatty Papers vol 1.* NRS CXXVIII, London 1988.

Report of the Barrack and Hospital Improvement Commission on 'The Sanitary Condition of the Mediterranean Stations.' Part I, HMSO, London 1863

Richmond, H W, *The Navy in the War of 1739-48.*F 3 vols. Cambridge University Press 1930.

Robertson, Terence, *The Ship with Two Captains.* Evans Brothers, London 1957.

Robertson, William, *Journal of a Clergyman during a Visit to the Peninsula in the Summer and Autumn of 1841.* William Blackwood, Edinburgh 1845.

Rocca, Gianni, *Fucilati gli ammiragli.* Arnoldo Mondadori Editore, Milan 1987.

Rohwer, Jurgen, *Axis Submarine Successes 1939-1945.* Patrick Stephens, Cambridge 1983.

Roskill, Stephen W, *The War At Sea.* 4 vols. HMSO London 1954-61.

Russell, Jack, *Gibraltar Besieged.* Heinemann, London 1965.

Salas, Ramon, *Historia del ejercito popular de la Republica.* Editora Nacional, Madrid 1973.

Salmon, Edward, *Life of Admiral Sir Charles Saunders KB.* Isaac Pitman, London 1914.

Semmes, Raphael, *Cruise of the Alabama and the Sumter.* 1864.

—— *Memoirs of Service Afloat.* Blue & Grey Press, Secaucus New Jersey, 1987.

Sherrard, 0 A, *A Life of Lord St Vincent.* Allen & Unwin, London 1933.

Sierra, Luis de la, *La guerra navale nel Mediterraneo (1940 1943).* Mursia Editore, Milan 1987.

Sims, William S, *The Victory at Sea.* Naval Institute Press, Annapolis Md 1984.

Slocum, Joshua, *Sailing Alone Around the World.* Dover Publications, New York 1956.

Smith, Peter C, *Destroyer Leader*. William Kimber, London 1968.

——*Pedestal: the Malta convoy of August 1942*. William Kimber, London 1970.

—— *Fighting Flotilla*. London 1976.

—— *Hit First; Hit Hard*. William Kimber, London 1979.

—— *Action Imminent*. William Kimber, London 1980.

—— *HMS Wild Swan*. William Kimber, London 1985.

—— *Battleship Royal Sovereign*. William Kimber, London 1988.

Smyth, Denis, *Diplomacy and Strategy of Survival*. Cambridge University Press, 1986.

Somner, Graeme, *Bland Gibraltar*. World Ship Society, Kendal 1981.

Spilsbury, John, *A Journal of the Siege of Gibraltar*. Gibraltar Garrison Library, 1908.

Spinney, David, *Rodney*. Allen & Unwin, London 1969.

Taylor, J C, *German Warships of World War I*. Ian Allan, London 1969.

Thomas, Hugh, *The Spanish Civil War*. Hamish Hamilton, London 1977.

Thompson, Kenneth, *H.M.S. "Rodney" at War*. Hollis & Carter, London 1946.

Tucker, Jedediah S, *The Memoirs of the Earl of St Vincent*. 2 vols. London 1844.

Tunstall, Brian, *The Byng papers*. 3 vols. NRS LXVII, LXVIII, LXX London 1930-32.

Tute, Warren, *The Deadly Stroke*. Collins, London 1973.

Vella, Philip, *Malta: Blitzed but not Beaten*. Progress Press, Malta 1985.

Vere, Francis, *Salt in their Blood*. Cassell, London 1955.

Villar, Roger, *Merchant Ships at War: The Falklands Experience*. Conway, London 1984.

West, Nigel, *MI5*, Triad Grafton, London 1988.

—— *MI6*. Grafton, London 1988.

Whiteley, E A, 'Warburton and PR from Malta.' *RAF QuarterlyReview*, Spring 1978.

Whitmore, George *The Travel Memoirs of General Sir George Whitmore*. Alan Sutton, Gloucester 1987.

Winton, John, *Carrier Glorious*. Leo Cooper, London 1986.
—— *Convoy*. Michael Joseph, London 1983.
—— *Warrior: The First and the Last*. Maritime Books, Liskeard Cornwall 1987.
Wood, Alfred C, *A History of the Levant Company*. Cass, London 1964.
Woods, Gerard A, *Wings at Sea*. Conway, London 1985.
Ziegler, Philip, *Mountbatten*. Alfred A Knopf, New York 1985.

GENERAL INDEX

Hewitt, Rear-Admiral H K, USN, 210
Hicks, Captain Jasper, RN, 16, 17, 19
Hillgarth, Captain Alan, RN, 206
Hill-Norton, Rear-Admiral Nicholas, 243
Hoare, Sir Samuel, 208
Hollins, Vice-Admiral H W E, 243
Homaslevi (Hammersley?), Thomas, 12 n6
Home Fleet (formerly Atlantic Fleet), 136, 147
Hood, Admiral Viscount, 65
Hopsonn, Vice-Admiral Sir Thomas, 31
Hospital of St John of God, 6, 27-28, 34, 222
Hotham, Vice-Admiral William (later Admiral Lord), 65-66
Howe, Admiral of the Fleet Earl, 60-61
Hughes, M, RN, 222
Hutcheon, David, 223

Iachino, Admiral A, 185
Inglefield, Captain John N, RN, 71, 241
Intransigentes mutiny, 95-96
Italian submarines, deficiencies, 192

Jackson, General Sir William (governor), 227
James, Rear-Admiral T M, 242
Jamieson, Rear-Admiral I W, 242
Janvrin, Lieut RN, 76
Jennings, Admiral Sir John, 27
Jervis, Admiral of the Fleet Sir John, Earl St Vincent, 66-76
Jumper, Captain Sir William, 16, 17, 18

Keats, Captain RN, 78
Keen, James, 222
Keith, Admiral Viscount, 72, 75-76
Keyes, Admiral of the Fleet Sir Roger, 134
Knowles, Cecil, 223
Knowles, Captain Sir Charles, RN, 62
Kvaerner, 229

Lagos, Battle of, 37-39
Lake, Captain Atwell P M, 241
Lane, John, 222

Langara y Huarte, Admiral Juan de, 48, 65
Lantery, Raimundo de, 10, 13 n21
Lathbury, General Sir Gerald (governor), 227
Lawson, Admiral Sir John, 10
Leake, Admiral of the Fleet Sir John, 22-24
Leech (explosive device), 168-168, 170, 172, 174
Leslie, Captain RN, 51
Levant Company, 2
Lisbon, 11, 14, 22, 66-67, 70, 169
Lloyd George, David, 127
Lobb, Captain William, RN, 241
Lopez Cordon-Cuenca, Luis, 177
Louis XIV, 14
Louis XVI, 65
Luna, José Carlos de, 19

McGrail, Alfred, 223
Macintyre, Captain Donald, RN, 199
Mackenzie, Rear-Admiral D J, 243
Macmillan, Harold, 224-225
M'Crea, Captain John, 241
Madcats, 214-216
Maiale see SLC
Malaga, 31, 76, 169, 207, 220
Malaga, Battle of, 21-22
Malta, 90-91, 92, 107, 129, 139, 151, 160, 167, 184, 194-198
Malta, Chapel of Knights of, 18
Malta, Knights of, 65 79 n2
Mansell, Admiral Sir Robert, 6
Marbella, Battle of, 23-34, 25
March, Juan, 124, 206
Mark, Purser William, RN, 90
Marlborough, Duke of, 14
Martin, Admiral (French Navy), 66
Martin Amador, Francisco, 222
Martinez Muñoz, José, 177
Mason, Captain D W, 197
Mason-MacFarlane, Lieut-General Sir Noel (governor), 205, 208
Mateos, Juan, 6, 27
Mazarredo, Admiral José de, 69, 75-76
Mazri Bay *see* Tetuan Bay

259

261

INDEX OF SHIPS

MINELAYERS

DESTROYERS

GERMANY

BATTLESHIPS

CRUISERS

SUBMARINES

ITALY

BATTLESHIPS

SUBMARINES